THEORY MATTERS

THEORY MATTERS

Vincent B. Leitch

ROUTLEDGE
NEW YORK AND LONDON

Published in 2003 by
Routledge
29 West 35th Street
New York, NY 10001
www.routledge-ny.com

Published in Great Britain by
Routledge
11 New Fetter Lane
London EC4P 4EE
www.routledge.co.uk

Routledge is an imprint of the Taylor & Francis Group.
Printed in the United States of America on acid-free paper.

Figures 2 and 5 appear courtesy of *Back Beat*.

10 9 8 7 6 5 4 3 2 1

Library of Congress Cataloging-in-Publication Data
Leitch, Vincent B., date.
    Theory matters / Vincent B. Leitch.
        p. cm.
    Includes bibliographical references and index.
    ISBN 0-415-96716-3 (HB : alk. paper)—ISBN 0-415-96717-1
(PB : alk. paper)
        1. Criticism—History—20th century. 2. Literature, Modern—History and criticism—Theory, etc. I. Title.
    PN94.L394 2003
    801'.95'0904—dc21
2003007397

CONTENTS

PREFACE

WHAT MOST CHARACTERIZES POSTMODERN CULTURE from the 1970s onwards is "disorganization," a word that suggests chaos, but in my usage means disaggregation, resembling geological formations with historical strata in disarrayed kaleidoscopic layers.[1] Neither economics nor politics nor culture today escapes this form. Recent political examples might include all the schemes implementing privatization and deregulation and the simultaneous antiquation of both the welfare state and large mainstream political parties, the latter in conjunction with the rise of numerous new social movements. Slogans depicting these phenomena are, on the political right, "small is beautiful" and, on the left, "coalition and micropolitics are best." Well-attested instances of disorganization in other domains range from the deconstruction of Western philosophy and the reconfiguration of identity theory as "multiple subject positions" in psychology to the incredulity toward metanarratives of historiography and the construal of tradition as infinite intertextuality in literary theory. Common words and phrases in the critical lexicon—difference, heteroglossia, contending interpretive communities, rhizome, polylogue, multiversity, and pastiche—all point to various kinds of disaggregation. In *Theory Matters* I argue that culture and in particular theory during postmodern times are marked by disorganization.

The progression in literary studies during recent decades from formalism to poststructuralism to cultural studies, from high theory to posttheory to cultural critique, marks a broad path of disaggregation, which to some implies the death of theory. To an earlier generation, recent theory often looks like advocacy rather than disinterested objective inquiry into poetics and the history of literature. There are a number of "deaths" one can single out here: the death of theory as poetics and as *literary* criticism at the hands of various nonliterary tendencies (feminism, race studies, postcolonial criticism); the death of theory as objective disinterested inquiry in favor of cultural critique; the death of the theory of literature as high- or middlebrow aesthetic artifact undermined by lowbrow popular culture, media, and pulp genres; the death of theory as supplier of a professional lingua franca, a set of foundational principles and normative methods of analysis; and, most revealing, the death of theory as a coherent enterprise, field, or subfield given the recent rise of cultural studies.

In retrospect, the formalist period from the 1940s to the 1960s and the poststructuralist period from the 1970s to the 1990s appear comparatively coherent, though one can trace across these decades a line of disorganization in the fields of literary and cultural theory. It is in the 1990s, with the flowering of cultural studies, notably in the United States, that theory has entered a stage of dramatic disorganization so much so that the usual orderly "schools-and-movements" approach in depicting as well as in teaching theory no longer works. Interestingly, advocates of Birmingham cultural studies, a relatively coherent earlier project coalescing during the 1970s, complain bitterly that U.S. cultural studies has become a front for a wide range of disparate practices.[2] What most strikingly typifies this recent phase of theory disorganization is the rise of numerous discrete subfields more or less associated with cultural studies, such as media studies, science studies, subaltern studies, trauma studies, whiteness studies, fashion studies, food studies, disability studies, leisure studies, narrative studies, globalization studies, indigenous studies, border studies, urban and community studies, queer studies, visual culture studies, animal studies, and body studies. Add to this list more established fields such as film studies, American studies, gender studies, and postcolonial studies, plus indeterminate fields, for example, legal studies and cognitive studies, and you have a cursory inventory of today's cultural studies. In this way, I would argue that cultural studies is the postmodern discipline par excellence, disorganized in the extreme.

Most of the fields and subfields just enumerated have their own key terms, leading texts, research problems, major figures, archives and histories, journals, conferences, university press series, theoretical wings, and so on. Few are departmentalized or well-funded, existing in various "flexible" margins of today's *modern* university, which itself has undergone disaggregation since the 1960s. I do not dwell upon the disorganization of the "multiversity," a topic much written about in recent years.[3] Suffice it to say, insofar as each subfield named above is interdisciplinary or transdisciplinary or antidisciplinary, it contributes to the postmodern disorganization of the modern bureaucratic departmentalized university.

How is theory positioned in relation to all these recent reconfigurations, particularly of cultural studies? To reiterate, each field and subfield has its own distinctive theoretical corpus. On the other hand, there exist numerous overlaps between and among fields, as, for example, the work of Michel Foucault, which finds use in philosophy, literary studies, body studies, queer theory, and more. In this connection, there is also the noteworthy rise to prominence of the "crossover text" that innovatively links multiple segments of (sub)fields. Gayatri Spivak pioneered this genre when she grafted onto deconstruction both Marxism and feminism from a Third World perspective.[4] Numerous such complex combinations are possible and everywhere in evidence. The point is the disorganization of theory is not another sad contemporary instance of death by Balkanization, but rather of expansion through combination and proliferation. It is also worth pointing out, however, that certain *theorists* regard the recent expansion of theory as a sad spectacle, implying dilution, vulgarization, loss of vigor, and death.

The new postmodern interdisciplines challenge the autonomous discipline or, more precisely, each discipline per se contains, it turns out, ineradicable elements of other disciplines. And although discrete disciplines may conveniently join like biology and chemistry, biology and chemistry themselves change in the process. Physics has mathematics, astronomy, and chemistry as both neighbors and unwanted guests. Literary studies by its very nature is entangled indissolubly with a half dozen or more disciplines from history and mythology to linguistics, anthropology, and beyond. Interdisciplinarity during postmodern times designates the unstable intermixtures of the disciplines. Where does this leave theory? If I say, "all over the place," I am sure you will at this point grasp my argument, one that I develop at greater length in chapter 12 on postmodern interdisciplinarity.

Inevitably, the question arises about whether theory, in the new era of cultural studies, isn't just one more example of late postindustrial, post-Fordist capitalist culture—flexibilized, imploded, preoccupied with popular culture, market-oriented, driven by rapid innovation, dedicated to vanguardism and countercultural ideas, and housed comfortably inside the new university. In one sense, how could it be otherwise. But in another sense, projects of cultural critique, rooted in various critical traditions ranging from Marxism to psychoanalysis to such new social movements as women's and civil rights, Third World reparations, and environmental justice, invariably promote an ethicopolitics steeped in egalitarian ideas, often setting it at odds with mainstream practices and values. The politics of theory and also of cultural studies are routinely identified today as too "politically correct," too antithetical, and too affiliated with various subaltern and marginal groups like people of color, queers, greens, Third World radicals, exploited workers—the usual suspects. In other words, theory is mired in commodified, coopted, cooperative moments, however, it regularly presents contestatory discourses. Hence one of the main meanings of my title: theory still matters, certainly as much as ever, in intellectual and political struggles.

* * *

Part 1 of *Theory Matters* offers personal commentary on the changing situation of literary and cultural theory during the past thirty years, the postmodern period, mapping in chapter 1 the broad shift from formalism to poststructuralism to cultural studies, and then in chapter 2 discussing key elements of two dozen theory texts that have been most influential in my as well as others' development over these three decades. Chapter 3 argues that developments in contemporary theory constitute a renaissance and not a simple-minded capitulation to the latest fashions, and chapter 4 critically examines the standard ways of portraying contemporary theory change, advocating a disjunctive mix-and-match postmodern mode of historical representation.

As general editor of *The Norton Anthology of Theory and Criticism* (2001), I spent nearly six years collaborating with a team of editors in putting together what turned out to be a large volume (2,625 pages), spanning from Gorgias and Plato to bell hooks and Judith Butler, complete, I hasten to add, with several hundred pages of bibliographies and an Instructor's Manual (an additional 200 pages). The inside story of this complex project is told in chapters 5 through 7, something no other Norton anthology editor, as far as I know, has ever done. Chapter 7 also offers observations about the current and future state of theory, literature, and literary studies.

Part 2 focuses at the outset on the development of globalization studies within the context of cultural studies. Specifically, chapter 8 assesses the influential works and concepts of Pierre Bourdieu, highlighting the last decade of his life when he became a formidable critic and engaged vocal opponent of neoliberal globalization. Chapter 9 surveys disparate new forms of economic criticism, focusing on their similar critiques of mainstream economic doctrine and globalization, showing how they connect to the recent rise of "Lilliputians," an emerging disaggregated postmodern front advocating transformation of the current global political economic order. Chapters 10 through 12 offer three case studies in cultural studies, exploring key elements of the postmodern disorganization of, to begin with, contemporary fashion, then of today's blues subculture, and lastly of interdisciplinary studies. To be more specific, chapter 10 gives a survey of the main topics and premises of critical fashion studies, going on to argue that fashion today numbingly reiterates beautiful destructive stereotypes, norms, and ideals while, in addition, it provides materials for positive reinscription, resistance, and transformation. Chapter 11 applies some tried and true cultural studies concepts and methods—especially theories of subculture, popular culture, fandom, and participant observation—to a local blues music scene (framed within the broad contexts of blues history and scholarship), demonstrating the progressive nature of today's blues music *in situ.* Chapter 12 develops four points, stark propositions, about the disciplines today, contrasting modern and postmodern conceptions of interdisciplinarity while sketching along the way the situation of cultural studies in the contemporary university.

* * *

In our era of fast reading, the preferred genres of literary and cultural criticism are gradually changing to shorter forms often cast in personalized modes. *Theory Matters* reflects this postmodern shift by foregrounding in most of its chapters, all deliberately short, a prose style based on personal perspectives, in spoken language, sometimes in interviews. Early versions and parts of certain chapters, here revised, appeared originally in journals: Preface in *Hungarian Journal of English and American Studies,* chapter 1 in *Massachusetts Review,* chapter 2 in *Genre,* chapter 3 in *Literature and Psychology,* chapters 4 and 6 in *minnesota review,* chapter 5 in *Symploke* and *College English,* chapter 7 in Finnish in *Kulttuurintutkimus (Cultural Studies),* chapter 10 in *Modern Fiction Studies,* and chapter 12 in *Profession 2000.* I am grateful to the editors for permission to reprint. For assistance I thank the Oklahoma Humanities Council, which provided research funds for work on regional blues, and the University of Oklahoma where in 2000 I received a Big 12 Visiting Faculty Fellowship, allowing me to develop some of my ideas. For help I am thankful to research assistants Mitchell Lewis and Nyla Khan, and for support I thank colleagues Eve Tavor Bannet, Richard Dienst, Jim Johnson, Winston Napier, Patrick O'Donnell, and Jeff Williams.

PART 1
Theory Personalized

1

THEORY RETROSPECTIVE

LATELY I HAVE BEEN WONDERING how I got here. I mean that I have been trying to map the stages of my profession's development during the past three decades, the time of my involvement in academic literary studies, particularly criticism and theory, my specialty. In retrospect, I see that it is a story, in large part, about U.S. university culture in the late twentieth century being Europeanized one more time, becoming self-consciously multicultural, and undergoing postmodernization. When I committed myself to literary studies as an undergraduate in the mid-1960s, New Criticism was the ruling paradigm, which had been in place, not without various telling challenges, for several decades. It was not until the mid-1970s that this oppressive formalism gave way to "poststructuralism" (as it was oddly called), a peculiar set of literary philosophical methods and frames of reference largely derived from Friedrich Nietzsche but filtered through Jacques Derrida, Paul de Man, and Michel Foucault, among others. Itself dominant for more than a decade—though not without significant challenges—poststructuralism mutated from its French roots in response to more local problems and challenges, particularly those brought to the surface in the late 1970s and early 80s by feminists, ethnic autonomy groups, and postcolonial thinkers. I have more to say later about the branches of poststructuralism. By the middle or late 1980s, various united fronts of literary social critics, feminists, postcolonial theorists, historians of culture, scholars of popular culture, rhetoricians, and left poststructuralists like myself began promoting cultural studies, many extending models developed during the 1970s in the United Kingdom's celebrated Centre for Contemporary Cultural Studies at the University of Birmingham. So what you had in U.S. university departments of literary studies through the late 1980s and throughout the 1990s was an ascendant cultural studies, increasingly capacious and broadly defined, simultaneously incorporating and displacing a once-dominant literary poststructuralism, both of which movements were held at arm's length by certain feminists, postcolonial theorists, ethnic critics, queer theorists, and leftists reluctant to join coalitions for fear of invisibility or cooptation. I hasten to add that New Criticism, to which many literary intellectuals trained in the 1940s and 1950s remained faithful, survived into the twenty-first century both as a besieged residual paradigm of "normative" literary education and a resurrected charter adopted by a small number of a young generation of new belletrists often associated with creative writing programs. To summarize using more emotional terms, in my experience U.S. academic critics and criticism can be characterized as comparatively complacent through most of the 1960s, frantic and expansive in the 1970s, embattled in the 1980s, and surprisingly ambitious yet generally glum during the 1990s. A detailed chronicle of everyday life during these years would enrich and complicate matters, needless to say, as would a less generalized more personal account of intellectual development, something I offer in chapter 2.

To simplify matters even further, I came into literary studies at a moment of extreme critical contraction and purification, and I have lived through an era of staggering expansion and hybridization. At the point at which in the 1980s cultural studies first grappled with the question of postmodernity, that is, when it started to map the global culture of the emergent "New World Order," academic literary horizons entered into a phase of extreme expansion, a time, still today, when popular music such as West Coast Afrocentric rap is scrutinized beside Shakespeare's Italianate sonnets; when contemporary global corporate practices such as downsizing and Renaissance patterns of aristocratic patronage both help explain publication practices as well as poetic themes and forms.[1]

Permit me to preview the trajectory of this chapter. First, I offer a personal retrospective on the tumultuous period in literary studies from the 1960s through the present, the time of my involvement as university student, professor, and scholar specializing in the history of literary and cultural criticism and theory. Second, I compare and contrast the three dominant critical paradigms of this period, namely, New Criticism, poststructuralism, and cultural studies, as a way to portray and assess the broad intellectual and cultural struggles of the times. I conclude with some personal reflections on theory now and in the future.

My overarching thesis is that the peculiar coexistence within literature departments today of different generational projects and critical paradigms reflects, in miniature, the wider disorganization characteristic of Western societies in recent decades, a form of disaggregation that renders pastiche arguably our dominant organizational mode. Not incidentally, the contemporary university itself does not escape this form.[2]

WRITING SCHOLARLY BOOKS: INTERSECTIONS OF THE PERSONAL AND THE PROFESSIONAL

One way or another, I have been entangled in all these historical developments I have been enumerating, as have virtually all members of university departments of English and, perhaps to a lesser extent, departments of comparative and national literatures. My book publications offer four case studies of my various involvements over the years, providing a retrospective on what has happened in the profession. When I published *Deconstructive Criticism* in 1983 (which was seven years in the making), it was, objectively speaking, a comparative historical account of first-generation French and American poststructuralist criticism but, speaking personally, it represented an anxious effort on my part to master certain innovative contemporary Continental philosophical modes of criticism as a way to get free of the enervated Anglo-American formalist criticism into which I had been indoctrinated as an undergraduate and then graduate student, and which I had been trying more or less unsuccessfully to modify and eventually jettison for almost a decade. Under the cover of an advanced introduction, this book facilitated an expansive practice of poststructuralist textual analysis. What it did not do was promote the shift of textual analysis to cultural critique, a project that younger French feminists and second-generation U.S. poststructuralists, intellectuals such as Gayatri Spivak, were undertaking at that time and that, as I noted before, culminated some five to ten years later with the emergence of cultural studies. Shortly, I'll have a word to say about cultural critique, which entails the explicit turn of poststructuralist styles of criticism to ethics and politics.

In the United States, departments of literary study were especially embattled sites during the 1980s as different paradigms of interpretation and of the curriculum were pitted against each other. The paradigm wars of those times are still with us, although usually in less disruptive forms. When in 1988 I published *American Literary Criticism from the 1930s to 1980s*, I sought to retell a complex segment of the history of criticism from the perspective of a left cultural historiography sympathetic to all manner of contemporary antinomian groups and forces, ranging from Marxism and poststructuralism to the new social movements (notably feminism, the black power movement, and the New Left). U.S. cultural history had a different look from this point of view, of course, but what preoccupied me personally was the effort to help change literature departments by telling graduate students and new professors, my main audiences, a story of their history culminating in the (momentary) triumphs of feminism, ethnic aesthetics, and cultural studies. This was my way of galvanizing myself and others toward transforming the institution of criticism and theory from its still powerful, yet too narrowly focused, formalist heritage to its expansive cultural studies future. To do this, I had to put myself step by step through an extensive education in the history of American criticism and theory, which willy-nilly helped me accrue a great deal of knowledge and become an authority, oddly an unlooked-for outcome.

It is one thing to write a partisan history and another to change the order of things through direct argumentation. I found in publishing *Cultural Criticism, Literary Theory, Poststructuralism* in 1992 that the effort to shape the emerging cultural studies project so that it took certain key techniques and solutions from poststructuralism on its way beyond poststructuralism offered narrow rewards. I personally worked up effective solutions to a number of key problems such as how to conceptualize "authorship," "genre," "discourse," and "institution" from the vantage of poststructuralist cultural theory and criticism. I also experienced an obvious truth: an emerging paradigm or vanguard movement is not necessarily interested in learning lessons from its immediate predecessors, nor in resolving its debts to more distant and less threatening progenitors. To the considerable extent that one writes books not just for audiences, such as fellow critics, scholars, and students, but for oneself (oneself always being at a certain crucial stage of development), this particular book has been for me the most important, even though it was poorly targeted and not well-timed. It forced me to move from understanding and promoting poststructuralism and cultural studies, through writing comparative histories, to theorizing poststructuralist solutions to cultural studies problems via scholarly polemics. It is a matter of doing—not just advocating—cultural critique, which entails investigating and criticizing contending positions and explanations with an eye toward not simply faulty logic, but questionable values, practices, and representations, requiring subtle yet frank ethical and political as well as aesthetic judgments. Robert Scholes nicely dubbed this "textual power" in a book with that title.

By the time I published *Postmodernism—Local Effects, Global Flows* in 1996, which offered a set of essays on different facets of post-1950s culture, cultural studies had triumphed, but in the limited way that most theoretical movements and paradigms succeed in university literature departments.

Here let me diverge to say a word about universities and educational innovation before I return to cultural studies. While contemporary university presses, scholarly journals, and academic conferences often welcome the latest developments, the curricula of both the literature major and the liberal arts core remain largely unaffected, accommodating change at a snail's pace by adding on yet one more option to a large number of preexisting options.[3] In my experience, curriculum innovation comes slowly and grudgingly—and long after the fact. Universities are strikingly conservative when it comes to undergraduate curriculum. None of this stops individual instructors or like-minded colleagues and students from making de facto changes, at first discreetly and then more boldly, often engendering in the process hostile enclaves and factions. During recent decades departments, or frequently segments of departments, refused or failed to change, with the result that at any given moment departments can be in very different stages of development, which is one more site of the disaggregation characteristic of postmodern times.

All this explains why I included for the first time arguments about curriculum theory in the book on postmodern culture. Not incidentally, this text also offered expected chapters on contemporary criticism, poetry, philosophy, and feminism, plus new material on recent painting, theology, historiography, and economics, especially finance economics, today a leading edge of globalization along with media and advertising. In our postmodern condition, culture is in the last successful stages of incorporating nature, including nature's wildest zones. Media constitute the vanguard, capital the engine.[4] I take up these matters again in chapters 8 and 9.

I want to circle back and comment on some important issues that I glossed over when discussing cultural studies. First, I prefer to think not that literary studies (or university education) was tragically politicized in recent decades, say since the 1960s, but that it was peculiarly depoliticized in the 1940s and 1950s as part of the "end of ideology" campaign waged during the early years of the Cold War, a period now noted in history for its reactionary cultural politics symbolized by Mc-Carthyism. In this scenario, cultural studies represents something like a return to normal after an aberrant period of reaction that tended to fetishize disembodied great works along with pure science and unending progress. Second, literary and cultural critics throughout the twentieth century have engaged in historical analysis and criticism, although historicism was largely out of favor during the mid-century hegemony of New Criticism. The return to historicisms in recent decades (if one can actually say "return") strikes me as a healthy turn of events, especially for criticism and theory. (I avoid discussing here today's contending modes of historiography, instead taking that up in chapter 4.) Third, the triumph of cultural studies is, to be sure, a complicated matter. At best such a "triumph" is limited insofar as university programs often bear skimpy evidence of such success. To the extent that cultural studies has mutated into a broad academic front under which almost any research goes, it serves as an example of innovation as mixed blessing. This is what I intimated when I suggested that a point of maximum expansion had been reached. Not surprisingly, cultural studies is in the process of segmentation, involving an as yet indistinct (re)constellation of the field around relatively autonomous new problems and hybrid subfields. The maturation of visual cultural studies in the mid-1990s provides an example: here fashion, art history, design, architecture, film, and television studies have been reconfigured so as to focus on "the look," that is, the historically constructed visual styling and modes of perception, characteristic of periods and cultures (or, more commonly, subcultures). Fourth, there is a tragedy unfolding in that many current graduate students are at once dedicated to cultural studies and effectively cut out of the profession because there are virtually no departments of cultural studies to hire them. Once in a while a literature department hires a token person. When the remnants of this new generation get into power a decade or two from now, departments of cultural studies will, no doubt, belatedly spring up across the United States. The glumness characteristic of literature departments starting in the 1990s had a great deal to do with both the depressed job market for new Ph.D.s and the institutional bottlenecking of cultural studies.

Let me sum up these comments on the changing historical situations surrounding my own research and publication by observing that, for good or ill, the professional conditions and shapes the personal and vice versa. One does not simply look into one's heart and write. To be heard and received at all requires submission to a period of training, credentialing, and professionalization. If in this case the personal is a much diminished thing, undergirded and determined (as it demonstrably is) by institutional and professional requirements, so be it: we might as well face the facts of our postmodernity, which seems at every turn to be closing in on the spaces of "individualism" so lauded during more Romantic periods. I for one refuse to be maudlin about this, since I find Romantic individualism to be an inadequate account of subject formation and identity dynamics. We are all post-Romantic, whether we admit it or not. None of this means that personal transformation or professional change has come to an end, but that their dynamics operate differently than traditional accounts allow.

ASSESSING READING PRACTICES: FROM NEW CRITICISM TO POSTSTRUCTURALISM TO CULTURAL STUDIES

It would be remiss of me in this theory retrospective not to spell out and assess the protocols and procedures involved in the different theories of interpretation advocated by New Criticism, poststructuralism, and cultural studies, respectively. This is the heart of the matter, the scene of instruction for several generations, and I like other academic literary intellectuals have had much to argue about regarding the formations and transformations of advanced reading practices during the past three decades.[5] As I portray and evaluate each of the three modes of interpretation, I am working from my experience of these professional paradigms. Critical methods are recipes for personal performance that tend toward ritualization, which is what I mainly expound upon here, although I do not mean to discount the innumerable singularities, innovations, and inspired eccentricities characteristic of much exegesis. The breakdown of method provides its own rewards. When it tends toward heuristics rather than dogmatism, method attains its best form.

To interpret as a New Critic—to revisit this primal scene one more time—is to demonstrate by means of multiple rereadings and retrospective analyses of short individual canonical poetic texts the intricacy of highly wrought artistic forms, whose meanings consist not in extractable propositions or paraphrasable contents, but in exquisitely orchestrated textual connotations, tones, images, and symbols, intrinsic to the literary work itself preconceived as an autonomous and unified, dramatic artifact separate from the lives of the author and reader as well as from the work's sociohistorical milieu and its everyday language. In order to display the complex equilibrium, special economy, and internal purposiveness of the well-wrought verbal icon (i.e., the ideal literary work), the New Critic invariably takes recourse in paradox, ambiguity, and irony, which are pragmatic rhetorical instruments used to harmonize any and all textual incongruities so as to ensure aesthetic unity, the endpoint and goal of analysis.

There is, of course, a lot to criticize in this dense and powerful mid-century reading formation still referred to honorifically as both "practical criticism" and "close reading." This type of textual explication remains for many critics not only a valuable norm, but, even for its professed enemies, a main method of classroom teaching and professional demonstration. For the record, it dogmatically rules out or just plain ignores so much, including most notably personal response, social and historical context, ethical and political critique, institutional analysis, and "meaning." It devalues the experience of reading, that is, the special unfolding and risky temporal flow, by calling for multiple retrospective analyses in the search for mandatory textual unity and spatial form through which means literature gets turned into impersonal sculpture, icon or urn, freestanding and monumentalized, meriting thereby critical adulation and special treatment. Let me recall, however, that the mid-century threats of ascendant academic science and social science, in part, prompted this severe sacralization of literature into a distinctive and miraculous discourse worthy of its own special department of study. And the politicization of literature by left- and right-wing governments during the 1930s earlier encouraged the trend to depoliticized formalist aesthetic theory.

It was, and was not, easy to call into question the widely successful reading practices and enabling presuppositions of New Critical formalism, which molded several loyal generations of readers, yet poststructuralists developed new points of departure and procedures that had successful impact on large numbers of university literary intellectuals, though not many undergraduate students. To read as a literary poststructuralist is to construct patterns out of the diffuse materials in a text and to impose meaning. Insofar as texts allow a wide range of possible meanings, they are, to recite the jargon yet again, "unreadable"; that is, they are not by nature explicable through a single masterful or totalizing interpretation. Given the considerable extent to which elements in a text are subject to free play, there can never be for poststructuralists a single correct reading, nor an interpretation that uncovers the original meaning of a text, nor an account that contains all the potential readings. As a result, all reading is misreading, although one misreading is stronger than another to the degree that it prompts subsequent counterreadings. Characteristically, poststructuralists of this kind focus on and privilege textual loose ends, contradictions, incompatibilities, discontinuities, gaps, and elusive rhetorical tropes. In addition, they observe that an interpretation of a text is itself not the text, but rather another separate later text, an assemblage, a paraphrase, a belated allegory. This deconstructive-style reading is for poststructuralists not, as is often thought, a case of undermining the stability, unity, or referential meaning of a text, but of demonstrating the inherent instability, heterogeneity, and referential aberration characteristic of language itself as well as its historical system of concepts. Poststructuralists, especially those influenced by Derrida, are particularly dedicated to demonstrating disorders and reversals in conceptual systems, putting on display the dependence of classical systems of concepts upon intertexts composed of prior linguistic conventions and cultural codes, which when aggregated overflow the much more strategically limiting traditional idea of context. An obvious anarchistic temper characterizes such poststructuralist reading, especially noticeable in its celebrations of randomness, unreadability, infinite abysses, and undecidable concepts.

The poststructuralist reading I have been talking about stemmed, of course, from the members of the Yale school (unquestionably the dominant poststructuralist group in the United States, if not elsewhere) who followed Derrida, but who were eventually challenged successfully by more politically oriented followers of Foucault and of French feminists (Julia Kristeva, Luce Irigaray, Hélène Cixous). My point is the various branches of poststructuralism went different ways relatively early in their development.[6] And while the Derridean–Yale line was and is highly influential among literary critics, the feminist and Foucaultian lines function as seminal elements for cultural studies groups.

The influential poststructuralist reading practices I have described merit, and have received, much criticism, the highlights of which I summarize here. To its discredit, the Yale-style of deconstruction shares much with earlier New Criticism. It favors canonical literary texts, keeping alive the habit of worshipping Great Books and especially dense modern texts to the exclusion of most other discourse. It prefers to focus on the text itself, discounting the author, reader, and milieu. It furthers the New Critical attenuations of literary "meaning" and linguistic reference in stressing textual free play, randomness, and undecidability. Reminiscent of its forebear, it privileges exacting explication, multiple retrospective reading, and rhetorical analysis of figurative language. It systematically avoids social and political subject matter, skirting institutional, ideological, and cultural critique. These compatibilities account in part for how it happened that poststructuralism was so quickly accommodated by literary critics. And yet it differs dramatically and decisively from New Criticism in its preoccupation not with unity but with heterogeneity and distortion, that is, with discontinuity, difference, incompatibility, and contradiction. In addition, poststructuralism proudly affiliates itself with such hostile critics of the Western humanist tradition as Friedrich Nietzsche, Martin Heidegger, and Sigmund Freud, all of whom were ignored, if not deplored, by New Critics. The poststructuralists' various emphases on misreading, on criticism as itself narrative text, and on the deconstructive transformation of once stable conceptual systems provoke widespread angry responses. This is also the case with the poststructuralist conception of the intertext as simultaneously (1) an inescapable and determining archive of historical materials and forces, and (2) an unlimited hodgepodge of sources, conscious and unconscious, infiltrating and disrupting all stable discourse. This radical formulation of the intertext ruins the cherished idea of the artist as a supremely conscious artificer, and it undermines the received notion of context, thereby disabling normative historical criticism.

To read as a practitioner of cultural studies, to complete this triangular account, is to employ a wide array of methods (often inspired by current literary studies and especially by sociology), including surveys, interviews, background inquiries, ethnographic descriptions, participant observations, discourse analyses, close readings, and institutional and ideological critiques. With each of its objects of inquiry, such cultural studies typically attends to the fundamental circuits of production, distribution, and consumption through which means it sets all objects inside cultural flows where occur formative processes of commodification, routinization, cooption, and hegemony as well as countervailing forces of resistance and subversion. By design, the analyst is located within, not outside or above, the circuits of culture, enmeshed in everyday life, and also positioned to assist coalitions involved in counterhegemonic activity. Opposed specifically to the aestheticism, formalism, and quietism of much contemporary literary criticism, cultural studies generally opposes reigning establishments, reflecting its roots in left social criticism. In particular, it castigates the isolation, monumentalization, and sacralization of the arts propounded by the arts and humanities disciplines, seeking instead to scrutinize and assess social foundations, institutional parameters, and ideological effects. It prefers to examine not elite genres and canonical works, but common culture and popular forms. Among the many objects it finds valuable to study are pop and underground music; youth subcultures; fashion;

shopping malls; popular dance; movies; advertising; gossip; race, class, and gender codes; magazines; television; working-class, minority, and postcolonial literatures; and popular literary genres (i.e., romances, thrillers, westerns, and gothic and science fiction). Potentially, the whole spectrum of cultural objects, practices, and discourses of a society provide materials for cultural studies. In its more self-reflexive moments, cultural studies also concerns itself with the social and political responsibilities of intellectuals; the political uses of education and literacy; the functions of institutions, especially the state and the media as well as the schools; the status of low and mass culture in the context of globalization; and the nexus of knowledge–interest–power.

There is much to question in the reading practices of cultural studies, which a considerable body of negative criticism makes clear. One major complaint singles out its politicization of method and subject matter: cultural studies makes ideological analysis compulsory, and it gravitates toward only certain kinds of discourse based on oppositional status and class affinities. Many of its materials and methods belong to sociology, having little to do with textual analysis or literary study. It is generally hostile to capitalism and market societies, siding with critics and opponents and celebrating resistance, subversion, and counterhegemonic activity. It renounces scholarly objectivity in favor of engaged activism. It largely ignores the great traditions and books of Western culture. It seems captive to social trends and fashions, attending to the latest television shows, ads, rock tunes, women's magazines, or romance novels. It is overly ambitious, even imperialistic, in the range and scope of its objects of inquiry. In its choice of educational materials and methods, it politicizes classroom teaching, engaging in indoctrination. Although it seeks a place in the university, it is critical of disciplinarity, departmentalization, and professionalization, making it antagonistic to the institution.

I have my own personal complaints about cultural studies. Its obsession with cooptation betrays a merely rebellious sensibility much too prepared to despair. A richer and more modulated account of cultural resistance is needed to accommodate innumerable types of life-enhancing activity. I am against academic loyalty oaths and mandatory political programs, believing the business of criticism is ultimately incompatible with party lines.[7] (I hasten to add that I have never complained about "political correctness.") However much aesthetics gets entangled with political economy and ethics, there is a demonstrable aesthetic dimension to cultural artifacts, which cultural studies risks ignoring. Cultural studies helpfully demystifies etherealized culture by insisting on underlying processes of commodification and hegemony, but frequently mystifies subcultural, countercultural, and minority resistance by exaggerating both their real impact and their compensatory symbolic significance. Elsewhere I have criticized the all-important Birmingham model of cultural circuits, arguing that production itself partakes of consumption and distribution: the result being that there is no justification for automatically assigning methodological priority to production, ironically a move characteristic of capitalist societies, which, furthermore, is out of step with capitalism in its consumer stage.[8] I end this critique of cultural studies with several admonitions for U.S. departmental colleagues everywhere that bear on the future of cultural studies: first, not everything is cultural studies; second, cultural studies' willingness now to incorporate all manner of historical scholarship is shortsightedly generous; and third, to appear paradoxical, the success of cultural studies should not require its too hasty and limited enclosure.

In its defense, I would observe that cultural studies, even when viewed from the dominant academic liberal perspective, offers life-enhancing balance to the rigidified and lopsided status quo operating in many places. For instance, it adds to the study of accredited aristocratic and middle-class "literatures" discourses of other classes and groups, which tend to be either ignored or denigrated. In doing so, it usefully highlights the different values, interests, and self-representations characteristic of these contending texts. (Incidentally, there is nothing in the tenets of cultural studies that excludes close reading of language or deconstructive analysis of conceptual systems—quite the contrary.) Its self-conscious promotion of critiques of capitalist societies is more than matched by the ubiquitous, largely unconscious affirmations of commodity culture, which is widely presumed to be an innocent eternal form of nature rather than a historical formation of recent centuries. If the job of criticism is criticism and not just silent approval of the status quo, then cultural studies is doing the job, however uncomfortable that may sometimes be. Admittedly, one tires of hearing about resistance, subversion, and counterhegemonic strategies, but then one grows weary also of being astonished at literary language, types of irony, textual unity, and heterogeneity. The claim that cultural studies engages in classroom indoctrination does not hold up, if only because a moment's thought shows that there is no undoctrinaire teaching. In my judgment, the scholarly focus of cultural studies on contemporary popular culture predictably and poignantly reflects the changing dynamics of postmodern mass society with its symptomatic new types of art and entertainment that antiquate older forms.

To close off this brief defense, the university has an obligation not just to study contemporary cultural discourse, according it as much support and prestige as the study of historical documents, but also to encourage the creation of new disciplines and departments, something that has not happened on a wide scale in decades.

THEORY CONSOLIDATED: DEFENSIVE MOVES

When in the mid-1990s I signed on as general editor of *The Norton Anthology of Theory and Criticism* (2001), I did so primarily in order to consolidate in a durable way and with maximum impact the many changes in the field of criticism and theory during recent decades. The way I see it, "theory" has gone through four recognizable stages during its contemporary development: rise of theory in the 1960s and 1970s, triumph of high or grand theory in the 1980s, posttheory in the 1990s, and now at the onset of the millenium "consolidation."[9] It is this last-named phenomenon that I address in these closing remarks.

I am, I confess, a staunch advocate of theory. And I admit that *The Norton Anthology of Theory and Criticism* establishes a theory canon, and that it, indeed, aims to do so. For me this canonizing project represents, in considerable part, a defensive move to conserve vital recent gains, to ensure the ongoing dissemination of theory, and to encourage the resultant transformation of literature programs and departments.

It is worth recalling that until the late 1970s and mid-1980s, depending on where you were located, graduate students could not specialize in criticism and theory. Only in a few select departments of comparative literature was it a recognized area of specialization. Before, say, 1975, there were almost no programs in this field. It would have been considered both odd as well as highly risky to study theory as a primary or secondary area of research and scholarship. This explains the special importance for my generation, the postwar "boomers," of such key institutions as the School of Criticism and Theory, opened in 1976; the Society for Critical Exchange, established that same year; the International Summer Institute for Semiotic and Structural Studies, started in 1980; and numerous National Endowment for the Humanities Summer Seminars on theory between the mid-'70s and mid-'80s (the years before the advent of the right-wing Culture Wars during the Reagan era and the resulting increased political surveillance of the NEH). These were recognized and respected meeting and training grounds for theorists, who at that time frequently had little or no formal training in the field. They were life savers for many theorists; I can personally testify to that. I summon up this background information from several decades ago in order to illuminate a large part of my motivation (and perhaps that of the other baby-boomer editors involved in the Norton anthology project): although theory has lately "triumphed," it is more certain to be here to stay with a substantial anthology and the accompanying imprimatur from W. W. Norton, the granddaddy of university textbook publishers.

I cannot recite here the contents of this comprehensive theory anthology, but briefly it covers the field from the pre-Socratics to the present with improvements over similar texts, notably in medieval theory, the history of women's criticism, and contemporary theory. I picture this anthology as something like a rainbow coalition, a tessellation of pieces in a polycultural mosaic and, as such, an example of postmodern disaggregation at the level of the university textbook.

A key part of the background for the project of theory consolidation is, of course, the Culture Wars started in the 1980s during the Reagan administration and reenergized with the conservative restoration represented by the election in 2000 of George W. Bush. Conservative attacks on theory and on "political correctness," that is, race, class, and gender sensitivity and analysis, often explicitly deplore the importation of foreign thought and philosophy, the academic study of popular culture, and the purported shift from literature to theory. So, for example, from the outset I persuaded W. W. Norton to include in the anthology a large-scale heavily annotated bibliography of the field and a wide-ranging subject index, feeling very much that I was engaged in a defensive project of consolidation as well as dignification. I could detail other features of the anthology that are explicitly designed as defensive consolidating operations, but I desist here, taking up this matter later in chapters 5 through 7. My first hope was, and remains, that anyone examining the anthology will conclude that there is no going back to some pre- or nontheoretical literary study.

It is my sense that U.S. culture broadly construed has been entering a phase of consolidation, a protective shoring up and display of strength, accompanied by an aggressive outreach campaign which, by my reckoning, predates the 2001 attack on the World Trade Center but has been made more evident by it. But perhaps not. In any event, my ruminations and speculations in this chapter have not pretended to be rigorous historical analysis, but rather testimony to some of what I have learned during three decades inside academic literary life.

2

THEORY FAVORITES

SEVERAL YEARS AFTER IT WAS PUBLISHED, an editor began encouraging me to do a follow-up to my book *American Literary Criticism from the 1930s to the 1980s* (1988), which during the subsequent decade sold about 10,000 copies, was translated into several languages, and garnered good reviews and a *Choice* award. From time to time I would contemplate two versions of such a sequel. The first, "After Theory: Criticism since the 1980s," envisaged a panoramic critical history of the major schools and movements of that energetic time with separate chapters on new historicism, postcolonial criticism, cultural studies, queer theory, personal criticism, and globalization studies, supplemented with several brief interchapters, one on the Culture Wars and professional guilds (left- and right-wing),[1] others on changes in publishing and the downsizing of the university, and a final one on the reconfiguration of the discipline. On and off, I contemplated additional interchapters about religious criticism, separatist race and ethnicity studies, the return of belletrism, the rise of the public intellectual, and the ubiquitous phenomenon of crossover and hybrid approaches. My thesis concerning the disorganization of criticism during the postmodern period would have taken the form of a refusal to propound a single theme or moral to cover the disaggregation characteristic of the times. The second sequel, "The Theoretical Discourse of Postmodern Criticism," envisioned reconsiderations and critiques of twelve or so often-cited and -taught classics of theory published after 1968, which I divide for convenience into thematic clusters: (1) Diagnosing Postmodern Culture—Jean Baudrillard's *Simulations*, Dick Hebdige's

Subculture, and Fredric Jameson's *Postmodernism, or the Cultural Logic of Late Capitalism*; (2) Reconceptualizing Literature—Julia Kristeva's *Revolution in Poetic Language*, Jacques Derrida's *Dissemination*, Roland Barthes's *S/Z*, Harold Bloom's *The Anxiety of Influence*, Paul de Man's *Allegories of Reading*, and Houston A. Baker Jr.'s *Blues, Ideology, and Afro-American Literature*; and (3) Critiquing Institutions—Gilles Deleuze and Félix Guattari's *Anti-Oedipus*, Michel Foucault's *Discipline and Punish*, Edward Said's *Orientalism*, and Judith Butler's *Gender Trouble*. Other texts I considered, but set aside, included, for instance, Frantz Fanon's *The Wretched of the Earth* (too early); Fredric Jameson's *The Political Unconscious* (one too many books by him); and Elaine Showalter's collection *The New Feminist Criticism* (a miscellany). Conceived initially as an introduction for students and as an antidote to a schools-and-movements narrative of contemporary criticism,[2] this proposed book kept worrying me on several counts: for example, it excluded miscellanies, textbooks, and collections (such as the *Heath Anthology of American Literature* and Lawrence Grossberg et al.'s proceedings *Cultural Studies*);[3] it dismissed poet-critics, literary journalists, and independent nonacademic critics; and, of course, it enthroned great works. As it happened, I signed up in the mid-1990s to be the general editor of *The Norton Anthology of Theory and Criticism* (2001), which took six years to complete, keeping me from other major projects. But an editor at Routledge continues to work with me on a followup, and I am in the process of coauthoring that along with Jeffrey J. Williams.

It is in this context that the editor of *Genre: Forms of Discourse and Culture* invited me, along with other critical theorists, to contribute to a 2000 special "Desert Island" issue of the journal then recently under new editorship. This invitation provocatively asked: "If you were marooned on a desert island with only a single contemporary critical text with which to work, which text would you choose and why?" It adds that this text must have been published or translated since 1966 and can be historical, interpretive, or theoretical; it can be a book, anthology, article, or other text. Criteria might include texts that are well-established or under-appreciated, foundational of a school or trend, or idiosyncratic, productive of imitators or strong misreadings. In the end, this task compelled me to single out my contemporary theory favorites.

* * *

When I first received the invitation for the "Desert Island" project, I had two immediate reactions: one practical, one theoretical. The practical took the form of mulling over what one text I would choose, which sent me to my notes for the work I had been contemplating on classic contemporary theory books. From that list I would pick Foucault's *Discipline and Punish*, although two decades earlier I would probably have selected Derrida's *Dissemination*. As have many academic literary intellectuals of the baby boom generation, I have moved over the years from formalism to deconstruction and poststructuralism to cultural studies, as I explained in chapter 1. Foucault is a key figure for such a trajectory, and *Discipline and Punish* is arguably *the* poststructuralist book by Foucault that best traces the transition from discourse analysis to cultural critique. This book has been broadly influential, having an impact on new historicism, queer theory, postcolonial criticism, and cultural studies. Three decades after its publication it reads well, remaining a rich and provocative text to teach in both undergraduate and graduate classrooms. It has contributed an array of indispensable concepts to cultural criticism: docile body, panopticism, the power–knowledge nexus, disciplinary institutions, the carceral, and the "disciplines" (i.e., such mechanisms of control as visibility, examinations, exercises, norms, and records). It contains productive problematics to grapple with such as its treatments of class, subjectivity, contract theory, reform, unequal development, illegality, and resistance. It is well designed and powerfully styled, as the opening depiction of the drawn-and-quartered body famously displays; and it is dotted with sentences like "Visibility is a trap."[4] (There are too few beautiful sentences written by contemporary theorists.) Most notably, *Discipline and Punish* offers an unforgettable genealogical account of modernity and the grim legacies of the Enlightenment.

My most immediate theoretical reaction to the Desert Island project took the form of questioning some of its accompanying concepts and presuppositions. On the mythical Desert Island, am I alone? (What does "alone" mean?) If so, why? If not, who are the others? Should I conceive this place classically as nature versus culture? What might a contemporary theory text be doing in such a setting? Why a single text? What is a text? Would one want, in order to while away the hours, a limit-text such as *Finnegans Wake* or, indeed, *Dissemination*? Maybe a more relevant work, say, *Anti-Oedipus*? Or perhaps a book for escape such as *S/Z* or *Simulations*? Possibly something on the order of *Subculture* to reminisce with? Or something to cater to a sour grapes mentality, *The Anxiety of Influence*? An examination of human errancy such as *Allegories of Reading*? What is one looking for? How long is one on the island?

I reconsidered and thought I would return to the practical approach, only focusing not on a text I admired greatly, but on one I disliked, and liked to dislike, such as Harold Bloom's *The Anxiety of Influence*. In my reading, this book makes a powerful indictment of modernity, but it seems desperately blind that it is doing so. Bloom's celebrated argument that Anglo-American lyric poetry from John Milton to Wallace Stevens simultaneously traces a devolution in quality and power and a dramatic upsurge in baleful poetic influence steadfastly refuses to consider the social and economic changes affecting lyric poets during the Romantic epoch (dated by him 1760 to 1960, the same period studied by Foucault). Without saying so, Bloom closes off the Romantic era, picturing it nostalgically in a heroic and tragic mode as a time of doomed and belated fading lights, with John Ashbery the last and the least of the great lyric poets. According to Bloom, "True poetic history is the story of how poets as poets have suffered other poets . . .";[5] and "art is the index of men born too late. Not the dialectic between art and society, but the dialectic between art and art . . ." (99). Here are art for art's sake and romantic psychobiography in their starkest forms. Bloom outrageously and programmatically neglects to link the growing sense of competition among major poets with the increasing competition permeating society. He does not consider for a moment eroding patronage or the economic position of lyric poetry in an expanding market-based, carceral society. As is well-known, there are no people of color, women, or minor ("weak") poets, but only "strong poets" in Bloom's true poetic history, a severe form of literary Darwinism and Great White Father cultural history. A summary indictment of Bloom would include such sins as aestheticism, bardolotry, Great Traditionalism, psychologism, and ahistoricism. Like Foucault, Bloom is melancholic, seeing no escape, except in his case for the few and fit Great Men of poetry.

What makes *The Anxiety of Influence* still worth rereading and teaching are not just its provocative sins and flagrant problems, but its aphoristic style, maverick mentality, inventive concepts, and experimental design (no notes, bibliography, or index plus a verse prologue and epilogue and also a wild little critical manifesto as an interchapter). Among the most inventive concepts are misprision/misreading as inescapable, the famous six revisionary ratios or stages of poetic development (an unselfconscious suggestive account of pastiche in its postmodern form), the notion of the precursor poet as a composite figure not necessarily read, and the phenomenon of apophrades (Bloom's sixth ratio, the uncanny sense in reading an earlier poet that a later master (and imitator) poet had written his characteristic work. As do his own most inventive precursors Northrop Frye and Kenneth Burke, Bloom revels in quirky terminology and ambitious structural charts, yet where he swerves from them is not only in his severely contracted view of literary history, but in his vehement Nietzschean antihumanism (a sobering trait): "the imagination's gift comes necessarily from the perversity of the spirit" (85), and "The strong imagination comes to its painful birth through savagery and misrepresentation" (86).

Because there would be no tranquillity on this island if I were holed up there for a long time with only Bloom's masterpiece, I began to think about more consoling texts, ones that had had a dramatic, yet more "positive" impact on my views. I found myself with a list of a dozen or so extremely heterogeneous items spread out over several decades: texts I had studied as a student; ones I came across doing research; others I encountered first in teaching; some recommended to me; books, collections, articles, manifestos, even a memo. Of these, two were classics that helped me early on get past formalism and its obsessive focus on individual works, Northrop Frye's *Anatomy of Criticism* and J. Hillis Miller's *Poets of Reality*. From the latter I first learned ways to write interestingly about an author's complete output that are still with me today; the former assisted me during my master's comprehensive examination to conceptualize Western literature as a complex orderly system like the Periodic Table of Elements in chemistry. Addison Gayle, Jr.'s edited collection of short pieces by many hands, *The Black Aesthetic*, opened my eyes poignantly to white racism in its many facets, especially the essays by Hoyt W. Fuller, Jr. and Mulana Karanga on the nationalist idea of, and social realities prompting, a black aesthetic. Later I would come upon Ngugi wa Thiong'o et al.'s "On the Abolition of the English Department,"[6] a powerful five-page memo on reconfiguring both "literature" and academic literary studies as a consequence of European racism and colonialism. Having first read both of these next two classics together for a chapter I was writing on U.S. feminism, I experienced Elaine Showalter's *A Literature of Their Own* and Sandra M. Gilbert and Susan Gubar's *The Madwoman in the Attic* as revelations: they offered admirably detailed, moving histories of women's literary subcultures whose productions challenged the canon and demonstrated unequivocally the existence of a historical feminine aesthetic. I especially admired Showalter's laying out three (really four) phases of development in British women's literature during the nineteenth and twentieth centuries,[7] and Gilbert and Gubar's innovative and daring counter-concept to Harold Bloom of the female "anxiety of authorship," as well as their documentation of literary women's historical illnesses: "patriarchal socialization makes women sick, both physically and mentally."[8]

The positive influence on me in the 1980s of Mikhail Bakhtin's "Discourse in the Novel" has made this text extremely productive to build on and to teach. It helped me move from Derridean and Foucaultian poststructuralism to cultural studies. It played this role for many other people as well. There are a handful of contributions it made. It presented language as utterances of embodied speaking subjects—as "discourse"—not as impersonal, asocial, prevocal signifiers, tropes, or grammar. It characterized discourse as stratified and centrifugal, composed of distinct dialects, speech genres, special group languages (age groups, professional groups, class groups, etc.). It portrayed these contending linguistic strata explicitly as social and ideological phenomena. It depicted literary language as only one of many strata that itself is divided by generic, stylistic, period, and other distinctive markers. And it showed the utterances of the individual framed by the discourse of society. This famous account of language as fundamentally dialogical and heteroglot has served poststructuralist-inflected cultural criticism in ways that the structuralist and poststructuralist concepts of arbitrary signifiers and self-canceling tropes could not, opening onto issues of social class, the body, multiple subject positions, and literary discourse and ideology.

There are, of course, problems with Bakhtin's as well as these other "positive" works, which are too numerous to catalogue in detail, but I single out here the major difficulties. Theorists are in the business of isolating problems, so I do not wish to skirt this aspect of my job here or elsewhere. Frye's notions of literature as a coherent closed system rooted in universal archetypes and of the famous four *mythoi* (romance, tragedy, irony, comedy) constituting a central unifying quest-myth have the oppressive effect of reducing individual works, genres, and periods to insignificance. And, to be sure, his "universal" poetics turns out to be unself-critically Eurocentric. Phenomenological criticism like Hillis Miller's is arguably most vexing in doggedly seeking a single unified, coherent voice (or consciousness) in its authors' works. (It's very unBakhtinian in that sense.) It programmatically renounces critique in favor of textual cocelebration with the author and blithely disregards the forces of history and the author's time. The project of a black aesthetic, articulated variously by Gayle, Fuller, Karenga, and others, runs into serious troubles with its reliance on racial essentialism ("blackness") and with the concept of the nation (the unified black nation). And too, this enterprise is notoriously sexist and heterosexist. The main limitation of contemporary first-generation Anglo-American feminism, which is manifested variously in Showalter and in Gilbert and Gubar, is its focus on middle-class white women to the exclusion of women of color and of other classes. In addition, the idea of "women's experience" tends to conceive "experience" too simply, discounting multiple differences, contending conventions and histories, conflicting interpretive standpoints, and discursive slippages and generalizations. A serious weak point for me of Bakhtin's work is the systematic denigration of poetry, which he positions at the opposite end of a spectrum from the novel. A stark set of binary concepts undergirds his view: novel/poetry, dialogue/monologue, real/artificial, decentralization/centralization, heteroglot/hermetic. As a lover of the Whitman tradition of American verse, I find this whole spectrum and its attendant concepts counterintuitive and wrong-headed. The celebration of the novel need not be at the expense of poetry.

There are several contemporary texts that have been positively important to me as a teacher, but I am not sure I should be thinking of them for my Desert Island sojourn. What irritates me, in this context, about the hypothesis of being marooned on an island is its deliberate foreclosure on community. Why this fantasy? Do I want to play along? I would prefer to imagine others, at least a few, tossed up in this place, ones who enter into dialogue, ruminating on society, education, the arts, and literature. (All of us would no doubt entertain fantasies of escaping the island.) I recall Lionel Trilling's grim judgment, "pedagogy is a depressing subject to all persons of sensibility,"[9] and I find now I very much disagree. Two books that have assisted me in articulating some helpful perspectives on pedagogy are Robert Scholes' *Textual Power* and Stanley Aronowitz and Henry Giroux's coauthored *Postmodern Education*.

Scholes usefully proposes a "professional unconscious" that contains an archetype of English studies, an arche-department, a repository of disciplinary conventions, practices, and values embedded in all members of the profession, which inventive concept importantly opens theory and teaching onto institutional analysis and critique. In addition, he distinguishes "reading" (literary explication) and "interpretation" (exegesis and textual puzzle solving) from "criticism" (evaluation and cultural critique). Of the latter, he suggestively observes "criticism is always made on behalf of a group."[10] Indeed, it is so, though I had never formulated it in so striking a way. The main problem I have with Scholes is his ignoring institutional history and genealogy in his rush to handle today's challenges, and his misleading idea that we should teach reading, interpretation, and criticism sequentially rather than simultaneously. In the name of sound pedagogy, let us not once again privilege literary explication over cultural critique. Scholes gains my admiration for steadfastly conceiving students as literate citizens in a media-saturated democratic society. Insofar as schools are hegemonic institutions that reproduce corporate ideology, students, especially "subaltern students" (poor, working-class, of color, and women), are not so much empowered as rendered docile citizens; that is a key point of Aronowitz and Giroux's book. Conceived heroically by them as public intellectuals, teachers must work against the grain to extend democracy by opening literacy beyond the Great Books to both popular culture and media analysis and critique, ways of fostering critical citizenship and promoting multiple literacies. What most bothers me, however, is that Aronowitz and Giroux ironically end up playing the venerable unpostmodern role of leading intellectuals, herding the multifarious downtrodden—their "subalterns"—into an unreal collective body. Yet they, like Scholes, persuasively make the case that students should critically evaluate mass media and popular culture as well as canonical literature; question norms, misrepresentations, and the unsaid; and discover alternatives and invent counternarratives to the status quo. Beyond Scholes, they advocate critical analysis of capitalism, patriarchy, and imperialism, political formations that literature teachers today are obliged to study and criticize given ongoing processes of globalization, the New World Order, empire formation, and wars on terrorism.

To bring closure to this account of positive texts, let me cite two powerful texts that influenced me during the 1990s, *New Times: The Changing Face of Politics in the 1990s*, edited by Stuart Hall and Martin Jacques, and Donna Haraway's celebrated "Manifesto for Cyborgs." Most of the nearly three dozen short essays in *New Times*, reprinted from a pair of earlier issues on "New Times" of *Marxism Today* (1988; 1989), explore the proposition that the late twentieth-century onset of post-Fordist, postindustrial economics signals an epochal transition in global culture. Of the half-dozen pieces that really crystallized my thinking on this topic, one in particular stands out, John Urry's "The End of Organised Capitalism," which is a succinct profile of modern organized Fordist capitalism and its aftermath in the disorganization of post-Fordism. It is a striking synopsis and postscript to Scott Lash and John Urry's *The End of Organized Capitalism* (1987), a full-length history and set of case studies of modern/postmodern economics and culture in France, Germany, Sweden, the United Kingdom, and the United States. In this synoptic essay of ten pages, I was struck by a handful of observations on political economy today, especially concerning changing class and cultural politics.

First, some observations related to class politics. The era of big government, big business, and big labor characteristic of the opening two-thirds of the twentieth century has in recent decades mutated into a period of comparatively minimal government; plus decentralized, small business forms such as franchising, subcontracting, small-batch production, and temporary workers; and an increasingly reactionary workforce that aims "to preserve or even return to outmoded patterns of industry, technology and values."[11] This last is what I call the Archie Bunker problem, namely, the working class projected not as revolutionary proletariat, but as reactionary hard hats. For people like me working on the left, this represents a moment of crisis, of partial disidentification with and loss of hope for the working class. From the 1960s onwards, progressive and innovative politics have noticeably shifted to the new social movements, a disorganized array of feminists, civil rights groups, radical environmentalists, gay and lesbian rights activists, antinuclear campaigners, Third World militants, animal rights activists, and anti-WTO and -IMF people. In chapter 9 I label them "Lilliputians." Within the context of such micropolitics, (working) class politics does not automatically represent the vanguard of political progress. And insofar as one occupies multiple changing subject positions at home, at work, at play, and in the marketplace, class allegiance is only one element of a fractured, complex political identity.

Second, Urry notes that popular culture as propounded especially on TV, in pop music, at the cinema, and in fashion displays strong opposition to authority, a mixed blessing since *all* modes of centralization and collectivity from government, the police, and political parties to schools and unions have come under suspicion in a culture promoting radical individualism and calculating hedonism. Incidentally, the best diagnosis of the ambiguities, weak points, and contradictions of popular culture appear, I believe, in the Chicago-based *Baffler* magazine whose finest pieces from the early issues are collected in *Commodify Your Dissent* (1997), edited by Thomas Frank and Matt Weiland, a wonderful set of articles to teach because it offers students an insider's view of pop culture with unrelenting critical eyes and biting humor from a rambunctious left libertarian perspective. The main problem with Urry (and the *Baffler* group as well) is not knowing what is to be done: so much hand-wringing and so little problem-solving. When Urry grandly sums up, "The structures of contemporary capitalism have thus been transformed by three simultaneous processes: of *globalization* from above, of *decentralisation* from below, and of *disintegration* from within . . ." (101), one wants immediately to assent, but then ask what shall we do. Unintentionally, Urry's magisterial observation provides an intriguing depiction of the newly "reengineered" postmodern university, and one wants perhaps all the more to hear of remedies. But perhaps there are none.

The most unforgettable passage for me in a manifesto sprinkled with such passages is the paragraph where Donna Haraway schematizes the three different forms that the family has taken during the past two centuries. The framework here derives explicitly from Fredric

Jameson's three stages of capitalism—commercial and early industrial; monopoly; consumer and multinational—which he ties explicitly to changing political and aesthetic forms, namely nationalism, imperialism, and multinationalism and realism, modernism, and postmodernism. The three forms of the family, in Haraway's account, are:

> (1) the patriarchal nuclear family, structured by the dichotomy between public and private and accompanied by the white bourgeois ideology of separate spheres and nineteenth-century Anglo-American bourgeois feminism; (2) the modern family mediated (or enforced) by the welfare state and institutions like the family wage, with a flowering of afeminist heterosexual ideologies, including their radical versions represented in Greenwich Village around World War I; and (3) the "family" of the homework economy with its oxymoronic structure of women-headed households and its explosion of feminism and the paradoxical intensification and erosion of gender itself.[12]

To simplify, I would reduce this conspectus to extended family, nuclear family, and single-headed household (with serial monogamy). What is striking here is less that the family is a social construct with a history than that the family form is linked with economic, political, and aesthetic forms. Haraway productively conjoins orthodox Marxian theories of ideology, of the successive modes of production, and of the dialectic, but qualified by the more recent Marxist concept of unequal development. "I would argue," she declares, "that specific forms of families dialectically related to forms of capital and to its political and cultural concomitants. Although lived problematically and unequally, ideal forms of these families might be schematized as . . ." (207). There follows the passage cited above describing the three forms.

On the one hand, I am enlightened by this map of modernity with its stages and forms. During recent decades the family form has mutated from the nuclear family into the single-headed household in an era of consumer and multinational capitalism and postmodern arts. Meanwhile, the old extended and nuclear family forms live on as residual entities. I can assent to this productive generalization. However, as a good poststructuralist, I feel incredulity toward Haraway's master narrative, which erases differences and singularities in a totalizing mode and which improbably speaks from the perspective of some known future (or *telos*). So here I adopt the twofold strategy developed by Aronowitz and Giroux: totalizing is heuristic; and we need "grand narratives" (not master narratives) of patriarchy and capitalism, as well as colonialism and racism and globalization, to make visible larger systems and to enable political transformation.[13] Haraway's model of the changing family forms is memorable largely because it brings grand theory and key crises of modernity convincingly into the home, including the living room, kitchen, and bedroom. For that I am grateful; it enables me to make sense in a broader historical and political context of my own experiences with "family."

* * *

The older generation of academic literary students and teachers coming up during the mid-twentieth century seem to have had a few key contemporary theory texts to cope with such as Cleanth Brook's *The Well Wrought Urn*, René Wellek and Austin Warren's *Theory of Literature*, or Northrop Frye's *Anatomy of Criticism*. Succeeding generations have faced an explosion and proliferation, which is no doubt a hallmark of our more advanced consumer culture. It thus appears nostalgic and old-fashioned to summon up a Desert Island where only one text is present. It is out of keeping with the times. My two lists of contemporary theory texts, each consisting of a baker's dozen, signal, I like to think, the breadth of the renaissance of theory in recent decades, and not, say, my inability to fulfill the assignment and winnow out the truly significant from the insignificant text.

Theory during postmodern times—even if one does not directly read it—has become at once so ubiquitous and multifaceted that we academics have almost all increasingly become critical pasticheurs mixing and matching heterogeneous strands into usable materials. This is what I call the "hybridization of theory," one part of which is the increasing number of "crossover texts" put together using a hodge-podge of approaches. One does not need to have directly read Derrida at all to have learned how to deconstruct binaries, or to have studied Foucault to analyze the mechanism of disciplines that render the modern subject docile, or to have examined any texts by feminist critics to detect unbalanced gender dynamics operating in a work. The most important "text" today is arguably this compound discourse channeled through many members of the academic community of literary intellectuals. My two baker's dozens of favorite texts select from this shared compound discourse, creating what, I have no doubt, is a somewhat quirky, personal mix. Still, what is most significant in this case is, I believe, the larger phenomenon of the contemporary archive of theory (or the professional unconscious, if you will) and less its innumerable customized forms and permutations. There is no way I can today occupy a Desert Island without bringing along this whole archive of hybridized theory, the postmodern professional unconscious.

3

THEORY FASHION

WHEN I BEGAN PUBLICLY IDENTIFYING MYSELF as a "theorist" back in the 1970s and regularly since then, I have experienced colleagues particularly in the humanities and social sciences as well as in literary studies asking me certain questions, such as "What's the next thing?"; "What's in today?"; and "How do you keep up?"[1] Any literary or cultural theorist will tell you that the comparison of theory with fashion is commonplace. And most theorists will admit that this comparison, whether earnest or lighthearted, is basically pernicious, however apparently flattering. The analogy insinuates that theory, unlike other disciplines, is unstable, ephemeral, and frivolous, and that it follows the rhythms of fads and related superficial media spectacles characteristic of our postmodern times. Let me explain my impatience with this matter as a way to map key aspects of the disorganization of contemporary theory and to clarify what I see as the renaissance of theory in our time.

Few card-carrying literary or cultural theorists construe it as a compliment when theory is compared, one way or another, with fashion. The comparison invariably disguises a wish to disarm theory or to make it disappear. The relations among theory, fashion, and the surrounding political economic order are much too entangled and complex for the theory fashion comparison to address adequately. If one seeks a rationale for the analogy, one might turn to the increasing aestheticization and the "becoming-fashion" of everyday life characteristic of our postmodern times. In any case the epochal scale of developments in "theory" during the recent decades is more on the order of a cultural renaissance than the expected seasonal changes in attire.

If we examine the fashion industry, we immediately encounter an array of defining features unrelated to theory. Among these are fashion's appeals to possessive individualism; its reliance on sweatshops; its broad use of dyestuffs and the resulting ecological destruction; its fascination with alluring physical commodities; its *planned* obsolescence.[2] Where fashion desires immediate acceptance and maximum profitability, theory aims at widespread dissemination and eventual triumph in the name of enhanced understanding, not increased profits. In all these instances, the breakdown of the theory fashion analogy underscores the incommensurability of fashion and theory, which possess their own distinctive materials, personnel, practices, histories, and dynamics.

Let me clarify what I mean by "theory." In its contemporary context "theory" refers to a body of texts, ancient and modern, concerned with poetics, interpretation, rhetoric, textual commentary, and models of culture. More recently, we have added to this list semiotics; media and discourse; race, class, and gender codes; and visual and popular culture. Yet "theory" also designates a mode of logical, skeptical, and judgmental inquiry. In recent times, theory, influenced by psychoanalysis, poststructuralism, and cultural studies, has added other dimensions, especially a "hermeneutics of suspicion," characterized by interest in ineradicable distortions and contradictions; distrust in common sense, social institutions, and hidden agendas; and preoccupation with linking up local phenomena to globalizing forces. That this "theory" has not provided a unifying method or disciplinary lingua franca has dismayed many people, including theorists.

The recent expansion and reconfiguration of theory, both as a body of texts and mode of inquiry, threatens some academics working in arts and humanities departments. In these circumstances, it evidently helps to think of theory as a passing fad, a mere fashion: here today, gone tomorrow. Theorists recognize that the kernel of this wish is hostile, whatever its outer coatings may be. To will theory to be fashion or like fashion is to want it, consciously or unconsciously, to pass away.

Many academics tend publicly to despise fashion, particularly haute couture and subculture styles as being superficial, costly, and narcissistic. Still, a moment's thought reveals there is no escaping fashion, not even by going naked or wearing rags. Whatever you are wearing (or not), it is part of the history of fashion, just maybe not the latest part. Chasing after the latest trend is what is especially despised, for only that which is lasting, permanent, and enduring is of true merit. Here we arrive at certain values, a conservative core, often motivating the hostile theory fashion comparison. The eternal truths of the Great Tradition constitute genuine value. From this perspective, the opposite of fashionable theory is the established canon of Great Books and philosophies. Moreover, the canons of proper attire tend in this realm toward the "classic" (as defined, of course, in our time). Self-adornment ought properly to take the form of respect for tradition, not a ceaseless pursuit of the "new," but a sober devotion to established conventions.

Not surprisingly, a certain amount of gender coding accompanies the theory fashion analogy. To be blunt about it, the analogy feminizes theory, placing it in opposition to more steady and serious, more macho, qualities.

Among themselves theorists recapitulate elements of this scenario, relying on the theory fashion analogy too. When, for example, new "trends" arise (instances in recent years might include, say, queer theory or body studies), theorists committed to preexisting models or movements sometimes react with what seems instinctive contempt for those "scurrying to the latest fad," which invariably appears outlandish and sure to fade. There is a flip side to this, namely the one-upmanship among certain theorists overjoyed to be catching the latest wave whatever it may be. In other words, some theorists themselves promulgate the theory fashion analogy, but they put a positive spin on it.

Despite some academics' expectations, theory has not emerged as a unifying terminology or method nor as a governor of professional practices. The opposite has occurred, that is, a division into many disparate and contending strands of theory. What is there, one wonders, in contemporary society that produces the disorganization of the disciplines, with theory being a severe instance? The most common answer is that in recent times a breakdown of master narratives and totalizing systems characterizes the postmodern condition in the West. As is well known, a panoply of analogies has been forwarded to account for the accelerating disciplinary changes and incommensurabilities common in the postmodern university: contending paradigms from physics, niche markets from commerce, species refuges from biology, chaotic systems from earth science, worldviews from history, currency markets from finance, and autonomy movements from political science. Just as we view the evening news on television with its rapid sequence of numerous disjunctive stories, we gaze upon the disciplines in disarray, and in both cases we are not surprised by disruptive patchiness, although we wish for common threads, some of us more than others. For those among us who tend toward paranoia, usually a small number, a conspiracy is clearly afoot in which the phalanxes of theorists out there are united in their trashing of cultural tradition, aesthetic value, critical independence, and common standards and methods. To the extent that theory has turned out not to provide a common thread and, even worse, to unstitch previous trustworthy materials, it is a disappointment and a menace.

But the premise that theory has begotten the division of literary intellectuals and humanists into disparate groups fails to take into account, at the very least, the new coalitions and realignments occurring especially in university-based journals, conferences, centers, institutes, and programs. Insofar as departments, the basic structural unit of most higher education, remain slow to change and resistant to overhauls, they impede the new formations, exacerbating the divisiveness and often becoming unhealthy zones of stress on this and other accounts. It is frequently left to the more "flexible" operations to deal expeditiously with change. As everyone knows, such entities fall prey, more readily than departments, to the theory fashion label.

It does not help that North American and Western European theory in recent years have been transplanted around the world, particularly into Asia and Central Europe, where numerous translations and visits have been made. Theory seems all the more fashionable, though perhaps not publicly enviable, for going global like Levi jeans or MTV. The commodification of theory, especially by commercial and university presses, has stirred up envy as well as incredulity among theorists and antitheorists, though obviously for different reasons. Because the world historical mission of Western capitalism and culture appears to be the commercialization of every nook and cranny of global space,[3] the university seems ever more destined to become business, which means the "new," the "different," and the "cutting-edge" as well as the "classic" will vie with one another in global educational marketplaces. The advertisements and blurbs for theory books will—and do—stress novelty, timeliness, and trendiness. Needless to say, many theorists are as bewildered by all this as anyone. In the New World Order, we are all recruits to markets in their transnational forms.

I admit the applicability, the limited applicability, of the theory fashion analogy. Compared to other periods, the pace of change in our time is accelerated. In addition, the rates and scope of change in contemporary theory evidently outpace those in other academic disciplines. Theory is changing at a rapid pace and bringing change to related fields. All this reminds people of fashion because, in modern times, fashion designers and houses mount new lines each season. But does theory, like fashion, change precisely each and every season? Does it outfit itself annually in four different sets of attire? Not at all. Here again, the theory fashion analogy breaks down, showing how tenuous is the link of theory to fashion.

We know there is a growing aestheticization of everyday existence across the globe that drags fashion along with it rather than fashion being the engine. Advertising and other visual media occupy the vanguard promoting a beautiful life. The "becoming-fashion" of many spheres of social life is part of this aestheticization typical of spreading consumer society, which proliferates choices and changes of all kinds. The logic of increasing product differentiation and innovation, as it affects disciplines in the university (including theory), may seem like a terrible giving in to superficial fashion, but it is something much larger that deserves to be properly named.

Still, I would not end this defense without observing that the changes in contemporary theory strike me, and others too, as a flowering equivalent to those that occurred in ancient Greece and in German Romanticism. Theory in postmodern times has become more sophisticated and more pluralistic thanks to psychoanalysis, poststructuralism, feminism, ethnic aesthetics, postcolonial criticism, queer theory, cultural studies, and the like. It is a serious category mistake to depict such significant epochal change as an instance of either the shifting market strategies of consumer capitalism or, worse yet, the seasonal comings and goings of mere fashion.

4

FRAMING THEORY

THERE ARE MANY WAYS TO "FRAME THEORY," as, for example, constructing
maps and models of the field; putting together packets, casebooks, and
anthologies of readings; compiling area bibliographies and reviews of research; writing histories of the discipline; composing glossaries of key
words; concocting syllabi, course descriptions, and pedagogical goals;
drawing up reading lists and exams; and producing specialized guides,
introductions, and handbooks. Each of these genres of scholarship engages in the work of framing. To be sure, there is always already, in Derridean terms, a play of frames in arbitrary and determinate relations with
one another. Invariably, frames turn out to involve linkages with matters
economic, social, political, and historical. When it comes to frames, there
are also questions not simply of inclusion and exclusion, concatenation
and configuration, but of privilege and prejudice, memory and amnesia,
highlights and blindspots, and profit and loss. Because the various academic forms of framing named above have separate histories and require
individual consideration, I limit the inquiry in this chapter to one: writing histories of literary theory, particularly of the contemporary period.
Given our present moment of restructuring and transformation, I believe in the merits of a disjunctive mix-and-match postmodern mode of
history writing, but I am getting ahead of myself.

* * *

To start, let me put forth a simple heuristic scheme. There are five
ways to construct histories of contemporary theory. One can focus on

leading figures, or key texts, or significant problems, or important schools and movements, or some mixture of the others. I comment very briefly on each of the four main modes of framing theory, mentioning strengths and weaknesses.

History of major figures scrutinizes the careers of a relatively few selected geniuses. Composed of a series of intellectual biographies, this kind of account suggests that cultural history and value are generated by gifted individuals whose special insights deserve care and reverence. It aggrandizes the concept of career and the associated idea of individual growth where the complete works afford evidence of decisive stages of development. Minor work can possess value in this context. Connections between and among luminaries may appear fortuitous or unimportant. In history as pantheon one is encouraged to admire. Not surprisingly, quotidian forms of theorizing don't register, and institutions seem vague backdrops.

One of the most salient features of the history of key texts is that it deemphasizes professional biography and preoccupation with complete works and lines of development. Also it opens space for outsiders such as, for instance, Martin Heidegger and Frantz Fanon, who work primarily in other domains, but who arguably have made significant contributions to literary and critical theory. History of theory here figures as a string of blockbusters, taking one's breath away. But as in a world-class art museum, the masterworks risk decontextualization. To counter this shortcoming, sequences must be fashioned, possessing at least minimal plot or sense of progressive movement. Chronological order, if nothing else, implies forward motion. Still, monumental works appear to emerge at random. Among the things that disappear in this framework are histories from below made by minor figures and collectivities. A partial solution to this difficulty is to expand the category of key works to include coauthored texts and collections by diverse hands. Sooner or later, however, one has to interrogate the idea itself of "great work," just as one has ultimately to put in question the notion of "major figure."

History of theory that focuses on significant problems—such as the conceptualizations of authorship, of literary language, or of reading—offers the "virtue" of coherence and the pleasure of managed variety. On the question of literary authorship, for example, one can trace intricate contemporary lines of reflection from, say, William K. Wimsatt and Monroe Beardsley to Georges Poulet, Hans-Georg Gadamer, E. D. Hirsch, Roland Barthes, Michel Foucault, Harold Bloom, and Sandra M. Gilbert and Susan Gubar. But the history of ideas approach, which often has a sequence of highly cohesive unit-ideas at its center, is open to existing critiques of intellectual history. It dwells in the rarefied realm of concepts, separating ideas from complex intertextual networks as well as from material contexts; it places too much emphasis on innovation; it privileges philosophically oriented theory, disregarding popular forms such as, in the present case, anonymous and collective modes of authorship typical of TV, cinema, advertising, street ballads, and compunovels. History of problems is, in addition, frequently committed beforehand to liberal pluralist agendas where the teleology of theory purportedly leads to both improved argumentation and respect for all points of view. The difficulties of position-taking tend to be deferred.

History of schools and movements, a favorite mode among historians of contemporary theory, has much to recommend it. It provides a means of assembling numerous major and minor figures, influential texts, key problems, and institutional issues within coherent spaces, although these diverse materials must be made to exemplify significant features in school portraits. With the postwar enclosure of theory inside the universities and the diminution in the ranks of nonacademic critics and theorists, history of contemporary theory has had to attend to such institutional factors as the formations of disciplines and programs, professional organizations, significant conferences, university presses, and journals. Histories of leading figures and major texts ignore such crucial matters programmatically. Given over typically to studying a wide array of groups, history of movements can dispense with teleology. Accordingly, history of theory need exhibit little evidence of any prearranged unity, evolution, cyclicality, devolution, or continuity. An obvious drawback of history of schools is its exclusion of mavericks, independents, and antidisciplinarians. Another limitation is its evident inapplicability to earlier eras, for instance, the Classical and Enlightenment periods. Also the categories "school" and "movement" can become so flexible that strange and strained configurations occur, as when a literary critic such as Jonathan Culler holds simultaneous memberships in three "schools," structuralism, reader–response criticism, and poststructuralism. What happens to a cross-disciplinarian such as Gayatri Chakravorty Spivak? Is she a deconstructor, Marxist, feminist, postcolonial theorist, or advocate of cultural studies? The schools-and-movements approach also exacerbates the contemporary tendency to valorize theory and metacriticism and to devalue "practical criticism" and scholarship (especially textual editing). Finally, like histories of leading figures, key texts, and significant problems, histories of schools and movements run the risk of skirting relations among theory and economics and theory and politics, not to mention other cultural spheres.

* * *

With the gradual restructuring now occurring inside and outside literary studies and the university, it is becoming less and less plausible to talk about *literary* criticism and theory. Literature is merging into the categories of discourse and culture. Departments of literary study are being transformed more or less grudgingly into departments of literary and cultural study. Framing histories of contemporary theory from this vantage requires contractions, expansions, and novel arrangements. A new array of figures, works, problems, movements, and sites comes to the fore, and doubtlessly new modes of history writing will ensue. Polemical histories are playing significant roles in this stage of transformation. The emergence of new disciplinary charters and paradigms entails historical re-visions, re-constructions, and re-framings. History of theory as a mixture of more or less incommensurable microhistories of precursors, texts, issues, schools, and institutions— variously intersecting with relevant social and cultural factors—strikes me as the best alternative for the times. However urgently and problematically, it is a matter of unevenly yet innovatively desacralizing/ resacralizing expanding archives of knowledge, a project outlined in chapter 2.

In my view, literary theory is undergoing less a simple expansion than a certain transformation. Not surprisingly, the agendas of current histories, textbooks, and other such framings often have more to do with memorialization and protection than charting vital knowledge. Meanwhile, the increasingly common reinscription of theory into new modes of practice signals the dissolution of ("pure") theory. Today theory is to be found widely scattered through the "new" fields of postcolonial studies, women's and gender studies, narratology, ethnic studies, many branches of cultural studies, rhetoric, queer theory, and, indeed, national literary studies. Here literary studies is reconfigured not as a master discipline but as a regional discourse amidst a host of others. And yet this scattering, this dissemination, signifies not theory's demise but a certain triumph through rhizomatous transformations, graftings, and hybridizations. The *modern* framers of theory have usually found it a semi-autonomous interdisciplinary field influenced by a limited range of established disciplines, particularly philosophy, anthropology, psychology, and linguistics. *Postmodern* framers, however, are discovering unstable and proliferating cross-disciplinary sites where new fields of inquiry as well as older disciplines (being restructured themselves) intersect in ways that render questionable the old terms "literary," "criticism," and "theory." In recent times "literature" has come for many intellectuals to mean not poetry or belles lettres but discourse. Similarly, "criticism" exceeds exegesis and approximates cultural critique. "Theory" increasingly designates neither method nor approach but both self-reflective practice and productive pragmatic tools gathered from hither and yon. Consequently, framing histories of contemporary literary and critical theory is, I believe, best done through disjunctive forms: such history approaches anarchistic romance, decentralized, carnivalesque, heteroglot, pluralized, irreverent, counterhegemonic, contentious, but not, for all that, laissez-faire.

Although theorists have encountered more allies in recent years, I do not mean to suggest that we are all theorists now (though everyone has a theory), nor do I wish to declare victory for theory. Although shrinking, the number of holdouts, old and young, remains large. The point is that theory among literary intellectuals has shifted from something like a relatively enclosed subspecialty to broadly diffused strands found in all specialties and subspecialties. This transformation testifies perhaps less to a happy destiny than to a moribund discipline seeking reinvigoration at numerous points. As a moment of "expansion," the shift in question strikes many commentators as a form of imperialism and others as a stage of Balkanization. It is neither. The incommensurabilities among different theory subfields, groups, and figures undermine claims of imperialism. And the singular mode of dissemination of contemporary theory has ultimately more to do with the proliferation of new territories than with the struggle over existing ground, which, of course, continues unabated. In these circumstances, framing theory as a scene of parochial turf battles misconstrues its mode of development. However disruptive they may be, departures are not simply takeovers. It is worth noting again that certain theorists regard the "expansion" of theory as a sad spectacle, signifying dilution, vulgarization, and loss of vigor. Writing histories of theory that take into account innumerable intricate conflicting perspectives and lines of development profits from both lateral multiplications and intercut frames. The politics of such form seeks to dethrone teleological history in the name of a seriality without guarantees. This postmodern history does not deny that events are determined, after the fact and subject to dispute.

5

INSIDE *THE NORTON ANTHOLOGY*
OF THEORY AND CRITICISM

IN 1995 I BEGAN WORK AS THE GENERAL EDITOR of *The Norton Anthology of Theory and Criticism,* a 2,600-page anthology published in 2001, which contains selections from 148 figures, starting with Gorgias and Plato and ending with bell hooks, Judith Butler, and Stuart Moulthrop.[1] From start to finish this large-scale six-year project developed through a range of discrete yet overlapping tasks and stages: drafting of a project description and guidelines; recruitment of the editorial team; drawing up of a Table of Contents; assignment of author headnotes; early outside review of both the project plan and sample headnotes; composition of the Introduction, Bibliography, Alternative Table of Contents, and Preface; writing, editing, and revising of headnotes; approval of the copyedited manuscript and of page proofs; and supervision of the Instructor's Manual and Index. Two of these tasks, constructing the Table of Contents and particularly compiling author headnotes, were intense collaborative enterprises marked by unexpected turns and revealing problems, and I want to reflect on them here as a way to examine the intricacies of anthology editing and headnote writing from an insider's point of view. No Norton anthology editor has ever offered written reflection on the experience.

Recruiting the initial four editors (later five) took several months, and involved the gathering of names, talking with experts, assessing selected writing samples, contacting candidates, and signing up the final team. Several months after that, we all met with our editor at the publisher's office in New York for two days in order to sketch a preliminary Table of Contents (TOC) and to assign headnotes, relying on a discussion and consensus approach in our sessions, then and later. Our dialogue continued over the next five years, however, it was, in retrospect, especially animated the first year as we faxed and then e-mailed each other back and forth about the merits and weaknesses of dozens upon dozens of potential figures and selections for our TOC. I have several fat folders stuffed with fading faxes and e-mail messages from our innumerable TOC interchanges.

When one of our editors had to resign two years into the project, we recruited a replacement plus an additional editor to make up for lost time. This second round of recruiting (like the recruiting a year later of an author for the Instructor's Manual) involved the whole team making lists of candidates, asking experts, locating writing samples of candidates, and providing the publisher and general editor short lists of names to contact. The whole process resembled a job search. The two new editors proposed changes to the TOC, suggesting drops and adds as well as different selections. More dialogue and consensus-seeking ensued, especially during the few months just after the new members joined the editorial board. And even as the anthology was entering the page proof stage two and a half years later and several months before publication, we ended up debating the entire contents as we discovered we had overshot our 2,300-page target by 600 pages, not the 250 we were expecting. At this last minute we needed to cut 20 figures, which entailed all of us making lists and arguments back and forth about those to be dropped. It was only during this last round of intense dialogue spanning two weeks that we, in fact, reached *final* agreement and established a fixed TOC. In my experience the contents are the most unstable element in anthology construction.

Dramatic and time-consuming as constructing the Table of Contents turned out to be, nothing was more continuously engaging and central to the work of putting together the anthology than compiling the author headnotes, requiring more sustained research, creativity, tact, and plain labor than the serial fine-tuning of the contents. Each editor was responsible for drafting about thirty headnotes with the general editor responsible for fifteen. The collaborative review process for headnotes involved several distinct steps. The general editor and the publisher's editor would separately read and mark up each drafted headnote twice, occasionally three times, and infrequently only once. From time to time an outside specialist would serve as a referee (or very occasionally coauthor) to ensure scholarly accuracy. The Plato and

Aristotle headnotes, for instance, were vetted by a classicist, and we had specialists look over the headnotes on Moses Maimonides, Giambattista Vico, and Martin Heidegger, to name just a few. Late in the process our copyeditor at Norton, a learned and rigorous reader, added copious refinements, corrections, and precision to the headnotes and especially to the textual annotations, which came as an unexpected and burdensome culmination. The headnotes, like the Table of Contents, involved intense collaborative work, and this was largely the case because, significantly, the figures and selections first decided on required agreement from at least three editors, the basis of our consensus approach and the foundation of all our later interactions.

Not incidentally, this key protocol of three editors agreeing on TOC items made us early in the project search high and low for the "right" selection. I read fifteen pieces by Houston A. Baker, Jr. and that many by György Lukács, for example, before finding what I believed to be the right one. Sometimes the other editors would agree with my own recommendations, sometimes not. A number of my favorite theorists as well as my favorite selections did not make it into the anthology. The other editors had similar experiences.

But let me back up at this point. My very first task as general editor was to draft a project description and set of guidelines to be used in recruiting editors. The centerpiece of that early ten-page project description turned out to be a one-page list titled "Protocols for Headnotes" (see Appendix), which contains a short preamble and fourteen numbered items. Here I look back on those protocols as a way to examine some unexpected intricacies of the venerable headnote form.

According to the protocols for *The Norton Anthology of Theory and Criticism*, which mostly codify long-standing composition practices, a headnote proper is to be an essay between 750 and 2,000 words, starting with the author's name, dates, and, where possible, a catchy quotation. The original protocols did not state, but we editors quickly developed, the practice of offering an introductory paragraph that summarizes the significance and relevance of the author and her selection(s) for our primary audience, undergraduate literature majors in North America. The protocols thereafter required a dozen discrete tasks on the part of the editor–writer. Unexpectedly, the final protocol on bibliography (which calls for one or more paragraphs of annotation covering standard editions or texts of the author, biographies on her or him, pertinent secondary sources, and bibliographies of the author's writings) added anywhere from 400 to 1,000 extra words to each headnote. As a result, our headnotes range in fact from 1,200 to 3,000 words, averaging

2,200 words, a short to medium-sized essay. (A few headnotes exceed 3,000 words.) Thus very early in the procrss the headnote emerged for us as a regulated, intricate genre like, say, the sonnet: numerous protocols and restrictions, yet ample room for the variations and writerly pleasures characteristic of the comparatively freer essay form.

The protocols did not (and do not) address, and the headnotes proper do not contain, any mention of the thing most dreaded by a headnote writer: textual annotations, a neglected and invisible subgenre. Consider *The Norton Anthology of Theory and Criticism*: any name, title, concept, or word unknown to the average undergraduate literature major was annotated in keeping with long-standing traditions of textbook editing, one especially honored by the W. W. Norton Publishing Company, we discovered. If a selection from an author contained the word "dialectical," for instance, it received a gloss appropriate to its use in that passage. "Dialectical: reciprocal interaction." If the name Philo Judaeus happened to appear, as it did, his dates were provided and a phrase or clause explained his textual significance. "Philo Judaeus (30 B.C.E.–45 C.E.), secular Jewish writer." The annotations, numbered like footnotes and located at the bottom of the page, take up a great deal of space and time, even though they are descriptive not interpretive and succinct, not to say clipped in style.

About the annotations—a very labor-intensive element of the headnote—I offer some further observations. First, a major effect of writing annotations is to keep the audience continuously in mind, constraining the headnote writer to be committed at micro as well as macro levels to a relentless project of clarification. Second, and more to the point, each "headnote" consists, in fact, of an introductory essay, a selected prose bibliography, textual annotations, and, of course, a selection or selections, some of which are trimmed and shaped by the editors to save space and to ensure relevance. (In this regard, consider the representative cases of Vico's *New Science* and Aristotle's *Rhetoric*, both many hundreds of pages; they require editing.) Thus when we members of the editorial team for *The Norton Anthology of Theory and Criticism* talk among ourselves about "headnotes," we almost always mean not the short to medium-sized essay on the famous figure, but this essay with all the trimmings, including the edited selection(s), the evaluative bibliography, *and* the annotations. For the headnote writer, an enormous amount of work gets put into these ancillary elements, frequently more than that involved in the essay proper. Much graduate student labor typically goes into the ancillary items as well, particularly the annotations.

But one protocol for drafting headnotes turned out to be more unexpectedly revealing than all the rest. This is the one that called for the headnote writer to offer a critique of problems in the selection(s) so as to ensure that students studying theory learn to look for problems as a regular aspect of the reading process. In contrast to what seemed the monumentalizing tendency of most headnotes, we wanted to stress that theory arises in the midst of dialogue and debate, with not everyone agreeing. We sought to alert students to the problem-oriented nature of theory as a fundamental part of doing theory, not just to prompt them to memorize key terms and concepts. One of the members of the editorial board provocatively argued, however, that nothing dates a text more than such critique, and also significantly that critique risks undermining a main goal of the headnotes: to motivate students to read the author and her or his works. In practice this observation got turned into a simple unwritten caveat, a key rider, to the original protocol: keep critique in proportion to explanation and praise. Praise is essential in explaining why a text is included. To offer three paragraphs discussing problems and complaints about a selection and, say, only one paragraph of praise or promotion is to disincline the student to continue on to the reading. What we headnote writers discovered, in the meantime, was that combining the protocol requiring critique with the one calling for discussion of reception and progeny helps solve the problem. In recounting the reception of an author or text, one really ought to mention hostile as well as friendly responses, dissensus as well as consensus. It works better in a headnote, for instance, to say, "Modern critics have complained that Plato is an enemy of open society" than to state flatly that "Plato is an enemy of open society." Upon reflection this "problem" with critique has to do in large part with genre; the headnote is by tradition unsigned, impartial, more or less objective, disinterested discourse. Critique, conversely, typically consists of a signed, partisan, interested intervention expressed in the name of a committed point of view usually linked with a group.[2] At the outset of the project, I had no idea I would be belatedly making so basic a discovery.

From everything said thus far, it is perhaps obvious that the headnote is an ideological form. But perhaps not. What, some readers may ask, are the ideological features of the headnote? A neighbor of the character sketch and the case study as well as the short essay, the headnote aims to set up for the uninformed reader a reading experience to come. In seeking to direct the reader, it typically links the text(s)-to-come with the author (a biography), her or his other work (an oeuvre), and a tradition or set of texts and topics defining a field of inquiry (a canon). The headnote tends to foreground what is common knowledge to the specialist, using a normative prose marked by accessibility, relative simplicity, and impartiality, that is, a certain kind of invisible ventriloquized style. It is part of a project of enlightenment, clarification, and demystification. As everyone knows, readers sometimes settle for the headnote, never arriving at the selection. Of course, sometimes readers skip headnotes altogether. Among the main ideological features of headnotes, in any case, are: they are rooted in personifications/authors' lives;[3] they are substitutes/ "supplements" for reading;[4] they rely on constraining historical and textual contexts/frameworks; they disseminate received opinion as a part of the certification process of educational institutions.[5] These features risk shutting down rather than opening up texts. And in projecting a retrospective tone and a sense of mastery, a headnote also risks taming the conflicts characteristic of cultural productions in their time. Perennializing problems has a way of dehistoricizing and tranquilizing them. By design, anthology and textbook headnotes quickly package and contain information as does a memo, valuing control, speed, organization, and clarity, values preeminent in today's market-oriented societies. So while the venerable anthology headnote is a humble genre fulfilling a minor service function,[6] it does cooperate with and further some larger ideological goals current in contemporary times. And although there is no clear and simple way around these circumstances, my experience confirms that one can and should productively teach about these ideological elements of the headnote to beginning as well as advanced students of theory and criticism.

Quite unexpectedly, I have been asked on several occasions whether I can tell a good anthology headnote from a bad one. Is there such a thing as a really bad headnote? As an insider, my answer is yes. Common to the headnote are a number of shortcomings and disorders, some obvious, some arguable. An inadequate headnote might contain insufficient, incorrect, or excessive information; offer a weak presentation of the big picture, especially the significance and relevance of the author's work; miss key elements, innovations, and strategies of the text(s) in question; overlook important continuities/discontinuities with tradition and the author's other works; leave out reception history and/or the sociohistorical context of the selection(s); over- or under-identify with the author and his or her project; minimize, omit, or overemphasize critique of problems and limitations in the work. Like any other essayistic writing, a headnote might have shortcomings because of flaws in style, design, or argumentation. In my experience some headnotes are better than others, and some more interesting or compelling than others.

Surprisingly, I have also been asked: Is it possible to write headnotes in a postmodern age? Is there such a thing as a postmodern headnote? My answer is yes. Some of the traditional elements of the headnote genre have in recent times been reconfigured, and new features have been added. Characteristic of recent headnotes, including a range of those in *The Norton Anthology of Theory and Criticism*, are forthright analysis of issues related to race, class, and gender as well as other aspects of social history. In addition, there is a willingness in our postformalist period to critique canonical and leading contemporary figures. And with the dissemination of social constructionist viewpoints in postmodern times, writers, including headnote writers, consider history, tradition, and biography to be narrative constructs, if not factitious totalizing tales, bringing a new openness to discussions of history, tradition, and biography. Given the widespread impact of deconstruction, moreover, there is now a willingness, often an eagerness, to isolate textual gaps, incoherencies, and contradictions in a nonaccusatory, occasionally celebratory, manner. Such faults are regarded as inescapable and ineradicable, revealing symptoms productive for analysis. Finally, ever since the advent of reader-response theory in the 1960s and '70s, when the reader and the intertext were born at the death of the author, a realignment has been occurring in the relations of power among the famous four elements of the critical pyramid long ago schematized by M. H. Abrams: the work, artist, audience, and universe.[7] If nothing else, the matrix of conventions underlying this commonsensical scheme has come into question, complicating and loosening the grip of a whole array of standard concepts, ranging from thematic unity and author's intentions to literary imitation, autonomy, and influence. So yes, there is a postmodern headnote, bearing the features just enumerated. Because the anthology headnote is, after all, a genre of literary criticism, it reflects the changes and trends of literary criticism: if there is a postmodern literary criticism, there is a postmodern headnote.

Let me tell a story as a way to conclude these initial reflections on editing a Norton anthology. I have more to say in the next two chapters. I remember vividly as a college sophomore stumbling onto the writings of Martin Heidegger. I was supposed to be reading Robert L. Heilbronner's *The Worldly Philosophers* for an economics course. Instead I ended up wrestling with *Being and Time*, which led me to deeper and deeper inquiries into Heidegger's work, existentialism, Jean-Paul Sartre, Albert Camus, Gabriel Marcel, and back to Heidegger. This lasted for several years and was a formative experience for me. But it was all an accident. It did not start with an anthology or a headnote, and I think I am lucky for that. It turned out to be a life-enhancing extracurricular pursuit unconnected to courses, exams, requirements, notes, and clear paths of inquiry. To the extent that headnotes and anthologies close off the chances for such productive deterritorializations,[8] they are pedagogical forms calling for a measure of wariness. For me nowadays critical reading and ideology critique extend to the headnote and the anthology form and not just to the texts of influential figures. Lately I have taken to asking students to write alternative and counterhegemonic headnotes or parts of them (singly and collectively). I encourage them to search out other selections, and to critique selected headnotes. Why not? Still, the best way to work against the headnote and the anthology as normative genres is by going through them, using them as material for information, for instruction, for critique, and for illumination. They are by definition preludes.

6

CONSOLIDATING THEORY
Interview

[Professor Clifford Manlove of Pennsylvania State University at Mc-Keesport Campus did this interview on July 7, 2001 in Norman, Oklahoma for *minnesota review.*]

Clifford Manlove: I guess we'll begin by talking about the nuts and bolts of *The Norton Anthology of Theory and Criticism* (2001).[1] You were invited by Norton to take on the project. How did it happen?

Vincent B. Leitch: The first thing that happened was I got a phone call from a W. W. Norton editor asking me if I'd review a proposal that had been sent to them for a theory anthology. So I did a standard, three- or four-page evaluation, and talked about the problems in the proposal and what would be a better way to do an anthology. A few months later, to my surprise, the Norton editor showed up at my office door, and I had a conversation with him about who, I thought, would be the right person to edit the anthology, giving him a list of the top candidates around the country. He asked me if I would be interested, and I told him only if it could be a team project. Previous anthologies had tended to be done by one editor or two coeditors, but it seemed to me that the way to do an anthology at this point would be to get a dream team of a half-dozen people. His initial response was that there wasn't enough money to spread around to half-a-dozen different editors, but I told him I didn't think that money was going to be the primary motivation for doing the project.

We went through a negotiation process, and I added some things to the contract, for example, that Norton would put up $5,000 for ancillary materials, such as the Instructor's Manual. No other anthology of theory and criticism has one. I also had written into the contract that they would pay for an Index, because I knew I couldn't do a sophisticated index for 2,300 Norton-sized pages! Actually, in the process of negotiating the contract, I had occasion to call up other Norton anthology editors to get their advice. I asked "If you had to do it all over again, what would you want in your Norton contract?" So that created a community of Norton editors who were back-up advisors and who were helpful later on.

CM: And this was 1995?

VBL: All of this happened within about nine months, September through May 1995–96.

CM: Did you expect that it would take five or six years?

VBL: We were projecting that it would come out in 2000, and it came out in 2001. We missed by a year because one of our editors, two years into the project, got an administrative position and quit, so we had to hire a replacement at that point, actually two replacements, in order that we would only fall that one year behind.

CM: You're the general editor; how did you select the other editors?

VBL: I made up a list of ideal candidates in consultation with the W. W. Norton editor. We got copies of their work, evaluated them, and looked at their vitas. It was a fairly standard search process. A few of the candidates weren't interested; they were doing something else. There was a list of maybe seven or eight candidates that I and the Norton editors finally agreed upon, and I started to call people, sending them a ten-page prospectus for the anthology, along with several appendices, such as the one-page set of protocols of the essential ingredients of headnotes, and a core list of theory figures. I signed on William Cain, Barbara Johnson, and Jeffrey Williams all at the same time during spring 1996. The second time we recruited, two years later, everybody on the editorial board pitched in on the search, and we added Laurie Finke and John McGowan. Peter Simon is the Norton editor who originally sent me the proposal, who came to my office, and who worked through the six-year process of putting the anthology together from beginning to end.

At the outset I made a list of a dozen criteria for selecting ideal editors. It was a way to help me because there were quite a few names floating around. I looked for—this is in no particular order—experience teaching theory; knowledge of the history of theory; ability to write clear, lucid prose, because most of the work was going to be writing headnotes, annotations, and bibliographies for undergraduates; and ability to get work done in a timely manner, so the anthology wouldn't take forever to get done. Those are pragmatic criteria, but there were others as well, such as the ability to see theory in a new way. If you examine some of the headnotes, they're beautiful original pieces of essayistic writing. Before I recruited people, I went and read their work. It wasn't, oh, I met so-and-so at a conference, I think I'll ask him or her to be an editor.

CM: How did you settle on a Table of Contents?

VBL: W. W. Norton had put together a core list. They went through several leading theory anthologies and made a list of about fifty figures that they thought should be in any anthology: the usual suspects, Plato, Aristotle, all the way up to the standard people in the twentieth century, such as Cleanth Brooks and T. S. Eliot. I added all the names I could possibly think of, several hundred names. I sent that to the editors as part of the prospectus, and then we had to work through constructing the Table of Contents, which was our first big job. We had to whittle down not only the names but the actual selections, and come to a consensus on all of this. I mean, everybody can agree, yes, we should have Plato, but which Plato? Which chapters of the *Republic*? What else by Plato?

CM: So you met and hashed these out?

VBL: We first met in New York at the Norton office in July 1996. We sat in a room for two days and drew up a preliminary Table of Contents, starting with the ancient Greeks and working up to the present. What we would do is debate who should be in there, which texts, why, until we had a consensus. We got up to about 1970, and ran out of time. We agreed that three of us would develop a contemporary list, a process that went on for probably twelve months, although fine-tuning the final list took another three years. We had endless debates about, okay, yes, we want Cleanth Brooks, but which Cleanth Brooks? Maybe a chapter from *The Well Wrought Urn*, or maybe this or that essay, and we kept mailing and faxing different selections to each other. Almost until the anthology was published, we were still discussing who and which particular selections should be in or out.

We included a lot of the expected figures, for instance, in the long eighteenth century, we included Giambattista Vico, Immanuel Kant, and Samuel Johnson, but we put a lot of other names on the table you might not have expected, such as Aphra Behn and Madame de Staël. The latter has this wonderful piece on women writers that shows there is a late eighteenth- and early nineteenth-century conversation on the topic, and it also resonates well with other texts in the anthology, such as those by Virginia Woolf and Sandra M. Gilbert and Susan Gubar. So it was much more than making a list; we tried to get mosaics.

When we met, it was a free-wheeling, wild conversation. People kept tossing names out. Sometimes everyone would laugh and say, oh, no, there's no way; other times, we would have pretty strong debates. Any figure in the anthology had to have at least half of the editorial team agree to go with it. If two people wanted to have John Locke but three didn't, that meant Locke didn't go. We had to have some process to adjudicate disagreements, and I adopted that key protocol based on my years of working on committees at universities. I designed the whole process (getting the team talking together, working through the Table of Contents, etc.) as a collaborative collective venture.

CM: It bugs me that consensus has a bad name, but one implication of working by consensus is that you lose personality and subjectivity. The other is that you get the lowest common denominator.

VBL: Well, very often an individual editor's eccentricities would be respected throughout the process of debate and discussion. When one of the editors proposed the Preface from Théophile Gautier's *Mademoiselle de Maupin* (1835), the rest of us looked at the editor and said, what are you talking about? We're not familiar with this text; it's completely eccentric. But when the others read the text, we said, yes, we have to go with this. It's wonderful on art for art's sake. I don't think that you get some lowest common denominator or a lack of individuality or originality.

CM: Were there ever times when you felt like you knew you had to have something by a figure, but couldn't agree on what, and even if a given text, which translation?

VBL: Sometimes it was hard to decide on a particular selection. For example, we went through perhaps ten different pieces by Kenneth Burke, not just from *The Philosophy of Literary Form* but from all over the place. We finally found one called "Kinds of Criticism," which Burke published in the 1950s in *Kenyon Review* as part of a series of theoretical essays called "My Credo." We also have, by the way, a piece by Cleanth Brooks called "The Formalist Critics," and one by Northrop Frye on "The Archetypes of Literature" out of that series. What "My Credo" did was to force people to say everything they believed was essential to theory and criticism in ten pages or so. I wish a journal editor would try something like that today.

The translations turned out to be not much of a problem. We were committed from the beginning to getting the best translations we could and to not worrying about permissions fees. For instance, in the case of the Aristotle, we pretty much knew we wanted to use the Richard Janko translation of *Poetics* (done in the late 1980s), which is highly respected by people in Classics. And it was easy enough for all of us to agree on that, even though we had to pay more for it than using, say, the Butcher translation, which is in the public domain. No other theory anthology, as far as I know, has ever used Janko, which mystifies me.

CM: And you cultivated a network of secondary readers.

VBL: Absolutely. If you look at the Acknowledgments pages of the anthology you'll see there are many names there. We editors had a lot of help from colleagues.

CM: What was the next stage after you had met as an editorial board, once you had firmed up enough of the Table of Contents?

VBL: In New York, just before we finished our two-day meeting, we spent an hour dividing up the headnote assignments, which was an amazingly easy task. I thought it was going to be a nightmare, but we started, who's going to do the Plato, who's going to do the Aristotle, and so on, and people volunteered. There were a few surprises. For example, Jeffrey Williams drafted the Paul de Man headnote, not Barbara Johnson, who was a student of de Man's. Of course, the headnote is an unsigned genre, which means it doesn't have an author attached to it, and some headnotes were collaboratively done with outside experts in special fields.

As the Table of Contents was modified, and then as we added new editors, we had to go back and trade some. Each editor had to do roughly thirty headnotes apiece. A "headnote" assignment meant you'd pick the selections and translations, you'd write the headnote proper, you'd compose the annotated bibliography, and you'd write the annotations for the texts. The editors did that in consultation with both the Norton editor and the general editor. If there were any disagreements, we'd bring in other editors. On the Plato, for instance, we had a discussion about whether we should include the last ten pages of Plato's *Phaedrus*. We decided to do that because it went very well with the Derrida selection "Plato's Pharmacy" from his book *Dissemination*, where Plato's views on speech and writing receive an exemplary deconstruction.

CM: So the flavor of each headnote would vary?

VBL: It would, although a person would draft a headnote and then send it to the Norton editor and to me. I would carefully go over the headnote proper, the text, the annotations, and the annotated bibliography, mark them all up, and the editor would then revise and resubmit to me and to the Norton editor. After that, the Norton copy editor, who was extremely meticulous, went through all the headnotes and revised them for style and accuracy. So every headnote had a minimum of five revisions, sometimes more. If there were a headnote we weren't sure about, we'd send it out to a specialist, who invariably offered some additions and subtractions, making it a better headnote. There were any number of times, twenty or so, when a headnote would go to an outside specialist. Occasionally, I would take an editor's headnote and send it to a second editor. So a minimum of five, but anywhere up to eight passes were common to each headnote.

CM: Wow! Did you also do thirty figures?

VBL: The editors had roughly thirty; I had fifteen. I drafted all the front and back matter, the Acknowledgments, the Preface, the Alternative Table of Contents, the Introduction, and the Bibliography. I did rough drafts of those and sent them around to everybody, more than once. Also, each of the sixteen schools-and-movements bibliographies were sent to two or more outside specialists in these fields. For instance, the one on cultural studies went to Larry Grossberg, Cary Nelson, and Richard Dienst. Even though I was assigned those materials, they were the most collaboratively done of everything, not surprisingly. Two graduate students did a great deal of work on the Bibliography.

CM: In terms of the construction and structure of the headnotes, was that preordained by Norton? Would you emend them in some way?

VBL: What I did early on was make up a sheet of fourteen protocols for headnotes (see Appendix). I went and studied headnotes in maybe three or four dozen anthologies of all different kinds, and I drew up what seemed to me to be the ideal rules for the genre. The Norton editor made a couple of revisions to go with the Norton house style. As we started to write the headnotes, we had to make some modifications to go with the realities of headnote writing. I added discursive annotated bibliographies to the protocols, which in retrospect was a good move. When you read the selection by Derrida, for example, you get a discussion of not only Derrida's texts, but the best and most useful critical materials on Derrida and whatever useful biographical and bibliographical sources there are, all in a succinct, readable prose format. Most anthologies don't have that. If you think about it, we have 140 headnotes with each having an annotated prose bibliography; consider how much labor and time went into that!

CM: So that was another benefit of having an editorial collective.

VBL: With a team you get the added advantage of the varied expertise of all the editors, plus their network of colleagues who are outside experts. To complete Althusser, we called an Althusserian; to do Eichenbaum, we called in someone who knows Russian formalism.

CM: Did Norton ever question the need for bibliographies? Do undergrads need all that stuff?

VBL: It seemed to me that there were three main audiences for the anthology: first, the undergraduate literature major, which is Norton's target audience. But second are the instructors who will use this anthology, some of whom might be seasoned theory instructors, but some of whom perhaps teach seventeenth-century literature and have been assigned to teach a theory course for the first time. Third are graduate students (future instructors). The headnote bibliographies are going to be most helpful to grad students and instructors, not undergraduates, whereas the general bibliography of contemporary schools and movements is primarily designed to help undergraduates. The latter has an autonomous feel to it, covering everything from structuralism to queer theory and cultural studies each in compact two-page bits.

CM: One of the things that strikes me about the collection is its width and breadth, but it also seems weighted toward the twentieth century. Did you go in with that in mind or was that just the way it worked out?

VBL: We didn't assign percentages or allocate how much would go to each period. I knew, because of the planned composition of the editorial team, that we would have a hefty medieval section and a substantial representation of women critics, both of which most other anthologies don't have. In fact, after we drew up the initial Table of Contents, one of the editors said that there wasn't enough twentieth-century material, so I went through and crunched some numbers to find out how much contemporary material we had. We have about twelve percent more twentieth-century material than our main competitor, David Richter's *The Critical Tradition*[2] and sixty-five percent more than Hazard Adams' *Critical Theory Since Plato*.[3] I would argue that the twentieth century is the great age of theory in a way that, say, the fifteenth century just wasn't. Maybe there's a "presentism" in that: we're more interested in our own period than other periods. What is also remarkable about the late twentieth century is the rise, scope, and creativity of women critics. At the end of the day, sixty percent of the people in the anthology born after 1934 turned out to be women.

CM: In the Preface, you talk about the fact that right now theory is still pretty much Eurocentric, but on the horizon theory is going to go global. How do you see this happening?

VBL: There are various traditions that we haven't tapped into yet. For example, there's a millennium-long tradition in Sanskrit, from the third century A.D. up to the thirteenth or fourteenth century, of theorizing the nature of poetry, interpretation, and the dynamics of symbolism. As far as I know, no theorist or theory anthology has ever included this. Around the world there are other traditions of criticism and theory. When we were putting together the medieval selections of the anthology, we included Moses Maimonides, who was a Jewish rabbi writing in Arabic, and who theorized rules particularly for how to deal with contradictions in texts. That slips out of Eurocentric lines into Middle Eastern ones. But my understanding is that a publisher would have trouble selling an anthology which had a great deal of such "foreign" material. The U.S. teaching corps is ready for that in world literature, but I don't think they're quite ready for it in theory.

CM: I'd like to see something like "world theory." What do you think of the reactions against theory, or the antitheory movement? I'm thinking of books like John Ellis's *Literature Lost.*[4]

VBL: The antitheory position you're referring to, which often comes from right-wing intellectuals who deplore the emphasis on theory instead of literature, first appeared in the 1980s and early 1990s, and I think they're going to have a second gust of energy in the next few years. With the election of George W. Bush, which is a neoconservative restoration, we're in for more of the Culture Wars, and one part of that is the antitheory position. We've already seen a bit of that in an attack on *The Norton Anthology of Theory and Criticism* in *The Chicago Tribune* in July 2001, which charges that theory sacrifices literature.[5]

There's also a prominent antitheory position centered within the university, which first coalesced in the 1980s, probably best represented by the famous Steven Knapp and Walter Benn Michaels essay, "Against Theory," which argues that the attempt to find a grand, overarching theoretical system, from their neopragmatic point of view, is a foolhardy endeavor. But that's antitheory in a very special antifoundationalist sense. We included that piece in *The Norton Anthology,* even though I think most theorists dislike it. The problem for theorists is the definition of theory: it's just too thin in that essay.

CM: To change gears, what in the personal realm and, on the other hand, what in your professional career helped prepare you to take on this project?

VBL: On the personal level, coming of age during the 1960s and 1970s with its antinomian tendencies led me to theory: questioning what literature is, how we define it, and who gets to define it and why, instead of dutifully analyzing texts formally à la New Criticism. What are the politics of interpretative conventions? As far as my own personal history, I grew up in a fairly strict Irish-Italian Catholic family and community and spent thirteen years in Catholic schools, wearing a tie every day, marching to class, and basically being in a paramilitary organization. That tends to create either really good Christian soldiers or really good anarchists and atheists. At this time, I was breaking away from the whole lifeworld of militant Catholicism. Now my turn to theory took four or five slow steps, from reading existentialism, especially Martin Heidegger, while moving on through formalism to poststructuralism, and then into cultural studies. I was an undergraduate and then in graduate school when the Vietnam War was in progress. During this time I went through three or four stages in my relationship to the war, ranging from personal uncertainty to draft dodging to opposition. That's part of the story too, of going from being a good, obedient, disciplined, tough Catholic boy from the working class to being an antiwar protestor siding with the New Left. And I think that theory—my commitment to theory—is entangled with all that.

CM: What was the professional scene like?

VBL: There were no programs in theory, except in a few Comparative Literature departments, in the 1960s and 1970s. It wasn't until the 1980s that you could seriously study or specialize in theory in a graduate program, so my generation of theorists went through a bunch of parainstitutions like the School of Criticism and Theory that was set up in the 1970s at the University of California at Irvine and is still going a quarter of a century later, and the International Summer Institute for Semiotic and Structural Studies, which was established by a group of Canadians but was taught in the United States and Canada, alternatively, each summer. There was also a cluster of NEH seminars which were theoretically oriented and taught by theorists, and the Society for Critical Exchange was a singular meeting ground for theorists in the 1970s and 1980s, developing collaborative projects with the idea that theory needs its own infrastructure. I was involved in all of those. I also had a stint at the Alliance Française in Paris to brush up my French, because a lot of the materials out of French poststructuralism still weren't translated into English. I wasn't the only one who was brushing up my French and German at the time, trying to read key contemporary theoretical texts that hadn't been translated yet.

When, in the early 1980s, I started writing *American Literary Criticism from the 1930s to the 1980s*, I aimed to write a detailed, thick insider's account of the history of theory in the last part of the twentieth century, which required the building and consolidation of an infrastructure that wasn't there.[6] The previous histories of American criticism were thin and inadequate.

So *The Norton Anthology of Theory and Criticism* was, I felt, a logical step. I see myself in a tradition of consolidating theory by means of large synthetic projects of one sort or another. René Wellek, who was born around 1900, did his massive, multivolume history of criticism and theory, and Northrop Frye, born around World War I, in his own way did his version, and Murray Krieger, who was born in the mid-twenties, did his own version. His setting up the School of Criticism and Theory in the mid-1970s was a particularly valuable consolidation of theory. There are more recent examples, many of which are recorded in the bibliographies of *The Norton Anthology.*

CM: Have you thought of doing a two-volume edition of the Norton?

VBL: I had this experience when I wrote *American Literary Criticism from the 1930s to the 1980s*: my editor at Columbia University Press said to me, because the manuscript was seven hundred pages, why don't we just publish two volumes? And I thought, oh great, I'll have two books. A seductive idea, but then I realized after a few minutes thought that, no, part of my motivation was to write a monumental account, and if you break it into two or three pieces, it's not going to have the same impact. So, I am reluctant to break *The Norton Anthology* up for the same reason. When you look at *The Norton*, it has all these different selections from different people and periods that don't necessarily go with one another, but they're in this larger consolidating enterprise. When you look at the United Nations, it's got roughly two hundred nations that don't necessarily go along with one another, but they're all sitting there hammering it out. However unified and monumental they appear, they are in fact assemblages and rhizomatic structures. They take a lot of space and they look really big, but their actual inner structure is very different from some sort of monolith.

My larger argument is that what characterizes postmodern culture is disorganization. But disorganization doesn't mean chaos; it means disaggregation. For example, one of the parts in the book I'm doing now has a chapter on postmodern fashion. There's a famous book by J. C. Flügel published in 1930 on the history of fashion, which observes that men in European culture near the end of the eighteenth century gave up wearing silks and feathers and all these colorful things, and took on the gray flannel suit.[7] This is referred to as the "great male renunciation." Now when you get to the 1960s, you can see an annuling of the great renunciation. Look at the cover of the Beatles' *Sgt. Pepper's* album and you see people in feathers and silk; it's a return to the late eighteenth-century kind of dandyism. This provides an example of disorganization: today there are many different styles of male dress, not one. But it's not chaotic; there's a finite set of permutations on a handful of conventions. You could do a structuralist fashion system for present-day U.S. male culture, for instance. The question about disorganization that characterizes postmodern culture affects not just fashion but literature and music and food and so on. I see the forms of organization across the arts and many of the other dimensions of society in this mode of disassemblage, disaggregation, and disorganization, but also then fusion, pastiche, and mixed media. The kind of structure you get when you look at *The Norton Anthology*, the whole thing, in toto with its Instructor's Manual attached, is an example of what I would call theory in its disorganized form.

CM: That resembles the thesis of your book on deconstruction, that deconstruction is a disorganized activity, but it has rules, and you try to lay out the rules.[8]

VBL: Part of the key to understanding poststructuralist thinking is to remember that poststructuralists, even though they're critical of structuralism, don't give up on the idea of system and structure. If you're doing a poststructural analysis, one of the first things you want to do is understand the system or the structure plus the conventions and codes that are operating, then go on about your critical deconstruction. That, to me, is part of the interesting thing about poststructuralism, that it doesn't renounce the notion of certain kinds of structure both preexisting and following its critical investigations.

CM: While you're a historian of theory, one strain that I've seen recurring in your books is Marxism as well as poststructuralism. Can you talk about the ways that the Left and materialism have informed your work?

VBL: Well, the traditions of the Left that I come out of are unionism and anarchism, in that order. When I was growing up, I joined a union while working on a dredge, the operating engineer's union, and then two years later, working construction in the summers, I joined Local 66 in New York for laborers. I was making a lot of money at the time; the equivalent would be something like $28 an hour. I was twenty years old making that kind of money because I was in the union. Construction was a slave-driving operation, and the company foremen got every nickel out of you, but there was always a union shop steward on site who would be looking out for the interests of the laborers. From that early experience I learned a lasting appreciation for unions and how they operate and what protections they can afford. Despite the problems with American unions—the link with the mafia, the misuse of the pension funds, and so on—it seemed to me that unions were a very good thing. So from early on I was committed to unions. I remember the big yellow poster in the union office: "Unionism is Americanism."

Ironically, my fate has been that I've ended up teaching in places where the antiunionism is so deep and pervasive that I've never belonged to an active teaching union. I was in Florida, then I went to Georgia, then I went to central Indiana (although northern Indiana has a strong union tradition), and now Oklahoma. All of these are de facto "right-to-work" states, which means they want to keep unions out so minimum wages can operate uncontested.

That's one answer; the other obviously goes through my Catholic upbringing and the Vietnam War and having to decide that yeah, if they insist on drafting me, I will go to Canada rather than stay here. The draft had a way of changing your relationship to patriotism and to authority, and it fostered the kind of anarchism I took up. In terms of politics, I think of myself as coming out of a syndicalist anarchist tradition. My maternal grandparents were Sicilians, and the mythical home of syndicalism and anarchism, for me, is the Sicilian tradition. Let's call it genetic predisposition. By the time I got to looking at deconstruction and poststructuralism and theory, I was trying to think of ways to get the more formalist dimensions in touch with the materialist dimensions of those projects. Of course, there's a whole group of people in my generation who, from the very beginning, were linking materialism and deconstruction. Gayatri Spivak and Michael Ryan are exhibit A in that match. The Marxism and deconstruction book by Michael Ryan is a beautiful working out, very early on, of some of the links. I myself was less interested in how one would take Derridean deconstruction and match it up with Marxism, and much more interested in Michel Foucault and Gilles Deleuze and Félix Guattari and how one would link poststructuralism, materialism, and post-Marxism. If you go back and look at my deconstruction book, it exuberantly yet dutifully marches through Derrida and the Yale School, but it ends up with more radicalized poststructuralism. The subsequent three books I published all start, progress, and end by grappling with Marxism/post-Marxism, poststructuralism, and Leftist cultural studies.[9]

One striking way that Leftism shows up in *The Norton Anthology* is the rich set of selections in the Left tradition of the history of criticism. No other anthology has anything like what *The Norton* does. Even just from Marx, we carry selections from seven different texts, all of which are key texts for cultural studies today. And it goes all the way through people such as Donna Haraway, Dick Hebdige, and Richard Ohmann plus the more usual suspects, such as Fredric Jameson, Terry Eagleton, and Gayatri Chakravorty Spivak. And it has a group of people who are doing Left projects, but are not strictly Marxists, such as Susan Bordo, who does a materialist analysis of the female body.

CM: What do you see ahead for the job market in the next few years in terms of theory and how does this anthology affect the job market? That's a difficult question, but how does theory relate to jobs?

VBL: The relationship of theory to the job market has gone through three or four, no three, stages. If you looked at the first *MLA Job List* from the early 1970s, you would see that there were no theory jobs. When you get to the 1980s, there are many jobs described as theory jobs. When you get to the 1990s, there are hardly any theory jobs per se; theory gets put into a secondary category, so the typical thing would be: "we are looking for an eighteenth-century person who does history of the novel, and we would prefer to have someone with any combination of the following secondary fields," and then you get a laundry list, "feminist criticism, history of theory, early African-American literature, and/or world literature." That illustrates how theory gets disseminated. Today, if you're teaching the eighteenth-century novel, or Shakespeare, or medieval literature, you're almost certainly doing theory in that course; theory is not restricted to a "theory" or "history of criticism" course. Oddly enough, the lack of theory jobs today represents a certain kind of triumph for theory.

Now, on the other hand, there are theory jobs at the upper levels, which don't always show up in the *Job List*. There is what I would call a relatively thriving theory job market on the senior level, but you can't quite see it. It's possible that the wave of retirements that will go on across the country in the next decade or so is going to have departments, particularly at the major research universities, looking to hire people explicitly as theorists as they lose some of their senior theorists. For example, when Hazard Adams retired a couple of years ago from the University of Washington, they did a search and ended up hiring Henry Staten. I expect that that model will not be uncommon. So I think there will be a theory job market in the future connected with retirements and senior appointments. Meanwhile, a lot of hiring is done in the name of other areas—medieval lit, eighteenth-century lit, nineteenth-century lit, twentieth-century American lit—where people get jobs in large part because they have strong theory backgrounds that shape their research and publication.

CM: What would you suggest to someone who has just finished their doctoral exams and really wants a theory job when they finish up?

VBL: I would offer these two thoughts, which don't go together. First, follow your passion and do what you really care about, and that will give you the energy to actually get things done, to finish your courses, complete your exams, do your dissertation, teach with enthusiasm, and do the projects you really care about. Second, most literature departments in their infrastructure remain extremely conservative. When they go about deciding what hires to make, they normally come up with the standard national literature, historical period, and genre grid (e.g., nineteenth-century British novel). Knowing all that as a graduate student, when you're taking your exams and concocting a dissertation and creating a professional image for yourself, you might self-consciously adopt a nation, period, genre, and topic, which it is hoped will go along with your passion, but maybe not. Opportunism has its dictates. You have to decide how to adjudicate these two different pieces of advice.

CM: What do you think is the next "hot thing" in theory?

VBL: In the time that I've been in the U.S. university, we've worked through three major critical paradigms. We've gone from formalism to poststructuralism to cultural studies. Right now cultural studies is dominant. That doesn't mean there aren't other practices; there's still plenty of deep-rooted poststructuralist and formalist work. But what's happened in the United States is that cultural studies from the late 1980s to the present has evolved and divided into many discrete "studies" areas, such as media studies, body studies, science and technology studies, popular culture studies, globalization studies, leisure studies, and so on. The most recent of those is, I suppose, transatlantic studies or possibly Inter-American studies, which looks at indigenous literatures in Canada, the United States, Mexico, and southwards in all of the Americas. What I expect is that the cultural studies paradigm will continue for a while, that new semiautonomous studies areas will be created as we go along, and that some of them will break away into autonomous fields.

CM: And some of those might appear in a second edition of *The Norton?*

VBL: Yes, but we may very well also end up going back into the eighteenth century or the medieval period, finding some precursors to, say, transatlantic studies. History is not safe from the present: when you discover or create something new in the present, you have to go back to configure it. That's part of the fun of it, and I expect there will be some additions to the anthology, but not just in the contemporary period.

CM: Norton asked you, at the last minute, to cut a substantial section of the anthology. How did that work?

VBL: The original contract called for the anthology to be 2,300 pages. Norton was willing to exceed that limit by several hundred pages. But about a month or two before publication, we realized it was 2,900 pages, so we had to cut some twenty figures. (The anthology right now in its published form is 2,625 pages.) The main problem was that we did not calculate the impact of the annotations. For example, the Said selection is the 28-page introduction to *Orientalism.* The headnote is about 10 pages long, but there were sixty annotations, which were 15 additional pages. Said refers to a host of nineteenth-century orientalists rarely heard of, all of whom are annotated. If you look at *The Norton Anthology of American Literature* or *English Literature* or *World Literature,* there aren't that many annotations. But for an anthology of theory you need, we learned, innumerable annotations.

A few months before publication I got a phone call, saying we had to cut three hundred pages. It was a devastating blow. Keep in mind that we were in galley and page proofs. I contacted the editorial team and said, look, we've got this problem, how are we going to handle it? So we started to make lists of figures we felt we might be able to cut, and we went back and forth until we got to a list of about twenty figures. In a couple of very close cases we actually voted. We had to revisit the entire Table of Contents and the history of theory. And in a couple of cases, we kept people but dropped selections. With Frantz Fanon, for example, we kept two chapters from *The Wretched of the Earth,* but dropped some other material by him.

CM: So, in a sense, the anthology is a snapshot of a moment in time in a process.

VBL: It is. But let me change ground for a minute. When I first got involved in this project, I said to W. W. Norton, look, why would you do a paper textbook when you could be going electronic with this? And the Norton people said, we think in the next ten years that the textbook is still going to be the dominant mode of pedagogy, and they turned out to be right. Damned little electronic textbook is in use. That said, when we had to drop the 20 figures at the end, the suggestion came up in a *Chronicle of Higher Education* online colloquy (May 2001) that we take those 20 figures, since they're already in page proofs, and put them online. Now if we think of the anthology as an archive of potential materials, why stop at those 20? Why not go back to the original lists of 250 +

50 figures and put all of them up online? So the anthology is just an impermeable selection of this larger archive, and if we were to do it tomorrow with a different set of people, even the same people, it might be a different configuration. It is not permanent, although one suspects there are "permanent" elements: there's always going to be some of Plato, very likely the *Republic* where he tries to extirpate the poets from the ideal society. But Plato keeps changing. Witness the Plato of Derrida's "Plato's Pharmacy."

I should add Norton pointed out to me that none of our permissions had been cleared for electronic rights. That was particularly discouraging for my idea to put up the twenty lost figures, not to mention the giant archive of theory. There will be all kinds of electronic things in the medium term—blackboards, websites, chatrooms, e-mail, you name it—but they're basically going to be ancillary. No doubt electronic "things" will become less ancillary and more at the center of the teaching operation as time passes. But I don't see any publishers out there making substantial gains by going electronic right now.

CM: What do you make of *The Norton*'s reception to this point? Is it better than you hoped? Or worse? Are you surprised by the attention?

VBL: It's really too early to say. There was an article in *The New York Times* in May 2001 in the Saturday Arts and Letters section.[10] A week before that there was a long article in *The Chronicle of Higher Education*, talking about *The Norton* and the problems with the last-minute cuts.[11] And then there was the article in July 2001, in *The Chicago Tribune*, which was actually using *The Norton* to attack the presence of theory at the University of Illinois at Chicago. It singles out Jane Tompkins, Stanley Fish, Walter Benn Michaels, Gerald Graff, and Lennard Davis. I imagine that for the next two or three years *The Norton* will go through different stages of reception, but I can't predict what that will be like. I do know that two journals, *Symploke* and *Pedagogy*, have scheduled forums on the anthology for 2003.

CM: How long do you think it will take for someone like Longman or someone else to try to copy it?

VBL: There are several handfuls of anthologies of theory and criticism out there now. The main ones are the Hazard Adams and the David Richter anthologies, published by Harcourt, Brace, Jovanovich, and Bedford, respectively. Longman tried a theory and criticism anthology from the ancient Greeks to the present back in the late 1980s, but it didn't do that well. They may want to go back to the drawing board and try again. In part because we had six knowledgeable and talented people working on it more or less nonstop for several years, I don't know how one would easily do better than this.

CM: If someone called you up, who was beginning a project like this, what would you tell them?

VBL: Well, I would definitely tell them to use the protocol of having the majority of the editors reach a consensus on each figure and selection. We had to have three editors agree. That rule of thumb turned out to be mighty useful and extremely good for community building. It prompted dialogue and it solved problems. That would probably be my number one piece of advice. Another practice that I instituted about half-way through the project is a monthly count of headnotes. I listed the six editors and how many headnotes they had completed by that point, all on e-mail, so that everyone could see where we all were in the project. And the people who were slower would look at that list, invariably feeling they wanted to add some more numbers. Editors would call me up the day before I'd post the monthly list and say, could you wait a day or two because I have another headnote or two I want to send to you express mail? It was a gimmick that turned out to be amazingly effective for community building, informing everyone what was happening while providing incentives to people to keep moving ahead.

I would also give the practical advice that was given to me, which is if you want to have an Instructor's Manual, make sure you have it written into the contract. If you're going to have an Index, you might want to think about having that written into the contract. You might also want to talk about page size, layout, typefont, and so on.

CM: After it all, what do you think of editing? Did you like it? There are a lot of scholars who won't touch it with a ten-foot pole; they'd rather write their own books.

VBL: I had already published four books when I decided to take on this project. I would be wary about being an editor of a big project early in my career. I'm glad I did it; it's been enormously rewarding. For one thing, I had to relive the whole history of theory, because everything had to be read and reread, not just the material in the anthology, but the material we rejected, which was an enormous amount of stuff. I had to go through, two or three times, every one of the selections, not to mention everything else in the anthology. To take an example, when I read through Aristotle's *Poetics*, I had to make sure everything that needed to be annotated was annotated. That's rigorous reading of a strange sort. I had to go to school again; there's no substitute for such intensive, wide-ranging retraining, if you want to think of it that way. The people I worked with—it's a great team—wrote wonderful headnotes, and it was a surprise and a joy to read their work, and to help them make it a little bit better. Norton is a fine publishing company. So I don't have any regrets.

What would be interesting would be to get the editors to talk about their experience. I think you'd get fairly different narratives and fairly different emphases. Some people would tell you, look, what I found is that I really hate doing annotations, and I love doing annotated bibliographies. And other people might say, I hate doing annotated bibliographies, but I love doing headnotes, especially the first paragraphs. The headnote is a genre with rules, but with quite a lot of freedom to do what you want. It can bring out scholars' creativity.

CM: Having finished *The Norton*, it seems to me that you're in a position to do a big history of the twenty-five centuries of theory.

VBL: Well, there are histories of theory. There's the William K. Wimsatt and Cleanth Brooks history of criticism that was done in the 1950s, which goes from the Greeks to the formalists in five or six hundred pages.[12] Then there's the eight-volume René Wellek history of criticism from 1750 to 1950.[13] And there's my own five hundred-page history of American criticism from the 1930s to the 1980s, and many others. If I were going to do a history of criticism from the ancient Greeks to the present, it would not be a chronological, straightahead kind of history, because that's already been done. It would have to be some sort of thematic history, say, with a chapter on the roles the poet has been assigned, maybe starting with Gorgias talking about the orator being the stylist who can use lies productively to entertain a crowd, and then Plato trying to extirpate the Sophists and the poets because they lie, bringing it up to someone like Foucault, who talks about the changing author-functions in different periods. It would be a different kind of framing, of historiography.

7

THEORY, LITERATURE, AND LITERARY STUDIES TODAY

Interview

[Professor Matti Savolainen of Oulu University in Finland did this interview on November 13, 2000 in English and translated it into Finnish for the journal *Kulttuurintutkimus* (*Cultural Studies*).]

Matti Savolainen: In the United States, the 1960s and '70s witnessed the emergence and strengthening of theory and theoretical discourse, with some academics focusing solely on theoretical works and virtually giving up reading literature. This coincides with the influx of Continental theory, especially French, to the United States. At the moment, do you see that the craze for theory has waned or somewhat calmed down or has it found its place in certain enclaves only? Or is it possible to perceive the situation in terms of location so that certain prestigious literature departments cater to theory and the rest of the country go on about things more or less as they have always done?

Vincent B. Leitch: I recall in the 1970s taking a personal vow not to write about literature any more, but to focus solely on theory. That was the moment at which Continental theory, especially French and German theory, particularly structuralism and poststructuralism, were flooding into literary studies departments. It was a common experience for literary academics at that time to make a serious commitment to theory. The next generation, or the next two generations, coming up in the 1980s and 1990s, had a quite different experience. The way we talk about that 1970s phenomenon in the United States now is to label it retrospectively "grand theory," after which followed a period of "post-theory." To generalize, there are stages in the contemporary reception of theory: different generations of intellectuals responded differently to the upsurge of theory from the 1960s to the present.

If you want to study theory at the graduate level, there are some U.S. universities that are better than others, where, for example, they have more sophisticated programs and ample faculty. Some doctoral programs offer strong specialties in theory, for instance, the University of California at Irvine, Cornell University, University of Florida, and Duke University's literature program.

Still, theory is disseminated everywhere. If you were to take a dozen literature courses as an undergraduate or graduate student in the United States today, in just about every course you would encounter some sort of theory. Theory is ubiquitous, but there are certain universities where it is more self-consciously inserted into the curriculum and systematically studied.

I regularly teach theory courses. Yet when I teach literature courses, I teach theory in those courses, and I foreground that theory, as many professors in recent decades do. Theory has triumphed: the discourse of literary and cultural studies is permeated with it. Perhaps the posttheory phase of dissemination makes it looks as though theory has somehow diminished. But it hasn't diminished at all. Quite the contrary.

MS: Jonathan Culler has suggested that literature departments took on some of the load of philosophy or philosophizing of a certain kind—the model and mode particularly set up by Jacques Derrida—that part which philosophy departments "proper" did not accept in their confines. I know that at Purdue University you yourself were involved in a program that combined literary studies and philosophy. What are the advantages and/or drawbacks of this kind of "common-law" coupling?

VBL: It is certainly the case that contemporary English departments teach philosophical texts. In part I think that's a U.S. phenomenon, meaning that philosophy departments in the United States, with a few exceptions, are given over to analytical philosophy, often leaving out modern Continental philosophy. There are a handful of philosophy departments, perhaps a half dozen, that teach Continental philosophy in a thorough and systematic way. Richard Rorty, of course, talks about this problem. He was an analytical philosopher for the first two decades of his career, then he switched to neopragmatic philosophy and Continental philosophy, notably Heidegger, hermeneutics, and poststructuralism. Starting in the late 1970s, he pointed out that literature departments had picked up philosophical tasks and texts because philosophy departments had unwisely restricted the scope of philosophy. Late in his career, Rorty joined the Department of Comparative Literature at Stanford University, having publicly earlier fled academic philosophy in the 1980s.

For eight years (1987 to 1995) I was the codirector of a doctoral program in philosophy and literature at Purdue University. In that program students choose half of their course work in philosophy and half in literature. They take one of their doctoral exams in a traditional field of philosophy and one in a traditional field of literature. At any given time there are ten students in the program. As it happens, almost all of those students are specialists in twentieth-century literary topics, very often subspecializing in literary and cultural theory. On the philosophy side, of the four choices in the exams that they can select, most select the history of philosophy, particularly from Kant to Sartre. Or they choose an exam in "values theory," meaning aesthetics plus either social and political philosophy or ethics. Very rarely, almost never, in the eight years that I was codirecting that program did anyone take an exam in either epistemology and metaphysics or logic and analytical philosophy of language.

Not surprisingly, the Purdue faculty and administration regards this as an interdisciplinary program. The literature faculty meet regularly with the philosophers. Together they work out programs, read exams, and serve on doctoral committees. Nevertheless, each person's primary identity rests in his or her discipline. Each student is obliged to choose which discipline defines his or her primary identity and where she or he will be a job seeker, *either* philosophy *or* literature. You ask about advantages and disadvantages of this setup: I will let you decide.

At the end of my time at Purdue University, which was in the late 1990s, some of us on the literature side wanted to modify the literature and philosophy program in the direction of a cultural studies program, enabling the students to select courses not only in literature and philosophy, but also in sociology, film and media, art history, political science, or whatever field they wanted to, as long as they could put together a coherent rationale for enhancing their study of philosophy and literature. The philosophers steadfastly resisted that modification, both the Continental philosophers on the committee, of which there were four, and especially the members of the Philosophy department, of which there were two dozen. So, yes, the doctoral program was interdisciplinary, but everybody had a primary disciplinary identity that would evidently never change. At the point at which cultural studies (which is more of a transdisciplinary program in the United States today than this philosophy and literature one) became a possibility, it was almost instinctively refused. Thus I would not want to present that particular program as a model for future interdisciplinary studies. It is rather a model of certain problems endemic to interdisciplinarity in general.

MS: In your book *American Literary Criticism from the 1930s to the 1980s* you documented that in the 1980s Marxism had become respectable in American academia, with the implication that in most cases it didn't have any political weight or practical social aims any more. And yet, in the field of cultural studies or media studies it is almost impossible to find theories or programs that do not carry at least traces or undercurrents of Marxist theorizing. How do you feel about this "naturalization" of Marxism in literary studies and cultural theory in general?

VBL: The situation of Marxism in the United States is different than in other countries like Finland. From the late nineteenth century to the late twentieth century, Marxism was regularly repressed, and that largely explains why in *American Literary Criticism* I started the history of modern American criticism with a chapter on U.S. Marxism and finished with a chapter on cultural studies (which represents a certain return of Marxism). One result of the official repression of Marxism in the United States is that we have a long tradition of left politics—this would include anarchism, socialism, syndicalism/unionism, communism, and progressivism—that is not Marxist. Today if you look at some of our leading left intellectuals, for instance, Noam Chomsky, bell hooks, Edward Said, they are non-Marxist leftists. Our politics on the left tends to be loose coalitions of people, some of whom are Marxist; many of whom are not. With the triumph of the New World Order and capitalist globalization in the 1990s, it looked to many observers as though Marxism was finished. However, one can be sure that Marxism will return. Jacques Derrida makes that argument in his *Specters of Marx*, noting that there is a new International of workers being formed because of increasing capitalist exploitation around the world. We're not done with Marxism.

Within the fields of literary criticism and cultural studies, Marxist theory provides key elements of analysis. I'm thinking of concepts such as ideology, hegemony, base/superstructure, modes of production, commodification. All of these are essential tools in contemporary criticism and theory, including, to be sure, many non-Marxist kinds of theory. One might be doing postcolonial criticism or race studies and be using the routine idea of hegemony without quite recalling that it is coming from Marxism. In recent decades there has been a broad dissemination and naturalization of Marxism.

A number of leading critics in American literary criticism are self-identified Marxists. One thinks of Gayatri Spivak and Fredric Jameson, but there is a younger generation of people coming up who are self-identified Marxists. Many literary critics belong to the Marxist Literary Group (MLG), which has hundreds of members among academics who meet each June and December. On the one hand, one wishes that Marxism had not been repressed and that there existed some sort of healthy broad-based leftist, if not Marxist, political party. Yet "Marxism" in its various forms (including post-Marxism) is alive and well in the university, and my prediction is that it will continue to be so in the foreseeable future.

MS: How do you see the institutionalization of cultural studies in relation to literary studies? Do you see it as a threat or an incentive? And another question that always pops up when we are discussing the aims and functions of cultural studies: how do you perceive the claims to interdisciplinarity in this context? To what extent are they being achieved?

VBL: On the topic of cultural studies, several observations: to begin with, as far as I know, there is not one university department of cultural studies in the United States. There are programs, institutes, centers, but not a department per se. (Things are quite different in Britain, for instance.) Cultural studies has been received in the U.S. institution, but not in as significant or permanent a way as one would have thought or liked. Another aspect of this problem deserves note: there are numerous graduate students earning their doctoral degrees focused on cultural studies who can't find jobs because there aren't many such jobs in the United States.

If you look at the various forms of cultural studies on different campuses, you find that they are often a barometer of what's happening on those campuses. For example, when I was at Purdue University, as I mentioned earlier, we on the literature side of the doctoral program in literature and philosophy were not able to open up that program to cultural studies. The philosophers resisted. So what the literature group did was to propose a theory and cultural studies (TCS) semiautonomous program within the English department, in an administrative format self-consciously symmetrical to the already existing programs in that large department in linguistics, in creative writing, and in rhetoric and composition. We had preexisting models for what a semiautonomous program *within* the English department looked like. The theory and cultural studies program aped those models in order to make its proposal more palatable to the rest of the English faculty. Of the fifty faculty members in that department, there were quite a number who were, nevertheless, resistant to TCS as a separate program.

Now on the question of whether theory and cultural studies at Purdue is interdisciplinary: well, yes and no. No, in the sense that the faculty in that program are all people with Ph.D.s in English or comparative literature. They are not trained in other disciplines. (We tried to set up an interdisciplinary program involving the departments of philosophy, English, and others such as political science, sociology, art history, communications, and so on, but we were unable to do it.) Still, yes, if one looks at the work that people are doing in cultural studies within English departments as well as in centers, programs, and institutes, it definitely is a hybrid of other disciplines, conjoining sociology, media studies, theory, philosophy, and so on. As I see it, cultural studies is the postmodern discipline *par excellence*, meaning a crossover, hybrid field, an innovative pastiche. It is worth recalling here also that each discipline itself partakes, to a greater or lesser degree, of other disciplines, making interdisciplinarity as much a point of departure as some ideal future endpoint.

MS: In an anthology like *The Norton Anthology of Theory and Criticism*, on which you served as general editor, it is almost taken for granted that one begins with Plato and Aristotle, even if the chosen extracts may change from decade to decade. Looking at the Table of Contents, I felt that you have very carefully tried to cover the Middle Ages, or in more general terms, the period after Greek and Roman antiquity up to the sixteenth and seventeenth centuries, which is often skipped over very fast. Are you, perhaps in the spirit of Ernst Robert Curtius, trying to underline the Latin or Latinized literary legacy all the way up to our modern period?

VBL: As a child growing up, I heard Latin on a regular basis. I studied Latin in Catholic school, as did many people of my generation, who grew up in the Catholic tradition. (I spent thirteen years in Catholic schools.) Until the late 1960s the Catholic mass was in Latin. But consider also the history of education in the United States during the twentieth century: my father studied Greek and Latin when he was in high school during the 1930s; I studied Latin and French during the

1960s; my two children, who went to school in the 1990s, did not study Latin. They both studied modern European languages (German and French). The Latin tradition is coming to an end in the way that it operated into the twentieth century. I have mixed emotions about that, being simultaneously sad and nostalgic, but also enthusiastic about the triumph of the vernaculars.

Aside from the question of the language, there's a great deal of interesting work in the Middle Ages which, of course, medievalists know about, but which has not typically made it into anthologies of theory and criticism. That's an oversight on the part of previous anthology makers.

There's something else at issue here. For my generation the definition of "theory" is much broader than it was for earlier generations. One could take representative anthologies put together in the 1940s, '50s, and '60s and compare them with later ones, and one would see what I'm getting at. When I define "theory," I include not just poetics and aesthetics, but a whole set of other disciplines and subdisciplines, which explains in part why the medieval period then becomes quite interesting. That is, for my contemporaries, "theory" reaches beyond poetics and aesthetics and includes rhetoric, philosophy of language, the commentary tradition (exegesis), philology, and hermeneutics. This explains why we have selections not just from Thomas Aquinas and Dante, but from Augustine and Moses Maimonides, the latter of whom theorizes Jewish scriptural exegesis. Theory also includes political theory and pedagogy. What might I mean by political theory? The role of literacy in society turns out to be productive of some interesting selections in our anthology, and not only from *Republic*. If one looks at Christine de Pizan, one discovers a fifteenth-century person complaining that women are not educated, not given the right to become literate, and not allowed to be familiar with literature. We have several selections from related theoretical texts in which, for example, the issue of the vernacular surfaces, raising questions about hegemonic and minority languages and literatures. Education, pedagogy, language, and literacy, politics are all in certain significant ways part of the history of literary and cultural theory. They need to show up in anthologies.

By the way, *The Norton Anthology* starts with Gorgias, not Plato. The sophist view of discourse deserves reconsideration, and Plato needs to be recontextualized among theorists.

MS: Let us look at the twentieth century and your selections from Friedrich Nietzsche, Sigmund Freud, and Ferdinand de Saussure onwards. This is the time period that usually undergoes changes in various anthologies, the more so the closer to the present we get. One can see that the attempt to represent voices from the black or Third World or postcolonial perspectives is obvious (Zora Neale Hurston, Frantz Fanon, Homi K. Bhabha, etc.) and that the standard focus on French theorists continues (Claude Lévi-Strauss, Jacques Derrida, Michel Foucault, Hélène Cixous, etc.), perhaps at the expense of German authors, even though the Frankfurt School is well represented. I was slightly struck by the almost virtual absence of the European phenomenological–hermeneutic tradition: Friedrich Schleiermacher and Martin Heidegger are included but not Hans-Georg Gadamer or Paul Ricoeur, for instance. And as to semiotics, the name of Umberto Eco is missing. Would you like to comment on these inclusions and exclusions?

VBL: When I think of hermeneutics, I think of it broadly, so the representation of hermeneutics in the anthology, in my mind, would include people like Dante, Aquinas, Augustine, even Freud. We have some significant interpretation theory out of the latter's *The Interpretation of Dreams*, for instance. We also include E. D. Hirsch, Maimonides, Schleiermacher, Hans Robert Jauss. Hermeneutics is a tradition not limited to phenomenological hermeneutics. There is "general hermeneutics." Within general hermeneutics, one would situate biblical, legal, and literary hermeneutics as well as the phenomenological tradition of philosophical hermeneutics coming from middle eighteenth-century Germany to the present.

With regard to Gadamer and Ricoeur, we editors did look at selections from both of them and didn't find anything upon which to agree. If one looks at how much phenomenology is in the anthology, one could say that, with our selections from G. W. F. Hegel, Heidegger, Georges Poulet, Jean-Paul Sartre, de Beauvoir, Jauss, and Wolfgang Iser, we have ample representation of the phenomenological tradition. Although Ricoeur is not there, there are quite a few other representative figures. Of course, tough choices have to be made; not everything can be included even in a big anthology like this one.

One other observation regarding hermeneutics: in the United States hermeneutics, particularly twentieth-century hermeneutics, is a minor strand of theory and criticism, which is taught and written about largely by people who are coming out of the Catholic tradition. If one lives within that religious tradition, and if one is doing literary theory, hermeneutics is perhaps the most vital, long-standing, energetic strand of thinking. What happens, though, is that people operating in this tradition have to deal with apostates such as Heidegger. If one examines John Caputo—a leading Catholic philosopher and hermeneuticist at Villanova University—his books are on the roles of Heidegger, Foucault, and Derrida in reinvigorating the hermeneutic tradition for someone who's a believer and member of the Catholic church. One can glimpse there what I mean by dealing with apostates and non-Catholics in the larger hermeneutic project of postmodern Catholic interpretive theory. (I have a chapter on the phenomenon of "posthermeneutics" focused on John Caputo in my book *Postmodernism—Local Effects, Global Flows.*)

About the semiotic tradition and your surprise that Umberto Eco is not included in the anthology, let me say several things. There is quite a bit of structuralism and semiotics in the anthology, from Saussure, Roman Jakobson, and Lévi-Strauss down through Jacques Lacan, Louis Althusser, Roland Barthes, Northrop Frye, Tzvetan Todorov, and Hayden White. By the way, Augustine's sign theory fits in here. One of the things that I have not talked about that plays into this question is the matter of for whom *The Norton Anthology of Theory and Criticism* is designed. The primary readers are undergraduate literature majors. My experience with Umberto Eco is that his best theoretical materials are not generally accessible to undergraduate students. Also his influence in the United States is minimal nowadays, as is scientific semiotics in general.

Perhaps you are asking this other, larger question: What's the status of literary semiotics in the U.S. academy at the beginning of the twenty-first century? I would say that semiotics is now a minor strand of literary and cultural inquiry. The most vital component of it is narratology, which has a significant number of people involved who have their own organization, their own annual meeting, and so on. But general semiotics, my sense is that mainly media and film studies have kept that tradition going. Social semiotics has become a wing of cultural studies. One can look at some of the selections we have on media and everyday culture to get a sense of what semiotics has evolved into. I am thinking of texts by Barthes, Laura Mulvey, and Judith Butler where the critical diagnosis of cultural codes is naturalized and routinized by now, no longer flying under the banner of a vanguard semiotics.

MS: The dictates of "political correctness" may be hard to achieve in all their multiplicity and heterogeneity, but as far as I can see your scheme seems to be quite successful in this regard: African-American criticism (Barbara Smith, Henry Louis Gates Jr., bell hooks), Native American criticism (Paula Gunn Allen, Gerald Vizenor), Latina/Latino perspectives (Gloria Anzaldúa), gay/lesbian/queer theorizing (Adrienne Rich, Eve Kosofsky Sedgwick, Judith Butler). I was also happy to find Donna Haraway's "A Manifesto for Cyborgs." To what extent do you think it may have affected your present editorial work?

VBL: Within the U.S. context the term "political correctness" has come to be mainly a right-wing slur used to characterize the programs and values of liberals and leftists. I am uncomfortable with the term. In any case, the question is: if you're putting together a textbook today like a Norton anthology, and you're making up selections for your Table of Contents, how concerned should you be with representation of different races and ethnicities, genders and sexualities, and social classes?

My initial response is that criticism and theory, especially from the 1960s to the present, the onset of the postmodern moment, has had increasing impact from race and ethnicity theory, gender and sexuality theory, and theory of social class. If you're trying to represent what's going on in contemporary theory, you have to be engaged with "political correctness," whether you prefer to or not. That's the first thing. But once you set up a rich array of selections in contemporary theory of ethnicity and race, gender and sexuality, and class, the question arises about forerunners in the history of these areas. Are there any earlier theories of class or gender or race and ethnicity that might be worth retrieving? You will find in the pre-twentieth-century part of the anthology selections that have resonance with the later selections from the twentieth century. For example, in the Christine de Pizan selection there are feminist gender issues that obviously come up later in the nineteenth and twentieth centuries. This is one among many possible examples of a historically informed "political correctness."

What's my attitude to this? Hurrah! Today we postmoderns are thinking of literature and theory with regard not just to the antiquated narrow canon of the Cold War formalist period in literary criticism, but to the emergent canons of other races and genders. Now Native American literature, including the oral components of that literature, and African-American literature, including the oral components of that literature, can be thought about as part of an expanded multifaceted literary tradition. The narrow belletristic modern definition of literature that was refined from the eighteenth century to the mid-twentieth century is being questioned from many different perspectives today. For me that turns out to be a liberation, and I have no hesitation in saying it is a good thing.

MS: Stuart Moulthrop is the youngest of your critics (born in 1957) and has the concluding article in your anthology. His piece ("You Say You Want a Revolution: Hypertext and the Laws of Media") takes the reader to new forms and dimensions of textuality, digital production, and the Internet. Putting aside the anthology, is this the direction toward which you see literary studies heading? What happens to the old-time literature professor who has been teaching Nathaniel Hawthorne and Virginia Woolf most of his or her career or whose specialty is the Victorian novel?

VBL: My experience of U.S. literature departments is that when new things come along you add them on, and nothing drops out. The ubiquitous principle of coverage is not based on dropping but adding. If you look at the staff in a representative English department at any given moment, you have four generations of people or perhaps three generations, depending on how you want to define generations. Given that there is an annual five to ten percent turnover due to departures and new hires, faculty members are regularly going out and coming in. In most departments you can see the different generations operating simultaneously: today you will get people teaching the Victorian novel in a 1950s "traditional" way, while you have other people teaching hypertext in a twenty-first century mode. But my sense of it is—certainly on the research and publication front, if not on the teaching front—the kind of research that the "older generation" is publishing now, let's say in nineteenth-century American studies or in Victorian fiction, has been influenced by theory and criticism. You might now have an older generation professor doing a Foucauldian analysis of a Dickens novel. I don't find that rapid (theory) change is, in actual fact, creating an untenable situation for large numbers of old-time professors. Perhaps it should be? And also the phenomenon of uneven development comes into play here. There are departments (I won't name any) that in the 1970s resolutely fended off and refused the theory wave. In some cases, it wasn't until the 1990s that they woke up and decided to do something about this problem, namely, that they had excluded theory from their curriculum and faculty hires. You can look at a faculty in a department and see the past history of the department in light of what's represented and what isn't, including theory as well as standard period and genre coverage. Each department has its own singular history and configuration.

Where is literary studies headed now, you ask. I think that the canon of discourses we study and the approaches that we use will continue to expand, and also to segment into different types, areas, and modes. The definition of literature has been broadened and will continue to be so. It includes not only canonical literature, but also minority and pulp literature (popular romance, gothic horror, science fiction, mystery, detective, and western). In this expansion one can imagine hypertextual novels soon being added, not to mention whatever new forms may come along. The broadening of the definition of literature and the canon characteristic of the postmodern period, however, doesn't mean that the hierarchy of genres and forms is being overturned. Among literary historians the epic and tragedy still hold pride of place over lyric poetry and fiction. In recent decades we've entered into a time of extreme expansion, as opposed to the earlier time of extreme contraction that characterized the history of literature from the eighteenth century to the mid-twentieth century. One should expect some backlash. The more we expand the canon of texts and approaches, the more we're likely to have rearguard actions (e.g., people trying to restore the canon and narrow the approaches). But also there are going to be continual "reconsiderations." This typically entails going back to the tradition and making it new, for instance, a queer theory reading of Shakespeare as a way of revaluing Shakespeare and making him new. To respond directly to your question about where literary studies is headed, I think that a decade from now the old canon and the old genre hierarchy will still be there, but there will also be "enhancements" and "reconsiderations" and making it new. There will be new discourses added as well as rearguard actions seeking to restore literary studies to an earlier time. Further expansion and segmentation will continue.

What I sometimes worry and wonder about in the U.S. context is the possible breaking away of the semiautonomous programs within literary studies departments—departments of English, for instance—like rhetoric and composition, linguistics, creative writing, film studies, and cultural studies. If we start to see them striking out on their own in large numbers to set up their own departments, which may be a good thing, there is a possibility that in losing these components of its present operation the literary studies department will find itself truncated and narrowed through external forces, and it might very well develop ideologies to suit that new reality. The result could be retrenchment back to more conservative modes of literary studies.

MS: The 1980s was the decade during which the debate about the canon was at its peak. The issue of canon formation was "hot stuff" and the whole idea of universal values and timeless standards was challenged. In reaction to this, Allan Bloom's *The Closing of the American Mind* (1987) and E. D. Hirsch, Jr.'s *Cultural Literacy* (1987) expressed, in their different ways, concerns and anxieties about the state of Western civilization in general and American culture in particular.

Is the canon and canon formation still an issue in the United States? How is the question linked with the bigger question of cultural difference and multiculturalism?

VBL: In the United States the canon wars are "over"—the canon has been changed and expanded. Still, this work will continue into the future. Significantly, there are a number of issues we continue to wrestle with that circulated around the question of the canon. Allan Bloom and E. D. Hirsch, as you mention, wrote influential books in the late 1980s, both defending "great traditionalism," that is, arguing we should study the greats and that that's the most important thing. Now, those two books are very different books, although a core argument in both is to protect the great tradition. The Bloom book, for example, is very hostile, almost foaming-at-the-mouth hostile, to popular culture, especially rock music and television, and by implication Bloom has no use for cultural studies. The Bloom book raises up in a rather stark way the whole question of high versus low culture, what Andreas Huyssen refers to as the "great divide." I see the Bloom book as being anti-or pre-postmodern, as it were, in its attempt to preserve the great tradition and, on the other hand, to exclude mass, popular, middlebrow, and "low" culture.

A key motivation of the Hirsch book is his concern about what to teach precollege, preuniversity students, including both elementary and high school students. This is not the first time that a literary theorist has found himself preoccupied with preuniversity education and pedagogy. I. A. Richards in the 1940s went through the same kind of thing. Northrop Frye developed a whole set of textbooks for a sequential literary curriculum. Today what we have in U.S. high schools is a mixture of the great tradition and multicultural traditions. If you study American or English literature in the school system, you're going to get both; it's not an either/or. Hirsch continues to argue that there's too much exposure to popular culture and not enough focus on cultural tradition.

If you factor in U.S. immigration (we have a long history here and it is complicated) in the post-World War II period, there have been several large waves of immigrants coming from different countries than in the past. We have massive numbers of people entering this country, just short of a million each year. The sense of U.S. culture being multicultural is stronger today than it has been since the turn of the century, when my ancestors came from Ireland and Sicily. I don't see the canon being purged anytime soon on a wide scale, nor do I see a deleting of the whole postmodern multicultural turn that we took in the late twentieth century. I expect further expansions and differentiations to the canon.

The extreme nationalist, populist, racist, and antiimmigrant "English First" language campaigns will not stem this tide of change, although anti-Affirmative Action lawsuits from neoconservatives have succeeded here and there in checking progress.

MS: To celebrate the new millennium the leading Finnish newspaper *Helsingin Sanomat* set a group of people to read Volter Kilpi's famous *Alastalon salissa* (1933) and documented their exchange of ideas chapter by chapter every week in their Saturday issue. In this way the paper contributed to locating and securing a place for this epic in the Finnish canon. There seems to have been an attempt to find a Finnish modernist novel comparable in scope and linguistic innovation to Joyce's *Ulysses*. Can you think of any similar measures to affect canon formation in the United States? Can you think of, say, *The New York Times Book Review* starting to publicize and propagate a work of fiction of the twentieth century which is not widely read or appreciated and is maybe only a favorite of a select few?

VBL: With the opening of the twenty-first century and the end of the millennium, a great deal of looking back is happening, some of which involves a shoring up. If you add to that the end of the Soviet bloc and the Cold War (particularly in a European context and a specifically Finnish context), there is not simply an end of the millennium and an end of the twentieth century (where one would look back trying to figure out what holds Finnish culture together, what achievements there have been), but also a sense of having to redefine, even if that means to ratify the status quo, what is Europe, what is Finland. There are nationalist consolidation projects going on all across Europe at the start of the new millennium, which are different from what is going on in the United States. But there is also the European Union. In its own way Finland is caught up in such an enterprise. What is going to become of Karelia and Karelians, including those living in the diaspora? Laplanders? The European Union? NATO? I'm not surprised that *Helsingin Sanomat* would be going back trying to consolidate the sense of twentieth-century Finnish literature and culture. In my mind that's a good thing on balance. The choice of the Kilpi text is, of course, debatable.

In this kind of "looking back," which has various dimensions to it, there needs to be some weeding out. It seems logical that a newspaper would be involved in the project. Why? Because newspapers, magazines, and other print media are naturally affiliated with books and Great Books (literacy). It's not surprising that the official newspaper of

Finland would be engaged in looking back and sifting through twentieth-century Finnish literature as a way to define Finnish culture. Print literacy and nation-building go together, as we know from Benedict Anderson's *Imagined Communities: Reflections on the Origin and Spread of Nationalism* (rev. ed., 1991).

Consider this, the canon wars that went on in the 1970s and 1980s in the United States entailed a revaluation of past literature. It didn't have the feel of the millennium and the fin de siècle to it explicitly. It operated more along multicultural, political correctness lines. But, nevertheless, it involved looking backwards, shoring up, sifting through. There is a women's literature, a Native American literature, an African-American literature, and many other U.S. literatures. They deserve to be recovered, revalued, studied, and made part of the canon. Perhaps the United States experienced this process of sifting through the canon earlier than some other countries?

In 1999 there were, of course, media people in the United States making lists of the hundred best books, the ten best American novels, and what have you. Although there are examples of that, it is not quite the same as you evidently had with *Helsingin Sanomat*. In the United States we really do not have one national newspaper the way many other countries do. *The New York Times* is a national newspaper for a very small segment of the population. In Oklahoma, for instance, *The New York Times* is very rarely mentioned. When I lived in New York, it was the dominant newspaper only among segments of middle and upper (but not lower and working) classes.

MS: Let's get to the literary scene in the United States at the turn of the millennium. Certain contemporary authors may attract an immense interest as thesis topics, and academic scholarship or whole fields or subfields of literary production may emerge and gain in popularity. Is there something along these lines on which you would like to comment? After the African-American women writers in the 1970s and '80s, there has been a great deal of interest in other ethnic literatures such as Native American or Asian-American literatures, and also women writers in many cases have taken the floor. I'm thinking of people such as Leslie Marmon Silko, Louise Erdrich, and Maxine Hong Kingston.

VBL: I argue that what postmodern globalization looks like at the level of U.S. literature is a kind of "transnationalization" of our literature from *within* and *without*. In other words, if you are asking me what is U.S. literature today, I answer there are numerous literatures that make up U.S. literature. There's Native American, Asian-American, Hispanic-American, and so on. One could go through a long list. If you consider each one of those, let's say Asian-American, there are within Asian-American close to two dozen different traditions: Philippine-American, Chinese-American, Japanese-American, Korean-American, and so on. Some of the literatures within these categories are written not just in English, but in Asian languages. For example, in Oklahoma, there is a community of 30,000 Vietnamese people who came to Oklahoma City in the 1970s after the Vietnam war. There are people in that community who are writing stories and poems in Vietnamese. What do we want to call that? Vietnamese-American literature. If you go into Italian-American literature, Chinese-American literature, Mexican-American literature, you'll find the same thing. An anthology was published recently by Marc Shell and Werner Sollors of Harvard University, *The Multilingual Anthology of American Literature* (2000), which is a pioneering collection of U.S. literature in several dozen non-English native languages. This is what I mean by the transnationalization of U.S. literature from *within*.

Also there are postmodern globalizing phenomena going on from *without*: the creation of Anglophone literature, the Black Atlantic arts, Francophone literature, and Meso-American (Inter-American) literature. In this last category, Inter-American literature, you have Canadian, U.S., Central American, and South American indigenous literatures regarded as a unified regional block, having more in common with one another than with the "national" literatures that they happen to be part of now. That represents a transnationalization from *without*, if I can put it that way. So, yes, I do see new things on the literary horizon, and obviously new writers will emerge and are emerging.

MS: Shall we move over to the mainstream? If the most hectic days of the Pynchon industry are in the past, are there any authors to challenge his position? Don DeLillo perhaps? Or how does Paul Auster fare on the thesis market?

VBL: The question you are asking is who is the next great U.S. writer, the next great fiction writer, the next great novelist. Right? Much of the literary research published today, at least in the form of the scholarly monograph, is not focused on individual writers. Doctoral students are frequently advised not to write on individual authors because such books don't sell; they seem old fashioned; publishers lack interest in them. What you often encounter are books on schools and movements, like African-American women writers or Asian-American novelists, or books on themes and topics, like gender bending or passing in contemporary literature.

If one focuses on different genres, one gets very different pictures. For example, U.S. poetry, which up until the mid-twentieth century was centered in the Northeastern major cities and along the Eastern seaboard, especially New York, is now produced all over the place. There's been a real explosion. It's one example of postmodern disorganization in the arts. A parallel phenomenon would be what has happened with the creation of popular music. It used to be that in order for a rock group to be widely known by the public they had to get an agent, find a major record label, play a well-defined club circuit, do tours, and so on. But now people produce their own CDs at relatively low cost, book their own shows, and gain regional notoriety, all without too much trouble. The means of production for popular music have changed, and consequently there are bands all over the place producing their own CDs. It's the same with poetry. There are numerous small magazines for poetry and venues for poetry readings. The means of production for poetry have changed. There are many more people writing and publishing poems and poetry than ever before. Just consider all the creative writing programs in the United States. We also have lots of anthologies of contemporary poetry that bear witness to this dispersion. And note that I have said nothing here about poetry slams, rap, and other such vibrant phenomena. Meanwhile, single-authored poetry books produced and distributed in the traditional way by major commercial publishing houses are disappearing; they are not economical; they lose money. Now drama is a different story. It requires playhouses and ensembles of actors; it is very expensive to put on plays, although there is a much more thriving regional and community drama nowadays than, let's say, at midcentury. Contemporary drama has not gone through quite as much of a proliferation (disorganization) as poetry, provided we exclude television (cable TV especially) and movie drama. Fiction has its own complicated story, which I won't narrate here.

Your question asks about who is the next *great writer* in the world of U.S. fiction. Perhaps we should first investigate that category itself? But what is most interesting in U.S. literary circles right now for me is the continuing proliferation of poetry, the thriving regionalization and breakup of drama, the rise of ethnic literatures, the expansion of pulp literatures, the development of theory during postmodern times especially, and not so much who's *the* major fiction writer. In any case, you left out Toni Morrison and other Nobel Prize-level authors such as Saul Bellow. But I prefer not to pick a winner in who will be the next great American fiction writer. Paul Auster, to make one last comment on this topic, appears to have a much higher profile in Europe than he does in the United States. Perhaps Europe will be involved in picking the next major fiction writer.

MS: Would you like to speculate on the future of literary theory and literary studies in the United States (beyond the outline of *The Norton Anthology*)? What are the directions it will take? What are the fields of study that are just emerging? To take one example, do you see that environmental concerns in the form of ecocriticism along the lines of, say, Lawrence Buell's book on Thoreau, *The Environmental Imagination* (1996), are on the rise? Gary Snyder would also provide ample material for this kind of approach.

VBL: Allow me to play the prophet. There will be more impressive production of Internet literature and hypertexts. Cultural studies will be broadly institutionalized in a way that it isn't right now. Certain movements, approaches, schools, and groups will continue to develop in vital ways: among those would be most prominently queer theory, postcolonial studies, and new historicisms, as well as Native American, Asian-American, and Hispanic-American studies.

If I think about developments in criticism and theory in terms of dominant paradigms, the dominant paradigm from the 1930s to the 1960s was New Criticism (literary formalism); then in the 1970s and '80s it was poststructuralism. From the late 1980s to the present, cultural studies has been the dominant paradigm. Within those paradigms there are all kinds of alternatives and countercurrents. If you are asking me what is the next *dominant* paradigm, what comes after cultural studies, I cannot tell you; I cannot glimpse it. I think that cultural studies has a way to go yet.

That said, there are new fields and branches of study being developed as we speak. Body studies and queer studies would be examples. Science and leisure studies are others. And ecocriticism and visual culture studies would be yet others; globalization studies still another. These are all new fields (or subfields) in different stages of development, which shortly may emerge as "autonomous." You ask about ecocriticism in particular. My hunch is that it will become an important branch of globalization theory and criticism as well as a semiautonomous subfield.

One can also see developing a new belletrism (to use Jeffrey Williams' term) which takes several forms. Quite a few prominent critics are explicitly turning away from sophisticated theoretical criticism toward personal criticism and autobiographical writing. Henry Louis Gates and Jane Tompkins would be prominent instances. Another aspect of this new belletrism involves the baby boomers, who, as they age and head toward retirement, may be expected to go through a conservative stage in their view of literary studies, returning to traditional canonical literature. We saw a few years ago Frank Lentricchia coming out in the magazine *Lingua Franca*, saying that he's not going to do theory any more; instead he's going to focus on reading and teaching literature. That is suggestive of a turn that I will not be surprised to see develop further in coming years.

MS: The University of Joensuu in Finland recently organized an interdisciplinary conference titled "Cultural Identity and Its Global Manifestations." As the title indicates, the construction of identities in the crossfire of global and local attractions and pressures is on the agenda. This is a preamble to my final question: How do you see the problematics of globalization in the North American context? This is a paradoxical question because globalization, in a sense, has been taken by some to mean "Americanization" of the globe. For many of us living in Europe and in other continents, "Americanization" can be a threat, whereas to some of you it may seem like a victory. What does globalization mean for you and what would its ramifications be for literary studies?

VBL: I do not see globalization as simply Americanization. That would be a misunderstanding of globalization, which has a history going back at least five centuries. The cutting edge, the vanguard of globalization, is today multinational corporations, or perhaps finance capital, or maybe, speaking symbolically, the International Monetary Fund (IMF). A multinational corporation is not just an American corporation. When I look at many of the products and commodities that are flowing through daily life around the globe today, I see such representative phenomena as a car whose components are made about equally in Japan, America, the Caribbean, Korea, and so on. Such products are multinational products made by multinational corporations and workers. These corporations are not rooted in national economies; they move from one national economy to another, depending on the best deal they can get. There is a "race toward the bottom," a leveling down in search of low wages, taxes, and fewer legal restrictions. We see, particularly in recent decades, a number of "American" corporations moving offshore to Mexico and many other "hotspots" where they can get nice "incentives" from the local governments, lower expenses, cheaper workers, and the option not to fund employee benefits. This is a cutting edge of globalization, and it is not Americanization in any simple or direct sense. The workers, the materials, and the executives are not just transplanted Americans, nor are the stockholders one hundred percent Americans.

Also the American dollar is out of the control of the American central bank. It's become a global currency, and it's traded on global markets, particularly in London, with considerable abandon that has little to do with the politicians in Washington, D.C. (We saw something like this globalization of currency with petrodollars in the 1970s.) It is another form of globalization that appears to be purely American, but is not. By the way, currency speculation—so characteristic of globalization—has metastasized in recent decades: $1.5 trillion changes hands on world money markets daily, which is seventy times the trade in commodities and nonfinancial services. During the 1970s the ratio was 3.5 to 1. In the 1970s the economist James Tobin proposed a very small uniform international tax, from .05 to 1%, on all speculative transactions to reduce their number, providing more fiscal autonomy for nations and funding campaigns against disease and poverty. It never happened.

Perhaps today globalization, or maybe the European Union, is a more significant, more serious problem or worry for Europeans than old style 1950s Americanization? That would be something for you to decide. (NATO complicates things here, of course.)

With globalization, there are two well-attested simultaneous cultural phenomena going on: homogenization and differentiation. An example of that would be the rise of "world music," which is occurring alongside the trend toward the restoration and recovery of all kinds of local musical traditions. Another example is the establishment of teen fashion on a global level through MTV and other worldwide media and the simultaneous efforts to restore native costumes and tribal dress. Globalization entails a kind of homogenizing on a world scale, but also a differentiating and singularizing on a local scale. Those phenomena are co-occurring. Yet if you overlay the concept of Americanization onto that whole double-pronged dynamic, it doesn't quite match up or make sense. Perhaps, then, the easy equation of globalization and Americanization is a bit of a hangover from earlier Cold War paranoia?

That said, massive amounts of American capital are driving globalization, but not only American capital. Many nations are happily engaged in the process; relatively few are not. What can one say about China, for instance, which has experienced world-record economic growth for more than a decade? Economic globalization is triumphant, comparatively unregulated capitalism running over all borders and partitions worldwide, selling goods and services, making investments, changing local customs, inciting the "race toward the bottom" (exploitation and inequality), setting everything on a money standard (e.g., begetting IMF loans, debts, "bailouts"). For many people the quality of everyday life has improved: better and more varied food, clothing, housing, interior design, medical care, education, and entertainment. For many, many others, poverty has come and stayed. The effects of such globalization are obviously wildly uneven and unequal. Lastly, to the extent that the American military enforces global "free trade," it is the visible marshal of this New World Order, but, as in the Iraq War of the early 1990s and the more recent Iraq war of 2003, this force is supported by nations in Europe, the Middle East, and Asia.

Among the many disparate forms of globalization in current literary and cultural studies are, off the top of my head: postcolonial theory; theories of postmodernity and globalization; ecocriticism; worldwide feminism; Anglophone, Francophone, and Hispanophone literatures; emergent transnational and regional aesthetic forms such as Black Atlantic arts, Maghreb literatures, Inter-American literatures, Pacific Rim literatures, and so on. In what way are these new literary and cultural phenomena just forms of Americanization? In what ways not?

PART 2
Cultural Studies Practiced

8

CRITICIZING GLOBALIZATION
The Case of Pierre Bourdieu

LIKE MANY OTHER ACADEMIC LITERARY INTELLECTUALS and cultural studies researchers and theorists during recent decades, I have found the
multifaceted sociology of Pierre Bourdieu useful in my teaching and
research. His well-known concepts of "cultural capital," "distinction,"
and "educational reproduction," for example, have productively entered into the lexicon of cultural and literary studies, and several of his
books on these topics are now contemporary classics, including the
coauthored *Reproduction in Education, Society, and Culture* (1970),
Distinction: A Social Critique of the Judgment of Taste (1979), and
Homo Academicus (1984). Conversely, none of his considerable work
on precapitalist Algerian tribal people and only one of the many works
on social scientific methodology, *Outline of a Theory of Practice* (1972),
has influenced the fields of literary criticism or cultural studies. Author of several dozen books, Bourdieu is celebrated for three or four of
them. Outside of sociology, his reception has been highly filtered and
selective. Of the more than a dozen critical books about him, almost
all are from sociologists. And to the considerable extent that he focuses
upon social dynamics in France, his work possesses limited appeal. Yet
with his characteristic combination of broad philosophical reflection
as well as copious empirical data (laid out in numerous charts and statistical tables), he appeals not just to French social scientists but to
Western humanists in general. This is most especially true of the surprising spate of books published by Bourdieu between 1993 and 2001,
the last years of his life, which advance sharp social criticism aimed at

a wide public readership, self-consciously addressing while reaching beyond academic readers. (Upon publication some of these books became bestsellers in France.) I am thinking mainly of the coauthored *The Weight of the World* (1993), *On Television* (1996), *Acts of Resistance: Against the Tyranny of the Market* (1998), and *Contre-feux 2: Pour un mouvement social européen* (2001), particularly the last two "theoretical" (nonempirical) books, both explicitly addressing European readers and movingly attacking the advent of neoliberal globalization accompanying the post-Cold War New World Order.

In the past Bourdieu's best critics all lodged complaints about his delimited politics. David Schwartz stated, "Bourdieu's field analysis needs a sociology of politics that would examine the actual processes of political action and mobilization."[1] Bridget Fowler called for Bourdieu "to strengthen further the political implications of his scientific studies."[2] Richard Jenkins observed, "His social universe ultimately remains one in which things happen to people, rather than a world in which they can intervene in their individual and collective destinies."[3] Loïc Wacquant, collaborator and coauthor with Bourdieu, declared, "For Bourdieu, the genuine intellectual is defined by her or his independence from temporal powers, from the interference of economic and political authority."[4] And Nicholas Garnham summed up the matter this way: "The problem . . . is whether we can find any sources for willed social change, and thus for a politics, within Bourdieu's explanatory schema. I do not see any."[5] It was and is widely attested among critics that Bourdieu is a pessimist and determinist, offering little encouragement to political activists. The concluding critique by seven social scientists in their collectively coauthored introduction is typical: "Bourdieu is profoundly pessimistic politically."[6]

It is in this context that Bourdieu's *Acts of Resistance*, *Contre-feux 2*, and a handful of polemical essays written from the mid-1990s onwards come as a shock.[7] Unlike the most celebrated books (for example, *Distinction* and *Homo Academicus*), these late works, which are collections of short occasional pieces, address nonspecialist audiences, most often Europeans, ranging from trade union workers, protesters, and strikers to writers' groups, newspaper readers, and students. Unexpectedly, there are few citations of scholarship and no statistical tables, Bourdieu's stock in trade. And the prose style is relatively clear and straightforward. In the past, Bourdieu was widely and soundly criticized for his forbidding style, characteristically filled with long complex sentences, having subordinate clauses piled on top of one another, with qualifications upon qualifications forcing double and triple reading of many sentences, all slowing the pace of reading sometimes to a puzzled stand-still. With these late works Bourdieu emerged on a European (not just French) stage as a cogent public intellectual critical of the New World Order and its many depredations, calling for a new social movement—a large-scale set of coalitions in Europe—united against globalization. As such, Bourdieu presents a useful model for contemporary cultural studies not only in the innovative sociological theories he employs and in his role as public intellectual, but also in the powerful critique of globalization he develops and especially in the revealing problems he encounters along the way.

LOOKING BACK: HABITUS, CULTURAL CAPITAL, FIELD

The three main sociological concepts that Bourdieu developed over four decades include "habitus," "cultural capital," and "field." Bourdieu's critics agree with me on this observation. These analytical tools designed to solve problems as well as to develop research projects typically puzzle Bourdieu's first-time readers. I have been one of those readers. Like others in the Anglophone world, I first encountered Bourdieu's special terminology in his *Outline of a Theory of Practice*, a text on ethnographic methods translated in 1977 and fairly widely known among literary and cultural critics of the time and still probably the best jumping-off point for Bourdieu's methodology. These concepts (habitus, cultural capital, and field) are not only useful and illuminating for cultural analysis, but are indispensable to assessing Bourdieu's later wide-ranging criticism of globalization.

According to Bourdieu, social structures produce "habitus," dispositions to act, think, perceive, and feel in certain ways and not others, routinized ways of talking and moving (stance, gait, gesture), and unconscious modes of constructing the world, not so much self-consciously learned as picked up through early primary socialization. Among the Kabyle people in Algeria, for instance, the female code of modesty orients her body downward toward the ground whereas the male ideal orients his body upwards towards other men. Beyond "disposition," some useful synonyms for habitus include ways of being, habits, and generative social codes. Each social agent acts within the context of her or his habitus, a cultural unconscious common to his or her particular historical community. Members of different social classes and groups share different habitus. And class antagonism and resistance form part of habitus as well. Not surprisingly, a social actor is not free to change habitus. Rather, habitus produces and reproduces the social order and the practices of agents (who have limited latitude to innovate).[8]

With the concept of habitus, Bourdieu accounts for the underlying logic of individuals' social practices and strategies, merging structuralism with existential phenomenology (objectivism and subjectivism), yet visibly weighting the tension between structure and agency toward the former. The result is a certain determinism, which leads to perplexity about how social change can and does occur. "It remains difficult to understand how," one critic complains, "in Bourdieu's model of practice, actors or collectivities can intervene in their own history in any substantial fashion."[9] I come back to this problem in the next section when discussing Bourdieu's vision of a new European social movement.

Especially in his essay, "The Forms of Capital" (1983), but also in most of his earlier and later works, Bourdieu distinguishes various guises of capital, namely, economic, social, symbolic, and cultural capital. The first has to do with money and property; the second with obligations, prerogatives, and connections; the third with prestige; and the fourth with education and taste. Under certain conditions each of these forms of capital (resources) is convertible into the others. For instance, high class standing might turn into a high-paying job. Interestingly, Bourdieu distinguishes three "states" of specifically cultural capital: objectified, institutionalized, and embodied. The first exists in cultural goods such as paintings and books; the second in educational qualifications; and the third in special dispositions of mind and body, for example, the ability to appreciate and understand fine art.[10] Obviously, cultural capital is unevenly distributed throughout modern societies by virtue of family origin and upbringing, economic holdings, educational attainment (formal and extracurricular), and social trajectory, that is, habitus. (So much for the "perfect competition" and "level playing field" models of free-market philosophers.) Social classes and groups accumulate and possess more or less *cultural capital*, which for purposes of illustration can be divided into such subspecies as linguistic, literary, musical, artistic, and scientific capital.[11] Good manners and taste, to cite two examples, are acquired and not natural gifts. Furthermore, "to the socially recognized hierarchy of the arts, and within each of them, of genres, schools, or periods," observes Bourdieu, "corresponds a social hierarchy of the consumers. This predisposes tastes to function as markers of 'class'" (*Distinction*, 1–2). According to Bourdieu, culture engenders social domination as well as distinction. Education systems reproduce social inequalities, unconsciously and overwhelmingly privileging the amount and type of cultural capital acquired from family over natural talent or giftedness. Moreover, possession of cultural capital correlates with levels of success in the job and marriage markets.

Among the most puzzling aspects of Bourdieu's concept of cultural capital, three are regularly cited by his critics. For U.S. critics in particular Bourdieu's account overlooks the realities of cultural pluralism in favor of a much too monolithic picture of cultural consensus, perhaps accurately reflecting centralized French society, but ill-suited to U.S. culture. Bourdieu's cultural capital, in addition, addresses upper- and middle-class social dynamics, skirting the common experiences with culture by the working class and thereby continuing bourgeois scorn of vernacular culture. Bourdieu is sometimes accused of being an antipopulist, although he was a lifelong leftist with roots in and identification with the working class. And, too, however modulated Bourdieu's model of capital is, with its four forms and half dozen or so subspecies, it is given over to economism, picturing social space as a set of markets where economic capital rules in the last instance, a charge which Bordieu repeatedly denied.[12] I return to this problem in a moment.

What most characterizes modern Western social space, in Bourdieu's account, is a broad set of more or less discrete "fields"in which struggles go on for power, recognition, and resources (the different forms of capital.) Much more than economic capital is at stake. Among the relatively autonomous modern fields (social microcosms) carefully examined across Bourdieu's many works are law, higher education, politics, journalism, religion, housing, philosophy, art, and literature in France. The nation-state forms the context of modern social development. Within each field different configurations of constraint, demand, possibility, and opportunity operate. Players new to a field, say law or art, having undergone an apprenticeship and having assimilated a field-specific habitus, seek recognition (legitimacy) from those above and distinction from those below, more or less accepting the rules and stakes of the game. Authorities of consecration and players operate within networks of institutions that have regulated practices. To a large extent, fields operate as markets where "goods" and "services" are produced, distributed, and consumed; where forms of capital accumulate; and where actors compete for possession of capital. However, competition within fields is not free, and field-specific strategies are highly circumscribed. Among all the many fields composing modern social space, the two most powerful are, significantly, the political and economic, which often seek to, and partially do, control and dominate the others at any given moment. The strength of a field in modern society is related to its degree of autonomy from these two fields of power and money. (In earlier centuries, autonomy from religion assumed a key role in processes of Western modernization.) Significantly, within each field two tendencies, toward heteronomy and toward autonomy, are at work. The university field, for instance, not only serves the world of order, power, and stability, the task of medical, legal, and certain scientific faculty, but also confronts the reigning order by raising questions, offering alternatives, and critically examining history, the task of arts, humanities, social scientific, and some scientific faculty.[13] The contemporary literary field, to take another example of the heteronomy/autonomy axis, reaches outwards to (1) the commercial sphere of fame and success via book sales, media appearances, book tours, and the like and inwards to (2) the art-for-art's-sake world of peer esteem, specialized literary awards, and coterie recognition.[14] With all its modulations, Bourdieu's flexible concept of field effectively forestalls the change of simple economic determinism.

The concept of field seeks to jettison the hierarchical base/superstructure model of society, replacing it with a horizontal model. Still, each field pits against one another two principles of hierarchy: the social hierarchy of economic capital and political power versus the cultural hierarchy of intellectual accomplishment, gravity, and prestige. For Bourdieu, contending modes of legitimation are operating here: the temporal and political versus the scientific and intellectual. One glimpses this structural antagonism between, for example, university administrators and faculty as well as between members of single disciplines and fields. As Bourdieu tells it, the emergence of the modern autonomous intellectual during the nineteenth century entailed separation from the patronage and censorship of the Church and Court and, in addition, establishment of projects, criteria, and authority internal to separate fields, which were able to resist external pressures. For him the appearance of Emile Zola's "J'accuse" during the Dreyfus Affair brought these various developments to a symbolic head in France:

> "J'accuse" is the outcome and the fulfillment of a collective process of emancipation that is progressively carried out in the field of cultural production: as a prophetic rupture with the established order, it reasserts against all reasons of state the irreducibility of the values of truth and justice and, at the same stroke, the independence of the guardians of these values from the norms of politics . . . and from the constraints of economic life.

The intellectual is constituted as such by intervening in the political field *in the name of autonomy* and of the specific values of a field of cultural production which has attained a high degree of independence with respect to various powers. . . . (*The Rules of Art*, p.129)

And yet Bourdieu regularly assigns modern intellectuals the status of "dominated fraction of the dominant class." Although they hold considerable cultural capital and social privileges, modern intellectuals are subordinate to the holders of political and economic power. Intellectual autonomy is always relative.

The concepts of field and forms of capital played key roles in Bourdieu's critique of neoliberal globalization. Significantly, discussions of habitus all but disappeared and concomitantly Bourdieu's political pessimism moderated in the work of the last decade of his life, as I show.

LOOKING AHEAD: SOCIAL INSECURITY, COLLECTIVE INTELLECTUALS, THE WELFARE STATE

Bourdieu's *Contre-feux: Propos pour servir à la résistance contre l'invasion néo-liberale* (1998), translated loosely as *Acts of Resistance: Against the Tyranny of the Market* (1999), is a small book collecting sixteen occasional pieces from the mid-1990s. His *Contre-feux 2: Pour un mouvement social européen* (2001) (not translated as I write this chapter) is a similarly small follow-up collection of eight speeches and occasional essays delivered during 1999 and 2000. (The hyphenated plural word "contre-feux" in French designates fires made to head off a larger raging fire; it translates well enough as "fighting fire with fire"). The subtitles of those two angry polemical books indicate accurately Bourdieu's main goals for them: "Remarks Assisting the Resistance against the Neo-Liberal Invasion" and "For a European Social Movement." In the 1990s Bourdieu fully emerged as a committed public intellectual opposed to neoliberalism and advocating a European-wide social movement against globalization. This surprising move of France's preeminent sociologist was, of course, in response to the New World Order of transnational free-market capitalism following upon the collapse of the Soviet Union and the end of the Cold War in 1989.

During this immediate post-Cold War period, Bourdieu published a spate of books, some related closely to *Contre-feux* and *Contre-feux 2*. Let me briefly mention three. *The Rules of Art* (1992) charts the historical development of artistic autonomy in France from Charles

Baudelaire, Edouard Manet, and Gustave Flaubert to Emile Zola, high-lighting the exemplary *modern* separation of the arts from the fields of politics and economics. *The Weight of the World* (1993), coauthored with nineteen researchers and consisting of sixty-nine interviews and prefatory articles (fifty-four in the English translation), examines so-cial exclusion and suffering in contemporary France. *On Television* (1996), a brief pointed polemic, condemns both the corruption of the field of journalism by the economic field and the bad influence of cur-rent media on all neighboring intellectual and cultural fields.

In both *Contre-feux* and *Contre-feux 2*, Bourdieu unambiguously calls for a new European social movement to unite existing and future new social movements, unions, and intellectuals against globalization. In the process he denounces numerous evils of globalization, espe-cially its guiding neo-Darwinian philosophy of neoliberalism,[15] and he outlines the roles that writers, artists, and research workers—"intellec-tuals"—can play in the new movement. Although Bourdieu's call to arms, at many points addressed directly to cultural workers, is not without strains and contradictions, it does succeed in its goal of offer-ing encouragement to intellectuals to join workers (unionized and not), farmers, the unemployed, immigrants, social activists, and militants (what I call Lilliputians here and in chapter 9[16]) to struggle against the depredations of globalization.

Bourdieu, like many other critics of globalization, was particularly vexed by the retreat of national governments from adequately funding welfare, medical care, housing, public transportation, education, and culture. The neoliberal focus of the post-1960s decades upon privati-zation, deregulation, and self-help, characteristic of British, American, French, and other advanced economies (whether neoconservative or social democrat)—practices promoted globally by the unelected and nondemocratic World Bank, International Monetary Fund, and World Trade Organization (WTO)—begat and beget a wide array of prob-lems, as Bourdieu makes clear: new desocialization policies, promo-tion of a cult of possessive individualism, union busting, entrepreneurial downsizing, labor "flexibilization," economic inequality, and erosion of a broad range of protections such as those against foreign owner-ship, investment, and cultural hegemony. The quest for maximum short-term profits and reduced expenditures keeps seeping into every nook and cranny of life. And this economic regime, an "infernal ma-chine" in Bourdieu's words, employs a new mode of discipline and "domination founded upon the *institution of insecurity*,"[17] which con-tinues today to become a way of life (not just of labor) for increasing numbers of people across all classes. As a condition of work, this novel job insecurity affects communication, medical, and educational staff as much as ordinary laborers, low-level white-collar employees, and a growing reserve army of unemployed, dislocated, and part-time flexibilized workers. Across all countries workers are pitted against each other. Ironically, noted Bourdieu, this neoliberal *social insecurity*, in its transnational spread, provides a tangible foundation for the emerging solidarity of antiglobalization Lilliputians.

Dramatically, Bourdieu made the case that culture, namely, literature, theater, film, art, and music, is threatened today by money, commerce, and the spirit of the global free market, being submitted at every stage of production to criteria of commodification and immediate profitability. He deplored this postmodern turn of events away from the important and necessary autonomy of the arts gained during the long and uneven reign of modernity. Among instances of eroded autonomy via commercialization, Bourdieu cites the increasing concentration of bottom-line oriented book publishers, particularly in the United States, where a handful of media giants now dominates; the proliferation of multiplex theaters and the disappearance of art cinemas and independent movie houses; the mergers of global media firms such as AOL and Time Warner and Viacom and CBS; and the shifts of many university presses to bottom-line thinking. "Artists, writers, research workers, but also publishers, gallery directors, critics, from all countries," urged Bourdieu, "must mobilize today at a time when the forces of the economy, which tend by their own narrow logic to subordinate cultural production and diffusion to a law of immediate profit, find notable reinforcement in policies labeled liberalization that the economically and culturally dominant forces aspire to impose universally under cover of '*globalization*'" (*Cf2*, 85).

In Bourdieu's view, intellectuals today need to give up their neutrality and ivory tower mentalities and link their research, scholarship, science, and art to political commitments in solidarity with other engaged Lilliputians. And he believed they could raise awareness and help define worthwhile ends and means for the new social movement without compromising the structural autonomy of their fields. Against the dominant think tanks, paid experts, and journalists (Bourdieu regularly castigates these last-named), intellectuals can produce criticisms and alternatives based on their expertise. However, argued Bourdieu significantly, such wide-ranging critiques and solutions cannot come from Sartrean master thinkers nor Foucaultian specific intellectuals (isolated specialists), but only from "collective intellectuals" offering answers beyond those already propounded by neoliberal governments, established political parties, and mainstream unions.[18] In Bourdieu's vision, the new European movement (like its affiliated transnational unions) must include artists, writers, scientists, and researchers collaborating with workers and immigrants; with members of different professions, classes, ethnic origins, sexualities; and with unemployed as well as flexibilized workers. All must struggle against the programmatic "politics of depoliticization" that casts globalization as inevitable (economic fatalism) while paradoxically celebrating its strategically enacted policies with a deceptive rhetoric about "liberation," "deregulation," "liberalization," and "individual freedom."

Not incidentally, Bourdieu was increasingly critical of the field of contemporary journalism, as in *On Television*, the main body of which contains two lectures that he delivered on television in May 1996, craftily bypassing the commercial and political control of the networks by speaking to the nation from the campus station of the Collège de France where he held the Chair of Sociology. Journalism controls not only public information but the means to public expression and to the public sphere, having an inordinate power of consecration, as every politician and public figure knows all too well. Starting with the postwar period, television has come to dominate the journalistic field economically and symbolically. But nowadays the whole field of journalism "is much more dependent on external forces than the other fields of cultural production, such as mathematics, literature, law, science, and so on. It depends very directly on demand, since, and perhaps even more than the political field itself, it is subject to the decrees of the market and the opinion poll."[19] Vulnerable to growing external pressures, journalists increasingly lack autonomy and independence, being ever more likely to cooperate with the powers that be (state, church, advertisers, etc.), shoring up the status quo. What perhaps most worried Bourdieu is that all the fields of cultural production today feel structural pressure from the journalistic field so that intellectuals and their institutions often now seek to maximize media coverage, keeping their messages short and simple, valuing telegenic settings and faces, hoping for high ratings and broad exposure, thereby importing the laws of media and market inside their fields. "The journalistic field tends to reinforce the 'commercial' elements at the core of all fields to the detriment of the 'pure'" (*On Television*, 70). All of this explains why in *Contre-feux* Bourdieu was critical of the media's role in promoting globalization and its submission to it. Thinking about organizing the European social movement and about countering media fatalism (depoliticization), Bourdieu advocated new forms of communication (Internet, cell phone, etc.) and encouraged battles against media intellectuals: "it is no longer possible nowadays to conduct social struggles without having a specific programme for fighting with and against television."[20]

In both *Contre-feux* and *Contre-feux 2*, Bourdieu deemed the welfare state and its social entitlements as "among the highest achievements of civilization" (*AR*, 60), citing health, education, and welfare systems; its right to work and minimum wages; and successful public transportation, housing, and child protection policies. These accomplishments should, as far as he was concerned, be exported now today around the globe, not dismantled or privatized. He ended up calling for a defense (not uncritical) of the most advanced forms of the welfare state and also for transnational organizing that is paradoxically rooted in a commitment to this national form of governance. For Bourdieu, however, the defense of the welfare state is inspired not by its national legacy but, quite the contrary, its universal functions and future usefulness. "Resistance to the bankers' Europe—and the conservative restoration it promises—can only be European . . . freed from interests, assumptions, prejudices and habits of thought that are national and still vaguely nationalist. . . ."[21]

Tellingly, Bourdieu depicted the crisis of the welfare state as in part an internal struggle of the left and right hands of the state, not just involving external globalizing forces. The "left hand of the state" is composed of agents ("social workers") in the so-called spending ministries such as family counselors, youth leaders, low-level judges, and increasingly teachers. They are opposed to the "right hand of the state," technocrats from various ministries such as banking and finance who do not know and do not wish to know (or do not want to pay for) what the left hand does. In this scenario what we see is "the failure of the state as the guardian of the public interest" (*AR*, 2).

Some of the strains, not to say contradictions, in Bourdieu's many short pieces against globalization most strikingly manifest themselves in the various roles assigned his "collective intellectual": regular member of the new European movement yet spokesperson for it; autonomist specialist but coworker with intellectuals from other autonomous fields; member of a privileged class (habitus) yet collaborator with other classes and factions; and advocate of the national welfare state but committed to large transnational projects and modes of governance.

It is telling that the early twenty-first century spectacular antiglobalization protests against the WTO starting in Seattle and spreading elsewhere encouraged but worried Bourdieu, especially in their lack of organization, their ephemerality, and their merely symbolic success. Here he was caught between the realities of disparate antiglobalization groups and disaggregated new social movements and his goals of organizing and making permanent a single European social movement, a plan he himself labeled a "rational utopia" (*Cf2*, 23). The creation of such a movement requires, as he affirmed, a "universalist voluntarism" (*Cf2*, 23). At this point in his evolution Bourdieu seems anything but a fatalist: he does not believe that globalization is inevitable; or that we must all live through globalization and its failure on the way to a more advanced mode of production; or that today's Lilliputians, however insecure and paralyzed, are powerless; or that intellectuals must renounce universalist ambitions, which so many postmodernist thinkers argue. For him hope rests in transnational unionizing, activist restoration and protection of the welfare state, and highly public and readable criticism of neoliberal globalization policies and promises developed by expert autonomous intellectuals coordinated into multinational regional collectivities.

CONCLUDING REMARKS: STRENGTHS, WEAKNESSES, COMPLICATIONS

In its strengths, weaknesses, and complications Bourdieu's take on globalization is highly useful for today's cultural studies work. It theorizes while providing an encouraging example of the tasks of the public/collective intellectual. It gives a sophisticated account of the mechanisms of "commodification" by its careful mapping of the autonomy/heteronomy axis operating through differentiated social fields. It depicts with memorable force the ravages of social insecurity while defending the welfare state and elucidating its crises. It pinpoints the growing (bad) influence and dynamics of the media across the wide expanses of contemporary social space. It not only predicted but planned for the antiglobalization new social movement of transnational Lilliputians, focusing on the place of culture as well as economics and politics in the current struggles. It demystifies neoliberal rhetoric about liberation, deregulation, and individual freedom, highlighting its neo-Darwinian and Calvinist ideological roots.

In the problems it encounters, Bourdieu's critique of globalization provides useful warnings as well as vexing examples for cultural studies work. It severely limits the prospects for significant transnational and national change by conceiving social space as complexly intersecting more or less autonomous fields (specialties, professions, and subcultures) set within incommensurable national frameworks.[22] It productively multiplies the forms and the flows of capital, yet at times seems unwilling to acknowledge the foundational role evidently assigned economic capital. It gives a leading role to the collective intellectual while wanting not to do so, being motivated by a distaste for Sartrean heroicism and a preference for participatory democracy. It quietly leaves behind talk about the more or less deterministic habitus without saying why. It seems instinctively to deplore popular culture (television, films, music, fashion, etc.). It dislikes cultural studies, on occasion sniping at its populism, eclecticism, and syncretism, that is, its lack of autonomy.[23]

Most tellingly for me, Bourdieu does not credit the postmodern turn, meaning here the emergence of a distinct post-Fordist third stage of capitalism, as convincingly theorized by numerous writers from Lyotard to Jameson.[24] Rather, he identifies with the modernist avant-gardes and their having carved out zones of autonomy against the church, state, and economy. As a result, he appears at times to romanticize the old days, downplaying the competition among vanguard artists and seeking to protect a modernist vanguardist perspective. The defense of the welfare state is of a piece with the support of the historical avant-gardes. Not surprisingly, many well-attested features of postmodern culture are anathema to Bourdieu: the collapse of the great divide between high and low culture; the advent of a society of the spectacle and simulacra; the upsurge of new interdisciplines (women's studies, gender studies, ethnic studies, cultural studies); the implosion of artistic forms and the eruption of pastiche and mixed media such as telenovels, MTV, happenings, and high-budget musicals (he singles out *Jesus Christ Superstar* and *Evita*); the critique of the Enlightenment, scientific reason,[25] and the grand narrative of progress; the combined emphases on the local, on micropolitics, and on the specific intellectual; the emergence of fragmented subjectivities, multiple subject positions, and hybrid identities (versus habitus); as well as the global spread of consumer and finance capitalism over the borders of the nation-state. Here Bourdieu appears a self-assured modernist conservative critic of postmodern society, especially of its implosion of fields and forms, its commodification of culture, and its dissemination of social insecurity and suffering.

At the same time there are distinctive postmodern features of Bourdieu's project, although he himself would not have credited them as such: the multiplication of forms of capital; the central positioning of cultural capital vis-à-vis other forms of capital; the fracturing of social space into numerous incommensurable fields (often portrayed by him as games with strategies); the critique of universal reason and science from a culturally relative historical perspective; the dethroning of the master intellectual in favor of the public/collective intellectual; the promotion of presence in the mass media, however distasteful it may be, by public intellectuals; and the advocacy of new social movements as effective mechanisms of social change. With one foot in modernism and one in postmodernism, Bourdieu looms as an exemplary figure whose angry critiques illuminate the dynamics and negative outcomes of globalization for a contemporary cultural studies increasingly besieged by and preoccupied with globalizing phenomena.

9

THE NEW ECONOMIC CRITICISMS

The Rise of the Lilliputians

IN RECENT DECADES MARKET-ORIENTED ECONOMICS has emerged as the dominant discourse of everyday life displacing religion, politics, and entertainment. This discourse is, of course, overwhelmingly the laissez-faire neoliberal economics developed by the neoclassical tradition stemming from Adam Smith, not the regulatory, welfare state economics of John Maynard Keynes and later neo-Keynesians, nor the radical economics of Karl Marx and other socialists, nor that of non-Marxist progressives. Increasingly, this mainstream economics seems a truncated ideology whose doctrines are ever more broadly disseminated through all channels of social life, especially academia and the media. A market-oriented perspective conditions not only our thoughts and decisions, but our imaginations and futures. Nothing appears to exist outside its scope. Alternatives and countercurrents hardly register in the public domain, and when they do so, it is typically in the form of unmotivated eruptions and partisan battles such as impromptu boycotts, protests, unforeseen strikes, or mad terrorist attacks.

Given the hegemony of economic discourse in its neoclassical neoliberal form, it is no surprise that in recent times comparatively few progressive economists or cultural critics have developed critiques and alternatives deemed worthy of public attention. Presuming that the dissemination of market-based globalization continues apace, we should expect mainstream economic doctrines to become ever more globally hegemonic and ever more contested.

It is in this context that certain countercurrents and alternatives take on significance. Among these are the critical economics movement composed mainly of progressive, Marxist, and feminist economists in the university; the new economics movement among literary critics, many of whom are liberal neo-Keynesians; and the recent critics of globalization who tend to be reformers and cultural critics working toward new postcommunist liberal-to-socialist political economies. This chapter examines each of these three phenomena in turn, demonstrating that critical economists, neo-Keynesians, and progressives, both inside and outside the university, fault mainstream neoliberal economics for a recurring set of shortcomings. To be specific and to preview the argument, the *homo economicus* posited by orthodox theory stands accused of being self-interested, competitive, utilitarian, and calculating to the degree that little space exists for cooperation, altruism, family, or community. Economic man's macho obsession with consumption and maximization renders him a one-dimensional figure, occupying a single unhealthy subject position. In addition, mainstream economics slights an array of major concerns, especially environmental care, the rights of future generations, social justice, shared decision making, social safety nets, fair labor practices, and reciprocity between centers and peripheries. Not surprisingly, those critical of mainstream business-oriented academic economics often stage returns, sometimes unconsciously, to "political economy," retrieving the moral and political dimensions of this old discipline, joining up with recent traditions of cultural studies that refuse to leave economics to professional economists and market doctrine. I side with this cultural studies orientation throughout *Theory Matters*. Many of today's diverse countercurrents and alternatives encouragingly coalesce around the Lilliputian strategy, a disaggregated postmodern front of new social movements, nongovernmental organizations, unions, and poor people seeking similar reforms, restitutions, and transformations of the global political economic order.

CRITICAL ECONOMICS

Perhaps the most dramatic element of "critical economics" is its critique of *homo economicus* (HE), rational economic man, the self-interested, fully conscious, calculating maximum utilitizer of orthodox economics and its metanarratives, including college textbooks. This attack is part of the wider postmodern critique of Enlightenment humanism, particularly its promotion of the Cartesian subject, a masculine figure whose instrumental reason controls desire, privileging mind over matter, order

over chaos, self over society, work over play, and competition over cooperation. According to feminist economists, for instance, HE is a fictional
figure, a straw man, who construes altruism and community as irra-
tional and feminine, valorizing his own atomized and isolated possessive
individualism. Consider several examples.

In her "Robinson Crusoe: The Quintessential Economic Man?,"
economist Ulla Grapard criticizes Daniel Defoe's fictional version of
homo economicus celebrated by economists from Adam Smith and
David Ricardo onwards.[1] Shipwrecked and isolated on his primitive
but charming Caribbean island for thirty years, Crusoe (a former slave
trader and colonialist), a self-sufficient producer and consumer of
goods and services, is unrealistically not bothered with family, sexuality, society, politics, or history. (Before his adventure on the island, he
is an exile from stifling middle-class life.) HE improbably represents
man in a state of nature, optimizing work, consumption, and leisure,
keeping ledgers all the while. On this fantasy island, Crusoe owns and
controls everything, especially nature. There are no women to worry
about. Friday, a person of color and his slave, is a passive, childlike inferior, a feminized housekeeper. In Grapard's argument Crusoe is the
universal subject of Western science and philosophy, a socially constructed masculine figure, acting in exploitative, sexist, and racist ways
characteristic of neoclassical economics yesterday and today.

In her "A Portrait of *Homo Economicus* as a Young Man," economist
Susan F. Feiner offers a psychoanalysis of HE, delving beneath the
manifest to the latent repressed contents of his unconscious, using ob-
ject relations theory to illuminate his problems.[2] From Feiner's perspective, HE is a romantic young male figure whose consumption,
work, and savings act out aspects of a child's world divided between
the fantasies of good and bad mothers. Consumption in HE's world
rules over all choices and activities: HE works or saves to secure income so as to compulsively consume more in an unending romance of
ingestion and unfulfilled desire constrained by income, which is structured as a parental limit and social discipline. For HE every aspect of
life is a psychodrama of constrained maximization. HE "must renounce the immediate pleasures of childhood and enter an adult
world in which pleasures are not derived from the activities themselves, but are instead dependent upon satisfaction achieved in other
realms (sublimation). He does not work because work has intrinsic
value or merit or pleasure to him . . .; instead he works to get the income needed to act on his desires in the market for final goods and
services. Work, and thus wage or salary income, is one way to insure
access to the symbolic mother . . ." (204). Feiner goes on to identify the

renunciation of present enjoyments and bodily pleasures as anal be-
havior and to point out a set of related ambivalences. For HE, play is
good (gratifying), on the one hand, but also bad, since it limits his
ability to secure goods. Work and savings are bad (they constitute
withholding), yet good (they ensure future consumption). What most
characterizes HE for Feiner is the contradictory exaltation of consumption and savings, oral and anal pleasures.

Although neither Grapard nor Feiner says so, the values of *homo
economicus*—masculine, antisocial, contradictory, and problematical—very much resemble those developed by the Puritans at the onset
of modernity. Max Weber's *The Protestant Ethic and the Spirit of Capitalism* is never mentioned. The point is that HE has a specific history
(which has undergone transformations), or, put more broadly, that
neoclassical economics emerges from yet disavows Western religion
and morality as well as social philosophy and cultural history. Mainstream economists, who generally think of economics in a formalistic
manner as a separate scientific discipline, deplore this view, of course,
which harkens back to political economy and the days before the social
sciences, sciences, and humanities went their separate ways. Critical
economics, the postmodern cultural studies form of the discipline,
propounds a critique of modernity, the Enlightenment, and neoclassical economics, aiming to redefine economics so as to take into account
such phenomena as altruism and the social good as well as the historical roots and multiple subject positions occupied by HE. It amounts to
a certain return to and redignification of political economy, although
critical economists do not generally put it that way.

Many progressives outside the field regard the discipline of economics as dysfunctional, looking toward posteconomic alternatives.
As we saw in the previous chapter, Pierre Bourdieu takes this point of
view. The futurist Hazel Henderson, to detail here another instructive
instance, a decade ago reconfigured the key mainstream economic indicator Gross National Product (GNP), arguing that the accounted-for
private and public sectors of the economy rest upon unaccounted-for
("nonmonetized") natural resources as well as cooperative activities
and countereconomical ones such as sweat equity, do-it-yourself labor,
and unacknowledged "home economics" like care of children, sick
people, and the aged (see Figure 1).[3] In Henderson's graphic assessment, mainstream economics has discounted fully one half of the real
economic cake (GNP). Among other things, she, like many other critics, contends that price setting should take into account the long-term
environmental and social costs of production. Her critique of GNP

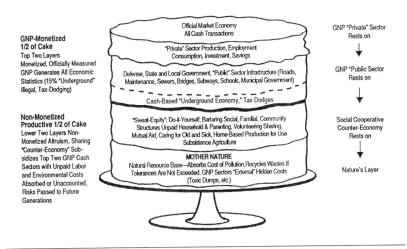

GNP-Monetized 1/2 of Cake
Top Two Layers Monetized, Officially Measured GNP Generates All Economic Statistics (15% "Underground" Illegal, Tax-Dodging)

Official Market Economy
All Cash Transactions

"Private" Sector Production, Employment Consumption, Investment, Savings

Defense, State and Local Government, "Public" Sector Infrastructure (Roads, Maintenance, Sewers, Bridges, Subways, Schools, Municipal Government)

Cash-Based "Underground Economy," Tax Dodges

GNP "Private" Sector Rests on

↓

GNP "Public Sector Rests on

↓

Non-Monetized Productive 1/2 of Cake
Lower Two Layers Non-Monetized Altruism, Sharing "Counter-Economy" Subsidizes Top Two GNP Cash Sectors with Unpaid Labor and Environmental Costs Absorbed or Unaccounted, Risks Passed to Future Generations

"Sweat-Equity": Do-It-Yourself, Bartering Social, Familial, Community Structures Unpaid Household & Parenting, Volunteering Sharing, Mutual Aid, Caring for Old and Sick, Home-Based Production for Use Subsistence Agriculture

MOTHER NATURE
Natural Resource Base—Absorbs Cost of Pollution, Recycles Wastes If Tolerances Are Not Exceeded. GNP Sectors "External" Hidden Costs (Toxic Dumps, etc.)

Social Cooperative Counter-Economy Rests on

↓

Nature's Layer

Figure 1 Total Productive System of an Industrial Society (Three-Layer Cake with Icing)

and orthodox price theory rests on the explicit premise that mainstream economics is a form of "brain damage" (51) requiring an "*end of economics*" (77). The point, however obvious it may be, is that the critique of neoclassical neoliberal economics comes from both inside and outside the discipline. And although it sometimes focuses on such metatheoretical topics as *homo economicus* and GNP, at issue fundamentally are key values and goals, particularly shared decision making, social justice, diversity, cooperation, equity, and environmental care, all receiving short shrift in mainstream economics. In this light, the main limitations of academic critical economics are arguably its fragmentation into separate groups and maverick individuals; its lack of publicly disseminated creditable alternatives; and its divorce from public discourse and mass media. Ideally, it should link up with the Lilliputians and take to the airwaves and the streets.

NEW ECONOMIC LITERARY CRITICISM

In their historical introduction to *The New Economic Criticism: Studies at the Intersection of Literature and Economics*, a hefty collection of twenty-two papers growing out of a mid-1990s conference, editors Martha Woodmansee and Mark Osteen offer a wide-ranging and incisive overview of this interdisciplinary field (complete with bibliography). They briefly review the last three decades and then single out for preliminary discussion six main aspects of the movement: work on the economics of authorship, research on the relationship of money and language, the emergence of critical economics, theory of gift exchange, the main economic approaches to literature, and future directions. Despite its impressive range and sophistication, there are some limitations to this introduction and collection, as my commentary below on the new economic literary criticism makes clear. In a nutshell: the exclusion of significant cultural studies work weakens its enterprise. But allow me to explain.

Woodmansee and Osteen single out two stages in the historical development of the new economic criticism among literary critics. After the groundbreaking books by Marc Shell, *The Economy of Literature* (1978), and Kurt Heinzelman, *The Economics of the Imagination* (1980), they cite a flurry of New Historicist and some cultural studies texts from the late 1980s to the present, featuring as a prime example Walter Benn Michael's *The Gold Standard and the Logic of Naturalism: American Literature at the Turn of the Century* (1987). But they overlook work in many key areas, notably research on subaltern literatures; critiques of the canon and its economics; studies of ethnopoetics in relation to ghettoes, reservations, and other impoverished enclaves; British cultural studies of popular culture and its commodification; attacks on the class system in academe, especially concerning part-timers, the star system, and unionization of teachers and teaching assistants; and Marxist and post-Marxist studies of global capitalist culture. It is perhaps worth recalling also that the economic analysis of literature does not start with Marc Shell in the 1970s: one could go back to, say, Giambattista Vico or Hippolyte Taine or Georgii Plekhanov or any number of later Marxists, not to mention non-Marxists from, for example, the interwar period.

The separate discussions of authorship, money, gifts, and critical methodology are illuminating: they are key issues for recent economic literary criticism and cultural studies. Let me take these topics up in order very briefly.

In the context of new modes of electronic discourse and the Internet, problems concerning copyright, intellectual property, and authorship have become increasingly public. Woodmansee and Osteen helpfully propound a typology having four historical economies of authorship: patronage (including self-patronage), writing for hire, freelance writing, and writing on the side. In the interesting category of self-patronage, they include writers who support themselves through day jobs like Wallace Stevens and Anthony Trollope and those who have parental allowances or inherited money (Milton, Pope, Byron,

Keats, Shelley, Browning, and Tennyson). Although they do not mention it, one wonders where creative writing faculty fit, this being a historically significant new economy of authorship (mode of patronage?) that has arguably come to the financial rescue of contemporary poetry, if not fiction. And insofar as critics are part of the economy of literature, one also wonders how to account for their current economic position(s), particularly given the postwar disappearances of public critics and independent "men of letters" now enclosed and displaced by the university-based institutionalization of criticism. A number of related issues concerning contemporary authorship do not surface in this collection dedicated to the new economic literary criticism: for instance, the bestseller, the agent as entrepreneur, movie and subsidiary rights, mergers of publishing houses, and Internet publication. During postmodern times the economics of authorship have changed, but such changes too often go unnoticed.

When in the 1970s money went off any standard (gold or otherwise), it entered into post-Bretton Woods phases of dematerialization (cash, check, charge, credit), literally becoming a floating signifier devoid of a tangible referent or thing like metal. (The treasury stamp, a social convention, creates money, not metal or paper.) The existence of homologies between language and money underlies a great deal of contemporary new economic literary criticism from the work of Shell and Benn Michaels to Jean-Joseph Goux, notably his influential *Symbolic Economies: After Marx and Freud* (1990) and *The Coiners of Language* (1994). Recent research on money often muses on the problematic of the "universal equivalent": reminiscent of metaphorization, money renders unlike things commensurable during the time of exchange. This process of transubstantiation, violent and destructive, magically conjoins incommensurable things. As a process of representation, it simultaneously entails equalization, and differentiation, which Saussurean linguistics charted a century ago. Perhaps the most vexing problem in this whole domain, note Woodmansee and Osteen cogently, is the "viability of homologies between disparate cultural forms and types of representation" (*NEC*, 29). What they do not note is that research into the money/language nexus is goaded (sometimes unconsciously) by the changing parameters of finance in the post-Bretton Woods global era, a postmodern time in which a Platinum Mastercard not only ensures cash and banking contact anywhere in the world any time of day, but providentially provides omnipresent credit, currency exchange, teletransfers of scheduled household payments, and insurance against loss. This innovative financial "coverage" resembles our increasing everyday saturation in language effected by expanding mass media along with all the alluring advertisements they carry. There is still much work to be done with the ongoing transformation of money and the deconstructive linguistic turn characteristic of our postmodern era.[4]

Research on primitive exchange and gift theory, especially in the French line from Marcel Mauss to Georges Bataille to Jean-François Lyotard to Jacques Derrida,[5] has provocatively explored issues of altruism, obligation, reciprocity, and expenditure. Key questions for economic literary criticism, economics, and particularly cultural studies arise in this area. Is a perfect gift, one with no strings attached, possible? (Interestingly, men and women tend to answer that question differently.) Is there a gender dynamic to gifts? Do gift exchanges occur outside of economic accounting? How do the subject positions of gift givers compare to *homo economicus*? Do gifts disrupt prized neoclassical notions such as economic equilibrium? Don't gifts, insofar as they are unforeseen and excessive like panics, inject irrationality into the economy, and thereby strategically raise special doubts about the mainstream doctrines of maximum utility and rational decision making? Gift theory poses a number of significant challenges to mainstream economic doctrines, but characteristically from outside the field of economics. It is a topic mainly for anthropology. Most importantly, it introduces alternative utopian dimensions into economics, trying to imagine nonmonetized and noncommodified exchanges free of the baggage of *homo economicus*, GNP, and the rest of orthodox dogma. Is there anything before or outside (market) economics?—something we postmoderns can't help wondering.

On the practical side, the majority of new economic literary critics, in Woodmansee and Osteen's account and collection, engage in analysis of texts. The editors proffer a comprehensive typology of several critical approaches to the economics of literature.

1. Contextual or extratextual criticism, an offshoot of New Historicism and cultural studies, examines surrounding contexts, including author's biography, social history, "the economy," competing arts, race, class, and gender issues, and national and transnational forces, focusing on relevant economic issues such as the author's source of money, his or her literary labor in the marketplace, the impact on the literary work of industrialism and/or imperialism, and so on.

2. Internal or intratextual criticism, a mode of critical formalism, analyzes economies of texts, conceiving texts as containing closed systems of exchange embodied in characters, image pat-

terns, plots, and, of course, themes (such as debts, losses, gifts, savings, contracts).

3. Intertextual criticism explores a range of literary and nonliterary economic topics on the premise that individual texts inescapably partake of other texts, and that texts are relatable and related to one another. Exemplary topics of research include the marketing of literature, canonization, the dynamics of literary value, the commodification of literature, literary influence and reception, and intellectual property and copyright.

4. Metatheoretical criticism scrutinizes the terms, concepts, models, and practices of economic literary criticism, studying such phenomena as economic reductionism, overuse of the concept "economy," "exploitation of the homological method" (*NEC*, 38), and connections and rifts between economics and literary studies.

Beyond the descriptive and the heuristic value of this neat typology, these approaches in practice often appear together to varying degrees, and such approaches as intertextual, contextual, metatheoretical, and intratextual run into each other, deconstructing each other's boundaries. In other words, the underlying economy of critical approaches is more an open-ended series of interconnected zones of inquiry rather than a closed system with four flexible but nonconverging vectors. This latter alternative economy of critical approaches I am sketching is meant as a postmodern counterconstruction of the standard account of "economics."

In some ways the strongest contribution in the Woodmansee and Osteen collection, Paul Delany's "Who Paid for Modernism?" illustrates the new economic literary criticism at its most wide-ranging and its most limited. This is a case study of the special patronage system behind British literary modernism specifically between World Wars I and II. Delany reexamines the alleged anticommercial ethos of the major male modernists, their hostility to female culture stemming from Victorian times, their ambivalent relations with the influential rentier class, and their reliance on female rentier patrons either through subsidies or marriages (Yeats, Pound, Eliot). Rentiers were those men and women (some hundreds of thousands) without visible occupation who around World War I lived on money accumulated by earlier generations.[6] Free from economic necessity and disconnected from landed estates or local communities, rentiers promoted an ethos of refinement and sensitivity counterposed to the vulgarities of trade, mass-produced goods, and marketing. One gets glimpses of this urbane class in the celebrated work of Henry James and E. M. Forster. Delany argues that the ideal-typical form of modernist works such as *Ulysess, Finnegans Wake*, and *The Cantos* stems from the long-term support of rentier patrons. Instead of writing more numerous and simpler works, Joyce, Pound, Eliot, and others worked and reworked texts in a labor of "densification" very much against the grain of commercial literature. Yet however mystified the relations between money and art were in this situation, modernist works did become commodities in several stages, contends Delany. To begin with, objets d'art and avant-garde works, despite appearances, circulate inside markets. Markets exist for rare objects. Initially such artistic works and their appreciative subcultures are small, but often enough these works cross over into broader circulation, moving beyond the relative autonomy of their original sites of production and consumption. Delany further argues that patrons and clients in such prestige protomarkets look from the outset to the day of broader circulation, hoping for increased prestige and (sometimes) increased return on investment. The aesthetic and the economic for Delany are indissociable; it is not a matter of the pristine modernist artwork sadly entering the market in a dual process of commodification/cooptation. When key modernist works moved after World War II from the cultural margins to best-sellerdom, it was one more stage of their product cycle. And yet one more stage has involved the acquisition of first editions and manuscripts of modernist works.

Delany's article is exemplary of the new economic literary criticism in various ways, good and bad. It brings to bear on perennial literary topics a pluralistic array of approaches and illuminating economic concepts. Specifically, it examines the lives of the poets, literary style and form, literary subcultures and movements, and the dynamics of canonization. To illuminate literary issues, it employs such economic concepts as class orientation, class mobility, wealth, patronage, the economics of culture, and stages of commodification. At one point it briefly discusses the various global investments held in the investment portfolios of Joyce and Pound, noting the presence of capitalism inside the leading modernists' hearths as a way to foreground the inadequacy of the usual pro- and anticapitalist arguments about modernist writers. (For Delany, to see modernism as a critical backlash against a depredatory capitalism is to gloss over reality.)

The new economic literary criticism, Delany's included, is miffed about the left anticapitalist orientation of many New Historicists. New economic literary critics are not Marxists, generally appearing to be liberal pluralists with neo-Keynesian sentiments. (Yet consider Marc Shell who is studiously neutral.) In making common cause with "critical economics" these literary intellectuals loosely affiliate themselves with some Marxist economists, although they do not personally identify with the working class or socialism or the wider Lilliputian front. A main shortcoming of the new economic literary criticism, as configured in Woodmansee and Osteen's collection and in Delany's article, is the absence of discussion about the politics of economics. By ferreting out the politics at work in these many new economic literary studies, one can extrapolate a spectrum that runs from moderate to liberal political values, with more extreme ends absent. Why? The omission of much discussion about standpoint theory in the volume raises questions about the larger movement (not school) as configured by Woodmansee and Osteen. It is hard to know why they omitted the exciting work on postmodern culture, late capitalism, and globalization usually associated with, to name just three well-known texts, Fredric Jameson's *Postmodernism, or, the Cultural Logic of Late Capitalism* (1991), David Harvey's *The Condition of Postmodernity* (1989), and *New Times: The Changing Face of Politics in the 1990s* (1990), edited by Stuart Hall and Martin Jacques. Is this a political exclusion? The odd effect is that the pressing issues surrounding postmodernity and economic globalization go undiscussed. The new economic literary criticism appears, as a result, to be a middle-of-the-road branch of literary history and criticism largely focused on earlier times, unself-consciously rooted in the present-day political economy about which it has little to say. It is separate from, and evidently out of sympathy with, much of cultural studies, especially the influential British lines stemming from Raymond Williams, the *New Left Review*, and the University of Birmingham's pioneering Centre for Contemporary Cultural Studies, the latter of which continues to shape much of U.S. cultural studies.

GLOBALIZATION STUDIES

The field of globalization studies has been forming for a long time, although its contemporary origins date from the symbolic tearing down in 1989 of the Berlin Wall and the proclamation of the triumphant capitalist New World Order. This turn of events very much concerns the definition and the work of current cultural studies of all varieties. There are two well-recognized schools of thought about capitalist globalization, as Anthony Giddens, among many others, has argued.[7] The hyperglobalizers, associated with neoclassical economics and transnational business, celebrate the erosion of the nation-state and the formation of spectacularly profitable regional economic zones spurred on by market imperatives. The skeptics of globalization, affiliated with left-wing politics and economics, lament the collapse of the regulated welfare state and the spreading disorders of consumer-oriented society. A few skeptics regard globalization as a myth and dangerous master narrative. Overlooked by Giddens is an obvious third school, the reformers, usually liberals, who promote globalization stripped of its excesses. This final section of chapter 9 examines representative arguments of reformers and skeptics, highlighting the main problems and drawbacks of economic globalization, according to its critics. By way of conclusion, it predicts increasing concern with the dynamics of globalization among a broad mix of people, Lilliputians, singling out cultural studies scholars (whether nationalist or internationalist in orientation) who nowadays regularly encounter transnationalized postmodern forms of national culture such as "domestic" ethnic arts and literatures composed of foreign and hybrid as well as national materials and standard languages. But more on postmodern aesthetics shortly.

What do the reformers of economic globalization have to say? Liberal billionaire financier George Soros, to take one famous example, in his anxious 1998 *Atlantic Monthly* article on global society enumerated five main deficiencies of the global capitalist system: uneven distribution, financial instability, threat of monopolies and oligopolies, erosion of the welfare state, and absence of shared values to ensure social cohesion.[8] Along the way Soros, a neo-Keynesian, singles out other telling deficiencies of global capitalism such as its erroneous neoliberal laissez-faire beliefs in the self-correcting power of the market and in rational expectations and equilibrium; its asymmetries between centers and peripheries; and its inadequate protection of human rights, the environment, fair labor practices, social justice, and individual freedom. What evidently most concerned Soros on this occasion was his fear of a general collapse as in the 1930s, much more so than his worry about trade protectionism rearing its head and cutting into profits.

Given Soros's damning indictment, one can understand the sardonic yet completely serious slogan uttered by the left-wing economist and skeptic of globalization Robin Hahnel: "Bring back the Keynesians. Any Keynesian!"[9] Hahnel's illuminating little book, *Panic Rules! Everything You Need to Know about the Global Economy* (1999), which originated as a series of articles on "Capitalist Globalism in Crisis" in *Z* magazine, was published by South End Press, a leading U.S. left-wing publisher, as a manual for progressive noneconomist readers. Although a professional economist, Hahnel is surprisingly straightforward throughout his book, as, for instance, in his admonition, "stop corporate-sponsored globalization by any means necessary" (*PR*, 106), although he believes economic globalization can be rendered useful. Given the current triumph of hyperglobalization, the return of reformist Keynesians of any stripe would represent, in Hahnel's view, measured progress at this point, yet not the ideal end state.

There are two schools of thought in mainstream U.S. economics, as Hahnel outlines matters, the "A Team" of free-market neoliberals in charge since the early 1970s and the "B Team" of Keynesian liberals in charge during earlier decades. Both teams support capitalism and corporate-sponsored globalization. What is needed now is a "C Team," a people's movement populated by progressives of all sorts, unions, farmers, members of new social movements and nongovernmental organizations, and the disenfranchised around the globe. (I would add critical economists.) This is the "Lilliput strategy" called for by left activists Jeremy Brecher and Tim Costello in their polemical *Global Village or Global Pillage: Economic Reconstruction from the Bottom Up* (1994),[10] and given form most dramatically in the public protests against the World Trade Organization (WTO) in Seattle in 1999 as well as elsewhere later.[11] Although a return of the B Team would bring temporary relief and practical restoration of social safety nets, ultimately the C Team must have a shaping hand in economic globalization. This parallels the argument made in France at the same time by Pierre Bourdieu as discussed in chapter 8.

Perhaps nothing in recent times represents more succinctly for C Teamers key issues surrounding capitalist globalization than the notorious "conditionality agreements" typically administered by the International Monetary Fund (IMF) to ailing Third World economies. Before the IMF will lend money to governments about to default on private international loans (and before it will restructure countries' debts among private international lenders), it requires such governments to increase tax collections, cut spending, sell off public enterprises to the private sector, tighten money supplies to raise interest rates so as to stabilize currencies to attract global capital, and remove restrictions on the flows of foreign capital and also foreign ownership. Faced with the prospect of no new loans and threats of asset seizures, individual countries regularly sign on to IMF (austerity) programs. Since the money the IMF lends comes from the tax revenues of member countries (as well as the interest earned on them), its bailouts enact public refinancing of bad private loans. That is, the IMF is a public insurance company for private international investors and banks, covering not simply past bad loans, but insuring their future profits and expanded international investments. IMF policies are not designed to foster economic recovery and development, nor do they, which is a shocking argument made very forcefully by Hahnel among other C Teamers. In the event, these policies, in Hahnel's account, administer a whole array of economic traumas: deregulation, privatization, foreign ownership and investment, lower wages, no domestic growth, unemployment, higher taxes, increased poverty, high profits for investors, and dismantling of welfare states and their social insurance programs. Western multinational (transnational) corporations and banks, thanks to IMF aid, purchase assets around the globe at bargain basement prices. Shareholders in these entities invariably encourage, or at least quietly profit from, such practices, none of which are arrived at democratically and none of which seek or promote economic equity for a nation's people. The IMF represents a vanguard of economic globalization with programs that engender "de-development," while interpolating one disabled country after another unevenly into the emerging new international economic order.[12]

A second key flashpoint in the Lilliputian critique of capitalist globalization concerns downward leveling or the so-called race to the bottom. Multinational corporations regularly "force workers, communities, and countries to compete to lower labor, social, and environmental costs . . . ."[13] When a multinational corporation considers opening or relocating a plant, it often seeks not only low production costs such as wages, benefits, and taxes, but relaxed regulations on workers' safety as well as on air and water quality. If a community or country contemplates increasing taxes, raising wages, strengthening environmental protections, or offering only skimpy "incentives," many multinationals threaten to relocate and often do so, seeking the lowest production costs elsewhere. As a result, living standards drop, job security vanishes, workers' rights erode, tax bases narrow, support for public services (transportation, education, health, welfare) shrinks, environmental degradation or destruction ensues, and governments' abilities to serve and protect their populations wither. Brecher and Costello conclude "downward leveling is like a cancer that is destroying its host organism—the earth and its people" (GV, 21).

For humanity's sake, economics should not be left to professional market-oriented economists—that is an argument of many anti-IMF and anti-WTO protesters, critical economists, neo-Keynesians, and C Teamers, though not of mainstream economists. Not surprisingly, political economy is making a public return under the pressure of economic globalization and the New World Order. Lilliputians are growing in numbers as problems with global capitalism spread and countercurrents mount. It is not surprising in this context that feminist critics, minority critics, ecocritics, postcolonial theorists, Marxists, and cultural studies scholars increasingly deal with economic problems, extending the potential ranks of Lilliputians as well as the scope of their separate projects.[14] But insofar as the emergent phenomenon of globalization more properly cooccurs with the upsurge of these critical schools and movements during the 1960s and '70s, it can perhaps be thought of as a "conditioning factor" then as now. As processes of globalization have intensified, critical engagements with their operations have intensified. The dynamics of globalization are increasingly unavoidable, seeping into all aspects of cultural life.[15] In his Preface to *The Cultures of Globalization* (1998), a collection deriving from a mid-1990s conference, Fredric Jameson prophesies: "What seems clear is that the state of things the word *globalization* attempts to designate will be with us for a long time to come; that the intervention of a political relationship to it will be at one with the invention of a new culture and a new politics alike; and that its theorization necessarily uniting the social and the cultural sciences, as well as theory and practice, the local and the global, the West and its Others, but also postmodernity and its predecessors and alternatives, will constitute the horizon of all theory in the years ahead."[16]

The dynamics of globalization concern contemporary literary theory and cultural studies projects everywhere, even when they have resolutely narrow nationalist orientations. This is clear with the recent coming to prominence of such postmodern cultural forms as Anglophone and Francophone literatures, the arts of the Black Atlantic, and Inter-American arts (indigenous arts from Canada, the United States, and Central and South America). Within national borders, the reconfiguration of culture(s), under transnationalizing pressures from globalization and backlashes, is increasingly common. Consider, for example, the United States, where the study of serious literature, not to mention the other arts, has recently expanded to include not just popular and pulp forms such as science fiction, romances, and dime novels, but numerous ethnic literatures written in foreign and hybrid languages as well as in standard English such as Chicano/a, Italian-American, and Vietnamese-American literatures. Speaking theoretically, all of this looks like the Lilliputian strategy on the level of poetics. The borders of the nation-state appear increasingly arbitrary and inadequate yet important as seeming guarantors of cultural autonomy, occasionally blocking from view other perhaps more significant current realities and histories as well as futures. By now it is well attested that globalization simultaneously "produces" both globally homogenizing and nationally heterogenizing effects as in the cases, mentioned in chapter 7, of world music[17] versus defensive national ethnic musical forms, or of world teen fashion versus native costumes, or of global English versus Jamaican or Irish or Black American English. Although mainstream market-oriented neoliberal economists do not concern themselves with such matters as the erosion around the globe of cultural autonomy and national traditions or the eruptions of indigenous groups defensively wedded to nationalist sovereignty, others ranging from neo-Keynesians reformers to critical economists to progressive critics of globalization to postcolonial and cultural studies scholars do so, constituting fellow travelers in the growing ranks of postmodern Lilliputians, most of whom, me included, advocate more cooperative, equitable forms of globalization from below and above.

10

POSTMODERN FASHION

MAKING PROPOSITIONS

One of the most distinctive features of visual culture during postmodern times is the disorganization and heteroglossia of dress codes and styles. The wide range and quality of fabrics, trims, colors, silhouettes, and particularly stylistic modes as well as the broad array of accessories spanning the spectrum from footwear and headdress to jewelry and hairstyle display an unprecedented openness and fragmentation in the history of post-Enlightenment Western clothing conventions. This is not to deny the existence of a fashion system complete with highly articulated rules and codes against which innovation, convention-breaking, revolt, reinflection, contradiction, and pluralization take place. Within the field of cultural studies these and related propositions are illustrated memorably in Dick Hebdige's pioneering book, *Subculture: The Meaning of Style*, which, it will be recalled, charts the differing styles during the 1960s and '70s of teddy boys, mods, skinheads, Rastas, and especially punks in relation to both the historical conjuncture of mainstream hegemonic culture and the contentious constellation of various male subcultural groups in England.[1] In postmodern culture, youth styles often combine dress with argot, dance, and music, creating shocking ensembles set against the reigning symbolic order; style is a way of being and of resisting. Innovation in fashion is less a matter of creativity ex nihilo than of mutation and pastiche. Punk fashion, with its torn T-shirts, orange hair, safety pin piercings, necklaces of toilet chains, plastic pants with multiple exposed zippers, and masklike

makeup, effectively demonstrates not only the spectacularized heteroglot visual culture characteristic of postmodern social regimes but
the simultaneous systematicity and disorganization of contemporary
dress codes.

There is little surprise in affirming that clothing and fashion are invariably connected with power, money, beauty, sexuality, and identity.
Still, I elaborate briefly here on these propositions, which, if uncontro-
versial, are yet significant for my subsequent analysis in this chapter.

Dress is, in part, frequently in large part, about cultural capital; it often
serves political designs; it consorts with hegemonic norms and domination; its regulating force incites mainly conformity but sometimes resistance. To adopt a style (or uniform) is to choose a socioeconomic milieu
and a future. Furthermore, the manufacture and maintenance of clothing involve domestic economies and various trades and guilds. Of all the
major industries thriving during late modernity and postmodernity,
fashion is most readily associated with the distinctive dynamics of late
capitalist political economy, namely, commodity fetishism; conspicuous
consumption; planned obsolescence; class envy; standardization and specialty markets; sweatshops, unionization, and professionalization;[2] possessive individualism; commercialization of art and culture; globalization
of production; broad ecological destruction (via dyestuffs); advertising,
mass media, and spectacle; blackmarket and graymarket distribution;
cooption, exploitation, and excessive profits; and critical vanguardism as
well as a range of other contradictory tendencies of modern and postmodern culture.

Aesthetic criteria play an essential part in clothing design and evaluation. However much they shift, there are finely calibrated touch-
stones, standards, and ideals for beauty. Whether at court or on the
street, in the marketplace or at the ball, in the past or the present, dress
exhibits both theatrical and performative dimensions. Fashion is typically staged in motion. Moreover, fashion's substances, particularly
fabric, texture, design, color, and drape, highlight its materiality, which,
significantly, opens onto long intertwined histories of costuming and
textile crafting. Every item of dress, no matter how humble, dignified,
frivolous, or vanguard, occupies space in fashion archives and the history of aesthetics.

Self-decoration is part of self-constitution, body image, and identity formation. To look in the mirror is to glimpse the embodied self,
but through normative grids related to nakedness and dress. We may
be too thin, too fat, too short, too tall, out of proportion here or there,
or in need of this or that enhancement (amplification, reduction, al-
teration). To stare at the body is to envisage the self through the inter-

nalized gaze of others inhabiting subjectivity. Fashion mixes socially conditioned fantasy with self-fashioning.

It is against the background of these propositions that I look back and consider *On Fashion*, edited by Shari Benstock and Suzanne Ferriss, a symptomatic collection of critical fashion studies pieces consisting of a brief introduction and bibliography by the editors, sixty illustrations and photographs, and wide-ranging essays by sixteen contributors.[3] In what follows I focus on three of a broad range of possible topics: feminist critique of women's fashion magazines, the politics of dress among disempowered groups, and the status of clothing in the formation of identity during postmodern times.

Let me forecast the findings and arguments connected with my three topics. First, contemporary fashion magazines are part of an extensive disciplinary apparatus that promotes unreal beauty norms, producing widespread anxiety and alienation among women. Although the carnivallike disorganization of contemporary fashion magazines takes place within hegemonic enclosures, strategic reinscriptions can create progressive alternatives and transformations. Second, the politics of strategic reinscription, especially among marginalized populations, typically employs pastiche to revalue in novel and sometimes liberating ways existing items of the reigning symbolic order. All the points along the social circuits of present-day visual culture from magazines to TV shows to music videos to films to carefully coordinated public spaces cooperate in propounding acceptable (yet challengeable) body images, clothing codes, and identity formations, all of which call for a cultural studies especially attentive to the subtle dynamics, global and local, of hegemony and resistance.[4] Third, identity formation is a function, in part, of multiple subject positions that cohere in contradiction and, in part, of continuous mirroring effects afforded by others: in both instances dress plays a central role in the social construction and maintenance of identity, particularly in contemporary societies increasingly dominated by images. This does not mean that for everyone self-transformation is possible through dress, in spite of fashion's general ideological appeal to a purchasable "new you." The potent wish among increasing numbers of people to become mannequinlike is a disguised death wish. The gaiety and promise of fashion offer costly compensations.

JUDGING FASHION MAGAZINES

Cultural critics often reveal vexed relations to women's fashion magazines, which, taken together, constitute an influential forcefield in contemporary visual culture. We enjoy the beautiful models, sensuous well-crafted photographs, and highly attractive clothing designs, yet we worry about the ubiquitous anorexic body ideals, the sexist voyeurism of the camera lens, the fetishization of both body parts and clothing commodities, and the narcissism and unreal beautification being promoted. To the extent that such magazines are uncritical vehicles of advertising, they engender suspicion, dismay, and wonder tempered by a more or less grudging admiration. We wonder especially what attitudes are being stimulated and what realities repressed? The underlying premises of such critical inquiries are that consumers/readers identify with fashion ideals, and that such ideals and identifications can be problematical. Here cultural critique characteristically aims to provide life-enhancing antidotes to seduction in its many registers. Not surprisingly, a certain sternness often emerges in this context, for we do not wish simply to be taken in. Critique requires that the wily fascinations and temptations of identification be, at some point, blocked, and that openness to pleasure, desire, and fantasy be ever vigilant of potential danger, exploitation, and illusion.

In the essay starting off *On Fashion*, "*Barbie Magazine* and the Aesthetic Commodification of Girls' Bodies," Ingeborg Majer O'Sickey offers a pointed and occasionally stern feminist critique of *Barbie Magazine*, which has appeared irregularly since 1959 and addresses itself to girls between the ages of four and twelve, promoting Mattel Toy Company's products that achieved earnings in the 1990s of many hundreds of millions of dollars per year. Unlike earlier critics of Barbie, O'Sickey focuses less on the celebrated 11-1/2 inch plastic doll (the blond and blue-eyed, ageless, perfect size six with couture dresses, affluent accessories, and well-tended body) than on the magazine's special role as a children's training manual within the context of the vast feminizing apparatus of American culture.[5] The discourse propounding the constant need for aesthetic renovation and beauty product consumption, constructing woman as commodity and consumer, provokes in O'Sickey a Foucaultian consternation, the driving ethicopolitical force behind her critique.

O'Sickey argues that toys are, and are not, us. As icon of the material girl, who is young, rich, thin, attractive (but asexual), Barbie models unrealistic norms of beauty, engendering anxiety and self-alienation among women of all ages, races, and classes. Adults and not just children widely emulate Barbie, which Madonna, Cher, Dolly Parton, Whitney Houston, and Jane Fonda variously reveal. The Black and Hispanic Barbie dolls introduced in the early 1980s do not disrupt the original homogenized racist demeanor, especially regarding the long slender body, straight curled hair, and delicate facial features.[6] As staged in the magazine, this toy (re)produces our social order and fantasies, requiring nuanced symptomatic analysis. Significantly, the fashion magazine is one part of an extensive disciplinary apparatus, linking together beauty salons, grooming schools, health clubs, spas, cosmetic surgery clinics, beauty pageants, and weight loss programs.

This is where Leslie W. Rabine's essay proves illuminating. In "A Woman's Two Bodies: Fashion Magazines, Consumerism, and Feminism," Rabine unearths a dozen contradictions embedded in leading post-1968 fashion magazines such as *Vogue, Glamour,* and *Essence.* Taken together such conflicts and incongruities testify to a certain disorganization of the commercial fashion system during postmodern times. Simultaneously, fashion magazines are instruments for global consumer capitalism and forums for feminism; they contribute to women's objectification through photography's male desiring gaze and to expressions of newly gained women's independence; they have fostered increasingly sexy styles and progressive social dialogue; they aid and abet gender constraints and display women's assertiveness; they warn women about systematic sexual violence and encourage them to develop sexual allure. Behind these irreconcilable but interdependent tendencies, Rabine finds two bodies characteristic of the "woman of fashion." Her body is caught up in a network of subordinating physical, economic, and political power relations, and yet it is free and powerful especially through its self-transformations by means of dress and makeup. The contradictions encountered in fashion magazines bear witness, in Rabine's account, to the enduring "subject-object binarism of Western masculine-feminine gender structure" (*OF,* 64), which structure remains basically unaltered during postmodern times. In this regard feminist assertions and transformations take place "within the commercial enclosure of the corporate publication itself" (68).[7]

Rabine identifies as typically postmodern the historical process that changes fashion contradictions into manageable ambiguities, instabilities, and oscillations inside the phallocratic capitalist order. Behind the randomly juxtaposed materials typical of fashion magazines, moreover, lies the struggle between domination and freedom enacted within an overarching framework of oppression. This figure of the dominated other/outsider working inside (blocked inside) hegemonic and symbolic orders describes, notes Rabine, the position of the academic feminist cultural critic too, who, in her personal case, oscillates uncertainly between radical separatism and liberal meliorism in a world increasingly dedicated to capitalist imperatives. What frequently characterizes postmodern culture, in my own observation, is a sense of paranoid enclosure within which we find a carnivallike schizophrenic disorder. Fashion magazines bear witness.

In their critical sternness, Rabine and particularly O'Sickey tend to downplay progressive reinscriptions occurring in fashion magazines. There are alternatives, variations, and negations worth considering. In her personal meditation on clothes, for instance, Iris Marion Young concludes, "female imagination has liberating possibilities. . . . The unreal that wells up through imagination always creates the space for a negation of what is, and thus the possibility of alternatives" (*OF*, 209). It is in this context that we should consider such liberatory phenomena as camp, resistance styles, voguing, parody, masquerade, and anti-hegemonic dress, little of which, evidently, ever gets outside profitable iconoclasm or market cooption. Nevertheless, consider the empowering mode of identification practiced by lesbian readers of fashion magazines, who, in Diana Fuss's essay, experience erotic stirrings and vampiric identifications when face to face with the fascinating photos of supermodels who, themselves, position spectators through fantasy as preoedipal homosexual women. As with so much else, the politics of fashion magazines admit progressive transformations, judged conjuncturally. Although contradictory challenges to the status quo manifest themselves often as instabilities rather than revolutions, this is not sufficient reason to minimize changes nor to succumb to romantic demoralization, two disorders common among cultural critics who await revolution.

DRESSING POLITICALLY

Fashion has violent political facets, a point brought home by Cheryl Herr's "Terrorist Chic: Style and Domination in Contemporary Ireland," which sympathetically decodes the resistance style of clothing worn by paramilitary groups and marching bands in Northern Ireland during the Troubles. The familiar IRA ensemble consists of black shirt and pants, wide white belt, black boots, black beret, dark sunglasses, and facemask. But to dress politically does not mean simply to don a (para)military uniform. The anarchism of punk fashion, for instance, politically repudiates social order and discipline as well as normative style and taste, employing a distinctive pastiche for purposes of communal and individual liberation. Similarly, Vietnam-era bra burning and the widespread renunciation of cosmetics among certain feminists attest to committed politics of dress, as do certain innovative practices of retro fashion, another mode of pastiche, which I discuss in a moment. Tribal costuming, which I also consider, preserves collective political identities, ensuring survival against the alienation and domination of imperial fashion dictates. As these different examples suggest, the politics of dress among marginalized groups more or less demands from cultural studies symptomatic conjunctural analysis attentive to the nuanced motions, both local and global, of hegemony and resistance. Clothing is not free from intricate political entanglements at all moments and levels.

In "Fragments of a Fashionable Discourse," Kaja Silverman roundly criticizes the sartorial reticence of early U.S. feminism, promoting instead vintage clothing for its purported life-affirming political efficacy. According to Silverman, retro reconceives the (patriarchal) past affectionately yet ironically and theatrically as in a masquerade; it gains critical distance from the tyranny of (this year's) fashion; it denaturalizes settled gender identity; and it recycles waste, reclaiming use values. As a distinctive type of contemporary pastiche, thrift-shop wear, in Silverman's illustration, "can combine jeans with sawed-off flapper dresses or tuxedo jackets, art deco with 'pop art' jewelry, silk underwear from the thirties with a tailored suit from the fifties and a body that has been 'sculpted' into androgyny through eighties-style weight lifting" (*OF*, 195). To elude current fashion is for Silverman to escape the reigning symbolic order, which depends on stability and coherence. Contestation through imaginative dress challenges class and gender demarcations, opening spaces for rearticulating subjectivity. To transform hegemonic dress codes successfully is to win not just a style skirmish but a cultural battle. Silverman favors gender bending and extravagant display over strict gender binaries and rationalized dress. Although she overlooks it, retro style does decisively displace the leading role of the fashion designer, enabling the impetus for change to come from below.[8]

Silverman amplifies her argument with an important observation: retro fashion is one part of "a cluster of closely allied discourses (painting, photography, cinema, the theater, the novel), it inserts its wearer into a complex network of cultural and historical references" (*OF*, 195). The visual cultures of particular historical periods differently territorialize and define the body: its posture, contour, movement, circulation, identity, and dress. The history of the female nude in Western art, as Silverman following Anne Hollander argues, "has always assumed the form dictated by contemporary fashion" (*OF*, 189).[9] On the one hand, then, clothing molds bodies and forms subjectivity; on the other, subjects shape bodies and identities through dress. The whole range of visual arts and crafts of a culture cooperate in propounding reciprocally sedimented and demarcated body images, fashion codes, and identity formations. This fundamental politics of dress plays itself out potentially everywhere in visual culture. In the cases discussed in this section, disempowered groups express political values through their use of strategic reinscription and pastiche of mainstream fashion.

Within the special context of present-day Amerindian life, Western dress belongs to the centuries-old operations of European colonialism whereas tribal costumes protect increasingly threatened indigenous cultures, especially ancient traditions of textile weaving, coloring, and religious design motif. This subject is explored by Barbara Brodman in "Paris or Perish: The Plight of the Latin American Indian in a Westernized World," a polemic sympathetic to the majority Maya of Guatemala, who in recent decades have experienced tens of thousands of state-sanctioned murders and disappearances as well as forced assimilations and for whom the imposition of Western fashion "is no less than a subtle form of genocide" (*OF*, 269). In this Central American setting, native costume is a highly visible, risky declaration of Indian identity, which remains rooted in rural village life centered on agriculture and textile production.

Revealingly, Brodman in her own handling of the politics of dress vacillates between separatist and integrationist sentiments. Moreover, she omits any critique of indigenous "backwardness." Brodman is dejected by the growing Westernization of Maya dress habits in the towns, buoyantly celebrating the ancient authenticity of remote hamlet costumes (of which there are three hundred recognized varieties). At the same time she accepts, and grudgingly advocates, adaptation in clothing style, which typically manifests itself in hybrid garb: "It is not unusual to see village men wearing long pants, a Western-inspired garment, made of hand-woven Maya fabric and topped with an overpant that resembles the peculiar, short, 'eared' trousers of ancient times . . ." (*OF*, 272). Because Maya men interact most frequently with Spanish and Ladino culture, their dress has adapted most, increasingly foregoing, for instance, the traditional turbanlike tzut for the cowboy hat and the sandal for machine-designed synthetic boots or shoes. These are sad compromises in Brodman's ambiguous treatment, but inevitable, she relents, if the Maya are to survive, which must happen through adaptation, activism, and selected radical engagements with the powers that be. Here the politics of resistance ideally springs from autonomous villages linked in pragmatic cooperatives that negotiate collectively to gain concessions from state and business interests, including transnational corporations. Brodman, like Herr, displays remarkably few reservations about the problems within the threatened and exploited groups (for example, unfair divisions of labor, land, and property as well as unequal fashion codes). The local politics, including the politics of dress, inside these communities seem almost off limits, a not uncommon omission among activist cultural critics, sometimes prone to romanticizing "premodern" communities.

The "tribes" considered in Andrew Ross's "Tribalism in Effect" refer to the numerous urban youth style subcultures formed in recent times all across the globe, although his emphasis is mostly on the early 1990s black hip-hop nation in the United States. This hip-hop fashion includes style ensembles of music, dance, speech, and clothing, divided into hard and soft core kinds based on such key binaries as violence-prone/fun-loving, gangster/entertainer, which are manifested in certain fashion details such as ski cap/dreadlocks and thick gold chains/beads. The street music of the hip-hop counterculture, rap, embodies communal fantasies and scenarios foregrounding the tribe's politics that ultimately derives from the devastating status of young black males in America. Hip-hop fashion is compensatory and defensive, asserting identity and affording protection in a hostile environment. Among the ways for the disenfranchised to challenge the social hierarchy is to reinscribe upscale dress such as designer sportswear, letting the price tags show, wearing caps askew, and leaving shoelaces untied. This is conspicuous consumption with a difference, and less a repudiation of Western consumer culture than a symbolic redistribution of wealth. Not unexpectedly, hip-hop style has been coopted by mainstream white youth culture and by segments of the fashion business.

Ross theorizes contemporary street styles in the following gnomic, yet telling way:

> Popular style, at its most socially articulate, appears at the point where commonality ends and communities begin, fractioned off into the geography of difference, even conflict. That is the point at which visual forms of creative consumerism, no matter how tidy or ingenious, are less important than the shared attitudes and social values that come to be associated with the willfully sundry use of consumer culture. Tribalism is then in effect. Everyone cannot be anyone. (*OF*, 289)

In Ross's account, people belong to separate, often fractious communities rather than to some commonality. This is why everyone cannot simply be anyone. No matter how imaginatively and variously street tribes reinflect articles of consumer culture, what is most important are the shared values and attitudes embodied in and signified by such popular styles. Tribalism is in its effects, some of which will be unforeseen.

A fascinating strand of Ross's argument, but downplayed, is that the disaggregation of the modern world leads to the disorganization characteristic of postmodernity, a disorganization visible in youth styles as well as in worldwide secessionist and autonomy movements, upsurges in ethnocentrism and race-baiting, breakups of mass political parties and unions, and the multiplications of new social movements including African-American nationalisms. The proliferation of localisms accompanies and characterizes globalization. MTV broadcasts sectarian youth fashions internationally; hip-hop style surfaces in Asian cities; the politics of dress is simultaneously local and global, following the stupendously expanding capillaries of consumer culture.

Mindful of such transformations, Ross concludes by recommending that cultural studies scholars practice subtle conjunctural interpretation of postmodern fashion: "if we have learned anything about the cultural politics of formations like style tribalism, it is that they cannot simply be read off as articulate statements of purpose, let alone as binding agendas for cultural justice" (*OF*, 299). And I would add that the internal politics (however polyvalent) of resisting subcultures should not be simply bypassed in the process of identifying with and defending them against hegemonic regimes. This goes for the IRA as well as the Maya, vintage-clad white feminists as well as the black hip-hop nation. Localism has its problems that are not just globally induced. To his credit Ross singles out many of the problems dividing the hip-hop movement, including misogyny, racism, and internecine violence.

What typifies the politics of dress among today's disempowered groups is a practice of reinscription whereby existing items from the reigning order are put together in innovative combinations and subtly revalued by members of the group. This operation of incorporation, at once economical and iconoclastic, characteristically manifests itself in the mode of pastiche wherein singular combinations of heterogeneous items construct novel aesthetic and historical assemblages.[10] Significantly, political resistance does not inevitably or often forego the sumptuous in disassembling and refashioning dress styles. My account of pastiche self-consciously runs counter to the hysterical and somber arguments of a large chorus of conservative critics, left- and right-wing, who regard this widespread pastiche peculiar to the postmodern condition as a cultural catastrophe and licentious implosion of categories, boundaries, and separate spheres. To the degree that the subversive political force of postmodern pastiche eschews challenging the broader political economy of late capitalism, however, it exhibits a telling tendency of postmodern new social movements, namely, the reduction of universalistic utopianism to micropolitics.

FORMING IDENTITIES

A key innovation of the carnivalesque, heteroglot, disorganized culture of postmodernity is the notion of multiple subject positions, in which subjectivity emerges as a sociohistorical construct cobbled together from the many roles and situations occupied, willingly or not, by "persons" whose agency and values, fantasies and desires, cohere in contradiction. Because the formation of identity, moreover, passes by way of continuous mirroring effects afforded by others, self-images are social constructions wherein dress plays an important performative role. In a world of looking and being looked at, clothing constantly undergoes coding and decoding in intricate processes of social interaction and judgment. The subject is clothed, and body images belong to monitored cultural inventories and practices. In the highly visual world of postmodern times, subjectivity unfolds in a play of images. For good or ill, fashion has become increasingly connected with identity formation and maintenance among all classes, races, and groups; its scope and significance are less and less restricted to upper and middle classes in metropolitan centers.

By way of exponentially expanding market and media disseminations, mainstream Western fashion has penetrated remote enclaves, extending the disaggregated postmodern phenomena of widespread shocking ensembles and strategic reinscriptions. Meanwhile, in the centers, the long-standing modern paradigm of drably clothed and accessoried males and decked-out females has eroded, generating not a simple reversal but unstable eclectic postmodern modes of dress.[11] This is not to deny holdouts, vestigial practices, and pockets of conservatism. At the same time vanguard fashion runways, music videos, and certain urban subcultures feature increasingly well-publicized gender bending, camp, masquerade, varieties of cross-dressing, and collapsed high/low dress distinctions, proliferating antifashion genres and pastiche styles. (Not incidentally, many of these vanguard practices are debunked in Robert Altman's movie *Prêt-à-Porter.*) What in any or all of these changes is progressive and regressive is difficult to decipher. This is a period of extreme outcomes and mixed results, not free from reactionary throwbacks and constricting hegemonic conventions, yet exhibiting new types of creativity and spaces of liberation for fashion.

It is against the backdrop of such transformations that Douglas Kell-ner sets his ambitious essay, "Madonna, Fashion, Identity." Surprisingly and convincingly, Kellner argues that, although the "Madonna phe-nomenon" bears traces of modernist and postmodernist elements, it is driven predominantly by a modernist aesthetic of iconoclastic and polysemic excess, shock, and theatricality steeped in self-expressive experimentation and designed to break down boundaries and create innovative forms. What is postmodern in Madonna's work are arguably her uses of camp, simulation, and pastiche; her broaching existing boundaries of sex, gender, and race; her disruptions of cultural hierar-chies based on high/low distinctions; her activism on behalf of an array of political causes, including rain forests, homeless people, AIDS pa-tients, and women's rights; and her staging of multiple subject posi-tions, rendering herself an exemplary "transformer."[12] More than either her (post)modernist practices or her separate roles as pop singer, music video star, movie actress, dancer, and businesswoman, it is Madonna's overall status as immensely successful, popular, and influential cultural icon that solicits Kellner's attention and, beyond his passionate enthusi-asm, his measured criticism, particularly regarding key elements of fashion.

Throughout the different stages of her career (initiated in 1983), Madonna's tours and videos have mounted spectacular polymorphous fashion shows. She incarnates transformation through dress. Regularly in the process of altering, her clothes, accessories, hairstyles, makeup, and body images have ranged from postpunk flash trash and vintage style to Hollywood celebrity evening dress and classic male suits to trampy streetwalker garb and bedroom wear to S&M chic to techno-fashion (the latter designed by Jean-Paul Gaultier). She has merchan-dized the Boy Toy label, Madonna-wear, Madonna makeup kits, the Slutco label, and innumerable tour T-shirts and memorabilia. Not in-frequently, clothing functions ironically with Madonna as, for exam-ple, when on the Blond Ambition tour she and her female backup singers while performing "Material Girl" wore bathrobes and hair curlers, singing with false voices and out of tune to subvert the song lyrics or when on the Virgin tour she sang "Like a Virgin" in a white wedding dress, suggestively thrusting her hips and screaming to the audience, "Do you want to marry me?" Consider also the humorous titles of her fashion labels. For two decades Madonna has represented the vanguard of popular youth fashion, which includes an irreverent sassy attitude.

Irony notwithstanding, a basic lesson Madonna teaches, stresses Kellner, is "that in a postmodern image culture identity is constructed through image and fashion . . ." (*OF*, 176). And he elaborates, displaying mixed emotions:

> Yet by constructing identity largely in terms of fashion and image, Madonna plays into precisely the imperatives of the fashion and consumer industries that offer a "new you" and a solution to all of your problems by the purchase of products and services. . . . Yet in becoming the most recognizable woman entertainer of her era (and perhaps of all time), Madonna produced works that have multiple and contradictory effects and that in many ways helped subvert dominant conservative ideologies. (*OF*, 178)

As the repetition of "yet" reminds us, the Madonna phenomenon characteristically calls forth qualifications to straightforward commendations and criticisms. Madonna is a subverter of normative culture, but she profits enormously (having earned hundreds of millions of dollars) without upsetting social relations of domination or offering alternatives. In Kellner's view, the cultural idea, the cult, of self-fashioning a "new you" is for many people a lie, an ideology: people everywhere cannot simply alter their bodies, ages, psychological and economic conditions, and images. Narcissistic schemes to refashion the self sell fashion items; in the process clothes and body parts become fetishes while any sense of community recedes into the background. Madonna makes things even worse, in Kellner's estimation, by deluding teenagers and by aiding in women's continued objectification. Yet by giving a prominent place in her work to Hispanic and black artists, to worthy activist causes, to interracial sex, to the image of a powerful woman, to alternative sexualities, to humor and fantasy as modes of cultural critique, and to the possibility of change, Madonna opens prospects and hopes not simply for self but for social transformation. Kellner does not disguise his approval.

I want to return to postmodern political economy as a way to situate more broadly the Madonna phenomenon and to bring this consideration of key topics in critical fashion studies to a conclusion. Processes of commodification within consumer society enclose and coopt radical actions, giving rise among most cultural studies people to a unique cluster of significant propositions about postmodern culture: there is no outside of commodity capital; revolution (a modern notion) is dead; internal transformation and strategic reinscription constitute viable political projects; and social contradictions offer productive sites for inquiry and activism. In this postmodern scenario, grandiose political schemes have had their day, although capitalism has without question recently entered upon another stage of grandiose global financial expansion.[13] Given the various vectors of political economy now in play, utopian thinking tends, when it is not blocked altogether, toward anarchism, identity politics, activist micropolitics, and limited coalitions. The Madonna phenomenon provides evidence of these tendencies: just when the scope of political communication is dramatically globalized, the reach and ambition of much political action are locally focused. But the demassification of political thinking entails less a simple surrender than the turn to certain "guerrilla" tactics. It is, however, often in the name of vague liberation, sometimes highly personalized freedom, that micropolitics gets enacted. Madonna is caught up in and symbolizes this complex array of forces and tendencies swirling around the intersection of postmodern fashion, political economy, and identity. While democratization spreads to formally excluded groups, economic security for all recedes from view. Meanwhile, a prized badge of democracy is the freedom to wear Western designer fashions, ever more ubiquitous commodities.

At the outset of their work the editors of *On Fashion* excitedly observe: "nothing stands outside fashion's dictates. Urban chic and urban violence, terrorism and tribalism, rage and rapture all have their mode—'attitude dressing'" (*OF*, 1). Postmodern politics and identity are clothed, so to speak, just as are contemporary mass fantasy and negation. As the scare quotes doubtlessly imply, fashion nowadays is more than (but also) a matter of personal attitude, posturing, clothing design, and haute couture; it encompasses and has impact on collectivities both First and Third World, urbanized and rusticated, disorganized and not; it is part of the contemporary aestheticization of everyday life. Accordingly, for cultural studies fashion invites allegorical and symptomatic readings, serving as an increasingly significant sociopolitical indicator, which we see in the cases of Barbie fashion and mass circulation women's fashion magazines, U.S. hip-hop tribes and Guatemalan Maya, and youth subcultures and the Madonna phenomenon. Within the confines of present-day fashion, clothing selections seem for most people generous; it is an expansive time in evident synchronization with an era of globalization and pleasure-inducing spectacle. And yet the images circulating through the fashion media, as I see it, numbingly repeat beautiful but destructive stereotypes, norms, ideals, and hegemonic views, producing alienated identification, anxiety, contradiction, and envy as well as death wishes: costly compensations and at the same time seedbeds of resistance, strategic reinscription, and personal and political transformation.

11

BLUES SOUTHWESTERN STYLE

WHEN I TEACH THE UNDERGRADUATE COURSE "Topics in Cultural Studies," I typically build it around five or six subfields or issues in the field that interest students, ranging from, for example, popular culture, media, technology, and science studies to nationhood and national identity, globalization, and postmodernization to fashion studies, body studies, and youth subcultures. With the last-named subject, a consistently popular one and a key area for cultural studies, I usually focus on Dick Hebdige's dated but still productive *Subculture: The Meaning of Style* (1979), highlighting its pioneering analysis of the punk phenomenon. In recent years, however, my views on subculture have become more personal and nuanced thanks to my participation in the blues music scene in and around Oklahoma City. It is this distinctive adult subculture that I explore in chapter 11.

CULTURAL STUDIES AND THE BLUES

I define "subculture" straightforwardly as a relatively small group of people sharing something(s) in common that distinguishes them from other groups in a significant, usually self-conscious, way. Subcultures often deviate from mainstream social values and practices, frequently occupying lower rungs on the social ladder. As such, they can provide telling perspectives on normative social values, offering compensations and respite, of course, but opening up alternatives and casting a critical light on the status quo. This critical perspective explains one of their main interests for cultural studies. In my work on subcultures, both in teaching and in studying this local music scene in the Southwest, I have taken inspiration from *The Subcultures Reader* (1997), edited by Ken Gelder and Sarah Thornton, which contains fifty-five selections, the most wide-ranging single source in the field and a good place for all researchers to start.

Speaking methodologically, much of the research on subcultures involves interviews, oral history, participant observation, ethnography, and autoethnography. My research is no different. Landmark books such as Studs Terkel's *Hard Times: An Oral History of the Great Depression* (1970) and Alex Haley's *Roots* (1977), not to mention pioneering academic texts such as Paul Thompson's *The Voice of the Past: Oral History* (1978) and the Popular Memory Group's *Making Histories: Studies in History-Writing and Politics* (1982) have not only inspired numerous imitator works, but helped ensure a respectable place for qualitative research. During my four years as a fan and a participant-observer in the blues subculture in Oklahoma City (OKC), I have carried out much qualitative research, especially informal interviews and oral histories. I tell students and colleagues (always in a hurry it seems) to start with the *The Oral History Reader* (1998), edited by Robert Perks and Alistair Thomson, which offers thirty-nine classic selections plus a useful brief bibliography. Perhaps my own favorite text on interviewing is *Perilous States: Conversations on Culture, Politics, and Nation* (1993), edited by George E. Marcus, the first volume in his series "Late Editions: Cultural Studies for the End of the Century," a sequence of books employing the "engaged conversation" as its signature format and demonstrating a surprisingly wide array of rigorous interview formats. Pierre Bourdieu's essay "Understanding," the conclusion to his coauthored *The Weight of the World: Social Suffering in Contemporary Society* (1993; trans. 1999), a book offering dozens of moving and telling interviews, is a tour de force on the subtleties and craft (vs. method) of qualitative research. He is especially useful on the complications of the induced self-analysis experienced by interviewees, on the well-being of interviewees, on the problem of interviewees' role playing, and on breaking through walls of clichés.

Cultural studies books on popular culture and pop music rarely study the blues and certainly not present-day local blues scenes, seemingly preferring mass as opposed to localized niche markets and culture. I have in mind such classic texts as Simon Frith's *Sound Effects: Youth, Leisure, and the Politics of Rock* (1983), Iain Chambers *Urban Rhythms: Pop Music and Popular Culture* (1985), and John Fiske's *Reading the Popular* (1989), as well as more recent scholarship. This is not to say that the literature on the blues is skimpy. The eight hundred large-format pages of Robert Ford's *A Blues Bibliography* (1999) document abundant material, including numerous sources on celebrated "regional variations" (Chicago, Mississippi Delta, Texas, etc.).[1] But cultural studies work has no noticeable presence in this domain, and the OKC blues scene of today has received no academic study.

What is popular culture? In *Keywords* (1983), Raymond Williams famously traces four connotations of "popular": it refers to phenomena liked by many people, it designates inferior (nonelite) objects and practices, it names work seeking to win people's favor and prompting consumption, and it applies to materials made by the people for themselves. Cultural studies definitions have generally stressed the subordinated, conflictual, and creative dimensions of contemporary popular culture, having in mind people's poaching on and resignification of mainstream cultural commodities such as television shows and mass music. "Popular culture," stresses John Fiske in a classic formulation, "is made by subordinated peoples in their own interests out of resources that also, contradictorily, serve the economic interests of the dominant."[2] By any definition, blues music, including early twenty-first century urban blues, is popular culture.[3] Globalization has not altered things in this regard, extending the reach of the music. Indeed, "'globalization' has heightened the localization of musical tastes and the appreciation of musical diversity,"[4] something that blues musicians, fans, and critics have long valued, celebrating regional variants with gusto and pride.

The postmodern moment, in my view, arrived for blues music with a third and fourth stage of development. The first stage covers the period of the acoustic country blues put on records between World Wars I and II: Picture the Mississippi Delta. The second involves the electrified urban blues of the period from roughly 1945 to 1965: Think Chicago. The third includes the broad spread of the blues outside the black community to whites and also outside the United States to Canada and Europe, especially England.[5] Two subgenres appear here: acoustic folk blues and electric blues-rock. The fourth stage occurs in the 1980s and thereafter marked by the explosion of reissues (in the new compact disc format) distributed to an increasingly internationalized niche market and catering to (and creating) a nostalgia for old-time "downhome" blues and its styles newly taken up (sometimes too respectfully) by the rising generation of musicians.

The class, race, and gender trajectories from modern to postmodern blues follow a broad historical path from poor black sharecroppers and songsters in the Depression-era South to the better-off black proletariat in the postwar urban centers of the Midwest to the white and black lower middle classes in the United States and abroad thereafter. (With the rise of rap music in recent years, there is well-deserved fear that younger black musicians and fans have abandoned blues music altogether, a recurring anxiety that first surfaced during the 1950s rise of rhythm and blues and the 1960s prominence of soul music.) At the outset remarkable women played a part in blues music, as Angela Davis (among others) ably documents in her *Blues Legacies and Black Feminism: Gertrude "Ma" Rainey, Bessie Smith, and Billie Holiday* (1998). The female blues tradition has continued intermittently, spreading into contemporary U.S. white blues from the 1960s onwards. Still, women blues musicians, composers, and producers (separate from lead vocalists) are perhaps only a bit less rare today than in the past. Queer blues is barely visible: heterosexism, especially virulent in early country and Chicago blues, dominates the blues with notable exceptions. Starting in the 1980s, blues scenes began dotting the globe, showing up in small European countries and across Asia, particularly Japan. In the United States, Native American blues bands and fans began appearing. Postmodern globalization for the blues has meant becoming multiracial, decentralized, international, and heterogeneous— that is my broad historical thesis in this chapter. The OKC blues scene is part of this transformation. Here is how William Barlow optimistically puts matters in the conclusion to his wide-ranging history of the blues: "An unusual cross-section of people are currently engaged in blues culture. Their race, class, and generational differences have made it one of those rare, eclectic, and in many ways utopian social experiments that can take place only on the fringes of the dominant culture."[6]

Blues people often define themselves, consciously and unconsciously, by contrast to devotees of other types of music, particularly classical, jazz, and rock music, but also country, gospel, and rap (Figure 2). Blues is neither highbrow like classical and jazz music, nor youth-oriented like rap and much rock. And, of course, it is defiantly secular, seeing itself at the opposite end of a spectrum from gospel. Preoccupied with urban life and problems, contemporary blues differs from both bluegrass and from country and western music with their focus on rural and small-town society and values. All such differences noted, there are most certainly innumerable examples of blues fused with these more or less neighboring forms of music. Blues regularly overlaps with country, folk, jazz, and rock. Yet other differences exist. Blues is consumed in characteristically small smoke-filled juke (jook) joints and not in upscale jazz clubs with well-dressed people, nor in churches, nor at country and western bars dotted with cowboy/cowgirl

How to Tell Blues Music from Rock Music

Here's How:

1. If the guitar player has one small amplifier, Blues Band. If he has a stack of them, Rock Band.
2. If the keyboard player only plays piano or organ, Blues Band. If he's used other sounds, Rock Band.
3. If the guitar player breaks a string and changes it on the spot, Blues Band. If a roadie comes out with a replacement guitar, Rock Band.
4. If the bass player's instrument has only four strings, Blues Band. More than four, Rock Band.
5. If there are wives and children around the stage, Blues Band. Scantily clad women, Rock Band.
6. If they play the same songs differently every night, Blues Band. Play the same songs the same way every night, Rock band.
7. If they make up the lyrics as they go, Blues Band. Recite the lyrics verbatim, Rock band.
8. If they arrive in a van, Blues Band. If they arrive in a school bus, Rock band.
9. If everyone is drinking liquor, Blues Band. Drinking beer, Rock Band.
10. If people dance together, Blues band. Mill about separately, Rock Band.
11. If people clap their hands to the backbeat, Blues Band. Pump their fists in the air, Rock Band.
12. If the male musicians are wearing Dockers, Blues Band. If they are wearing Spandex, Rock Band.

Tips:

1. Real Blues bands swing! No swing and all funk ain't the Blues.
2. You don't need electricity to play Blues.
3. You don't need Spandex pants to play the Blues either.

Figure 2 Blues vs. Rock from *Back Beat*

boots and hats, nor at huge sports stadiums with wild fans, nor at philharmonic halls packed with formally dressed, quietly seated people, nor at rave parties with disco lights and frantic mosh pits. In the jukes, adults of all ages dance, talk, smoke, and drink whiskey and beer, never wine, never artisanal beer, rarely exotic mixed drinks. (I myself drink wine and boutique beer, but not in the juke joints and not with the blues crowd.) Compared to rap, rock, country, and Top 40 music, blues is "noncommercial," which is both a sore point and a point of pride with its fans. According to a letter from the Blues Music Association published in *Blues Revue* 76 (June/July 2002), "the blues category makes up less than 2 percent of all music products sold . . ." (55). Given its links with juke joints, its small noncommercial fandom, and especially its historical ties with the African-American lumpenproletariat and working classes, blues is not mainstream but rather lowbrow entertainment associated in many white and black middle-class minds with a vaguely disreputable demimonde. All of these distinctions and points of view on blues, many of which are stereotypes, circulate today through the blues world as a source of identity, of cultural "distinction," of solidarity, and of humor.

OKLAHOMA CITY BLUES SCENE

The blues scene in Oklahoma City, a metroplex of roughly 800,000 people, is vibrant and multifaceted, much more so than other places I have lived. At any given time there are twenty or so blues bands and a dozen or so jukes hiring these bands. Although the scene is fluid, there is a more or less stable inner core of venues and groups. There are three weekly blues radio shows: one runs on the local National Public Radio station each Saturday afternoon from 1 to 5 pm and on Sunday from 1 to 4 pm, followed by a one-hour nationally syndicated show, *Beale Street Blues*, produced in Memphis by the Blues Foundation (founded in 1980). The third runs on a local commercial rock station from 9 to 12 on Sunday nights. Both local shows advertise blues events and disseminate news, serving as key sources of information for people in the OKC blues community. In addition, both shows interview local musicians on air and play locally produced compact discs (CDs) as well as the latest regional and national releases. The Oklahoma Blues Society (OBS), a group of 320 paid members (annual dues $15.00), publishes a bimonthly newsletter, *Back Beat*, containing twelve to sixteen pages of news, advertisements, photos, reviews of albums and shows, interviews, historical articles on blues greats, plus directories of local clubs, bands, events, and available musicians. (There are two other blues societies in

Oklahoma, one in Tulsa, 100 miles away, and one in the southern part of the state.) These directories of musicians list roughly fifty OKC artists and sound technicians prepared to play on short notice. OBS hosts an annual picnic; an annual twelve-hour marathon Blues Bash featuring a dozen local bands (Figure 3), an annual talent contest associated with the Blues Foundation (which organization has more than

OKLAHOMA BLUES SOCIETY
"BLUES BASH 2001"

"KRXO" 107.7

OCT 13, 2001
"CRABTOWN"
IN
BRICKTOWN
2nd floor
2PM – 1:30AM
$3.00 Members
$5.00 Non Members

"KGOU=KROU" 106.3 105.7

"Gazette"

2pm	The Blues Rockers
3pm	Shortt Dogg
4pm	Sweet Brenda & The Prison Guard's
5pm	Miss. Amy & Her Sho' Nuff' Blue's Men
6pm	Pinkie & The Snakeshakers
7pm	Doc Blues Review
8pm	Jesse James Cahn & The Hiway Sound
9pm	A. J. Johnson & Why Not
10pm	Blackhawk Blues Band
11pm	Harold Jefferson & The Show Biz Band
12am	Miss. Blues & Prime Choice

"Crabtown"

As usual, times and bands may vary & bands TBA.

"Terry's Guitar"

OUTSIDE STAGE

"Sherrie's Dinner"

2pm	Live to Tell
3pm	The Blake Street Band
4pm	Lee McWaters
5pm	Curly Jackwire
6pm	

Animal LoK Productions

Figure 3 Oklahoma Blues Society Blues Bash 2001 Flyer

100 affiliate Blues societies around the globe), monthly four-hour jams on Sunday afternoon with family and children welcome, open meetings monthly of officers and directors, a twenty-four-hour phone hotline listing bands and venues updated weekly, and an e-mail list and a website both spreading information on a continuous basis. Often when there is a large festival in the state (400 to 5,000 people) or a popular national or regional band performing locally, OBS sets up a booth and sells buttons, bumper stickers, canvas bags, bandannas, and shirts (tanks, tees, and long sleeves), all carrying its logo (Figure 4). On any given occasion, the gross receipts can range from $300 to $3,000 per event. The shirts, in particular, serve as something of a "uniform" in the local blues community. But there is more to the subculture than the regular playing of bands in clubs, radio shows, Blues Society functions, and paraphernalia.

In any given week there are usually a half dozen or so jams. These are generally four-hour events where a host band plays a one-hour set (50 minutes) after which a sequence of loosely formed groups plays three more sets. Unaffiliated, visiting, and new musicians are more or less welcomed at these events. At a good jam two or three of the finest players from different bands might work together, spurring one another to peak performances. Or an unknown person might break through and bring the house down with an inspired solo or song. At a bad jam the players might not quite jell, or the available talent is too thin, or one or two players dominate the event, or one or two groups might play songs too long, filling them with overextended solos (Figure 5). (In blues, unlike rock, musicians are expected to "respect the song" and keep solos short and controlled. However, such restraints do not apply in blues-rock.) It is the job of the jam meister (usually a musician-host paid a small fee) to quietly organize and manage the jam, lining up the players (both at the scene and days earlier), putting together the combinations, monitoring the equipment, supervising the sound mixing, and keeping things rolling. Jams are special occasions when many musicians, sometimes several dozen, are brought together in one venue and when unattached musicians get to play. At the monthly OBS jams, musicians sign up when they come in, but at most jams musicians must "network" with the jam meister. (There is a politics of jams.) Because working musicians rarely get to see or hear artists from other bands, jams provide a relaxed occasion for mingling, intelligence gathering, and community building. The Sunday night jam at Danny's Blues Saloon, the premier jam in OKC, which often packs two hundred people into a medium-sized smoke-filled juke, is the closest thing to a headquarters for blues musicians and fans. I often think the jam is what many blues people have in place of church.

P.O. Box 76176
Oklahoma City, OK 73147-2176

The
Oklahoma Blues Society

is a not-for-profit organization
dedicated to the preservation and per-
petuation of blues music

A Blues Foundation Affiliate

Figure 4 Oklahoma Blues Society Flyer (Front Page)

The typical blues band today consists of a drummer, an electric
bassist, a lead electric guitarist, and a singer. Often the roles of lead
guitar and singer are joined in one person. And many singer-guitarists
are also songwriters and harmonica players. Other instruments, in
order of preference and likelihood, include electric rhythm guitar, harmonica ("harp"), keyboards (electronic piano, sometimes organ,

Nine Pet Peeves of a Blues Fan

The following was provided by a donor who wishes to remain anonymous.

1. Guitarists cramming in too many notes.
2. Long solos.
3. Super loud bass drums.
4. Keyboards who can't manage boogie woogie.
5. Inaudible lead singers.
6. Sound mixers who bury harps.
7. Uninspired bass players.
8. Slow bartenders.
9. Rock fans.

Figure 5 Peeves of a Blues Fan from *Back Beat*

rarely piano), and brass (usually saxophone). Occasionally one encounters an acoustic guitar, standup bass, trumpet, and very rarely washtub base, washboard, spoons, or flute. A great deal of money is spent on equipment (instruments, amplifiers, microphones, etc.), and among musicians much conversation centers on the technical features of equipment. It is more or less an absolute requirement that the lead guitarist be a virtuoso. What is important in blues singing, however, is less virtuosity than style. A "good" or operatic voice can be a positive drawback; a strong, emotive, malleable "rough" voice is not only desirable but more or less prized, and this goes for female and male vocalists alike, as the famous cases of, say, Howlin' Wolf and Koko Taylor or Johnny Winter and Janis Joplin make clear. Among fans (as opposed to blues professionals) songwriting ability is widely disregarded in favor of stage presence and showmanship, instrumental virtuosity, captivating lead vocals, good song selection from the repertoire, and band tightness. Although at festivals the majority of fans tend to listen rather than dance, in the clubs much dancing goes on so bands generally play a high percentage of danceable shuffles ranging from three to six or seven minutes in length. Still, blues fans listen to song lyrics: clear enunciation, well-crafted verses, and high-impact themes are appreciated, except by devotees of the blues-rock subgenre, many of whom prefer extremely loud and long guitar solos that typically overpower singing and drown out lyrics.

Blues audiences occupy three spatial zones. Those fans closest to the band sway to the music or dance, with physical contact among audience members. It's carnival time. Farther back and usually seated are more or less attentive listeners, resting dancers, and people chatting. And farther back still, one finds musicians, club owners, sound technicians, jam meisters, and other cognoscenti in conversation, a conversation with one ear finely cocked toward the stage.[7] There is much "noise" in a blues club.[8] Respectful hush is unheard of. People move freely from one zone to another, listening, perhaps getting up and dancing, then drifting toward the edges for conversation. Traditionally, food, basic food like fried chicken, barbecue, greens, and the like, has been part of the blues experience, and all festivals and roughly half the clubs serve such fare, which is consumed either in a cordoned-off area or more likely in and at the edges of the listeners' zone. Food, drink, and merchandise (CDs, T-shirts, posters, etc.) are sold on the outer edges of the venues beyond which lie doors/admission gates and restrooms. And beyond that are parking lots and at some festivals camping grounds.

Blues fans in OKC range across age groups, excepting the very young and the old; most races, including African-Americans, Native Americans, and Caucasians, but generally not Mexican- and Asian-Americans, and both genders equally (lesbians and gays are not visible). Fans come from the well-paid working class and from the low-to-mid strata of the middle class. One occasionally sees "aristocrats" and lumpenproletarians at blues events, most of whom stick out like sore thumbs. Several of the clubs in OKC, especially Danny's and Strokers, attract leather-clad bikers, who tend to be middle-aged with obvious disposable income and who on any given night might constitute a noticeable portion of the audience in these two clubs. Despite their menacing reputations, the bikers, though peaceable, are clannish. On a busy weekend night a blues club audience of one hundred people (depending on the venue) would consist of half men and women; twenty to twenty-five percent or so from each age group—the twenties, thirties, forties, and fifties—with a few older and younger people mixed in; plus approximately eight percent Native American and five percent African American. (The 2000 census data for Oklahoma City show a five percent Native population and sixteen percent black.) There are several de facto segregated black clubs in the city, not frequented by whites, where blues gets played but mixed in with soul, rhythm and blues, and funk (no blues-only clubs). The substantial Mexican-American group, eight percent, very newly arrived in OKC, and the Asian-American population, four percent, dating from the 1970s, are absent from the blues scene. The blues audience, as far as I can judge, is more heterogeneous today than any other music fandom.

A certain small faction of the OKC blues audience, "regulars," both fans and professionals (full-time and part-time), share a common social space, knowledge, and set of issues. They are familiar with the loosely defined pecking order of local working bands and part-timers as well as with the blues repertoire dating from the Delta blues of the 1920s to the Chicago blues of the 1950s and the British invasion of the 1960s up to the various blues revivals of the 1970s, '80s, and '90s.[9] This entails a history of stars, record labels, famous sidemen, celebrated covers, technical innovations, and so on. They share the blues argot (for example, harp, ax, Strat, Marshall, green bullet, shuffle, slide, Muddy, SRV, etc.), and have generally been listening to local blues radio, playing recent CD releases, and perhaps reading blues publications, the latter ranging from local press to such national magazines as *Living Blues*, *Blues Revue*, and *Blues at the Foundation*. When these aficionados show up at shows, jams, festivals, or other blues events, they do not mention their day jobs and no one asks about what people do for a living. The line between daily life and music (work and leisure) is clean and firm. Politics and religion are very rarely talked about. After four years in the scene, few blues regulars know what I do for a living, and I know very little about their work or personal lives. Stature in the group does not derive from external sources, but rather from participation and from visibility within the local blues world. This leads to a high level of egalitarianism in the blues subculture.[10] Among blues musicians, as among other artists, there is a tension between "purists" dedicated above all to the art and "entertainers" robustly seeking external approval and rewards (money, fame, festival gigs, record deals). In addition, fans, like musicians, have more or less "rigorous" definitions of the blues, being ready to argue over authenticity. If a band performed a high proportion of rockabilly or soul or rock, it might be said disparagingly that it was not a blues band. Patroling the borders of the blues is a continuous occupation and game among some blues regulars.

LOCAL PROFILES

In August 1999 Pinkie & the SnakeShakers won the annual Unsigned Blues Talent Contest of the Oklahoma Blues Society, beating out seven other acts.[11] The band consists of five white thirty-somethings, dressed in black, including a drummer, electric bassist, amplified harmonica player, lead electric guitarist-vocalist, and lead vocalist, Pinkie (Figure 6). As I write during summer 2002, the band has been in operation for four years with several personnel changes (drummer and bassist). On average this combo, one of the two most popular in OKC (Figure 7)

Figure 6 Band Photo of Pinkie & the SnakeShakers

plays 200 dates a year. [12] Most of the band members hold down day jobs. A typical gig of three or four 50-minute sets lasting from 9:30 pm to 1:30 am earns anywhere from $250 to $600. Each set consists of roughly ten songs, many drawn from the standard blues repertoire, [13] although the SnakeShakers' lead guitarist (Chris Henson) and lead vocalist (Pinkie West) compose original songs together. The SnakeShak-

	July 7	*Planet Rock/Rockn' Horse Club*
		Ponca City
	July 10	*Woolly Bully's - 7628 N. May*
	July 11	*Dr. Feelgood's - Midwest City*
	July 13	*Woolly Bully's - 7628 N. May*
	July 14	*Harley Fest at Incahoots - 3:30 pm*
	July 14	*Concert - 8 pm*
		Bricktown Coca-Cola Centre
	July 14	*Classic Rock Cafe - Oklahoma City*
	July 17	*Woolly Bully's - 7628 N. May*
	July 22	*Classic Rock Cafe - Oklahoma City*
	July 24	*Woolly Bully's - 7628 N. May*
	July 25	*Dr. Feelgood's - Midwest City*
	July 27	*Park Tavern - Medicine Park, OK*
	July 28	*Galileos - Paseo District*
	July 31	*Woolly Bully's - 7628 N. May*
	Aug. 3	*Danny's Blues Saloon - 10th & Villa*

Figure 7 Monthly Schedule of Pinkie & the SnakeShakers

ers' one CD, the full-length *Shake These Blues* (Figure 8), self-released in 2001, contains eleven songs all written by West/Henson.[14] At $15 a copy, the band sold roughly 1,500 CDs in the first year at their shows and festival appearances. That's a large number by local standards. (They estimate production expenses at $9,000, a very high figure.) Club owners love the SnakeShakers: they come ready to entertain;

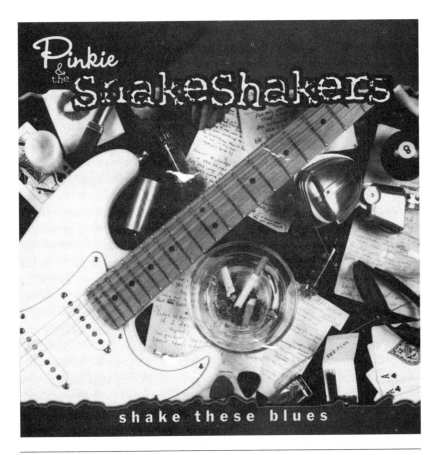

Figure 8 Pinkie & the SnakeShakers CD Front Cover

draw big enthusiastic, thirsty crowds; get people up on the dance floor; and play full, mixed tempo, tightly sequenced sets. People hearing them for the first time are astonished by their musical talents, big blues-rock sound, tightness, professionalism, enthusiasm, and high energy.

Pinkie West is a stage entertainer, the best in the OKC blues scene.[15] Dressed in black, occasionally mixing lace and leather, with ample, below her buttocks blond hair, which is often waving wildly in performance, she possesses a three-octave vocal range, with the ability to "distort" her voice in a blues manner, sometimes purring, meowing, yowling; sometimes shouting, screaming, growling; and sometimes whispering, warbling, and scatting. She can mimic flute and trumpet vibratos. First-time listeners think of Janis Joplin, an apt comparison. West is also the manager, booking agent, and public relations person for the band. Henson is the band leader. (Most bands divide up such chores.) On the debut album she penned the lyrics for all eleven tracks, and he composed the music. The song lyrics/narratives foreground a strong, sometimes vulnerable, woman dealing with the difficulties of love relationships, ranging from being cheated on, experiencing jealousy, and wanting vengeance to desiring attention from a handsome man, needing temporary separation, begging a lover to stay to advising a woman friend on how to keep a man. Although some of these songs are constructed as stories about other women, most are presented as personal experiences. But intuitively the audience reacts to this strong blues woman as a type and spokesperson.

Blues scholars such as Dennis Jarrett have noted that, although much blues music uses an autobiographical, first-person form, it presents a fictional, collective self, a persona, separate from the singer-songwriter, which is by now a widely recognized convention of the genre.[16] Steven Tracy puts it this way: "blues performers can be seen as purveyors of both personal and communal, contemporary and historical, realities and visions. First person singular on the surface, first person plural down deep. . . ."[17] Of early blues women, Angela Davis cogently observes they "forged and memorialized images of tough, resilient, and independent women who were afraid neither of their own vulnerability nor of defending their right to be respected as autonomous human beings."[18] Pinkie West follows in this line of strong, vulnerable, sexy, and provocative blues women whose troubles are part of everyone's experience. The difference, a contemporary postmodern one, is that this woman is white and comparatively well off. Long experienced by black women, the ephemerality of adult love relationships (call it "serial monogamy" in the contemporary white community) is, historically considered, relatively new for white women from nonelite classes. Not surprisingly, Pinkie is a favorite with women fans who vociferously (antiphonally) shout encouragement and agreement as she sings about the complications of love relationships.

For some blues purists Pinkie West is too much an entertainer and not enough an artist. Indeed, she gravitates fully toward the populist rather than the insider coterie position in the local blues scene. Her own songs and her song selections from the repertoire focus on love and little else,[19] a complaint which is true, but only about one-third of all blues lyrics focus on other topics. Her style of dress (lace, leather, black) strikes some adherents of the regionally normative jeans and T-shirt as pretentious. Yet fashion in the blues, now and in the past, occupies every spot on a spectrum from work clothes to finely tailored suits and dresses to lavish stage costumes, as attendance at any blues festival attests. (Festivals typically host anywhere from ten to forty acts over two or three days drawn from a mixture of local, regional, and national talent.) Pinkie leaves the stage for two or three songs each set to let the male guitarist-lead vocalist sing and to allow the other musicians to solo; she enthusiastically joins the dancers or wanders toward the edges of the audience where she greets people, energetically working the crowd. Some blues regulars consider the artist's joining in with the dancers a breach of decorum, and certainly this is unconventional, although the fans and particularly the dancers appreciate the gesture, which usually reenergizes the juke.

The SnakeShakers have many admirers, dozens of devoted fans, a few critics, and a growing crossover (nonblues) audience. More and more, they are invited to play at rock and country and western venues. This popularity generates great pride in the OKC blues subculture, which glimpses one of its most talented and flamboyant groups of musicians being widely admired while staying true to their blues roots. On this score there is, of course, some criticism and jealousy among musicians and cognoscenti, but paradoxically such negativity generates interaction and functions like glue for the subculture.

There are two esteemed Native American groups who play in OKC, Blackhawk Blues Band (Figure 9) and Blues Nation (Figure 10). In addition, there are ten or so individual Native American musicians playing with non-Native-identified bands. (The state of Oklahoma has a large Native population, several hundred thousand.) Although Blackhawk entertains at Native events and festivals, it operates for the most part in the mainstream: it plays predominantly in local OKC clubs and popular festivals, it covers primarily classics from the blues repertoire, and its own compositions focus not on Native themes specifically but traditional blues subjects, as is clear on both their first CD, *Gypsy Blue*, where four of the five originals out of the eight songs are about the usual experiences of love, and their second CD, *Rainy*, where nine of the original 12 songs are concerned with various typical aspects of love relationships.[20] The four forty-something males of Blackhawk generate a solid, skillful blues sound based on well-seasoned guitar and harmonica playing along with pleasing vocal harmonies. The song lyrics are unexceptional, while the original musical compositions are compelling. Some of the songs on their CDs are heavily orchestrated (sax, trumpet, keyboard), but Blackhawk at appearances is a simple bar band, not a studio quartet with gadgets and technical wizardry, much appreciated for their straightforward instrumentally polished live shows where the two guitarists-vocalists-songwriters often trade concise "licks" in intricate arabesques. The band attracts a small following of devoted Native

Figure 9 Blackhawk Blues Band CD Back Cover

American fans as well as the usual blues lovers (five to ten percent of whom are Native American in OKC). (This is the one time when I get to socialize with many Native Americans.) Batiste Jones, the working-class bandleader of Blackhawk, an easygoing much beloved person in the subculture, occasionally appears at jams, especially the monthly OBS ones. He is a bridge-builder of sorts, linking red, white, and black people as well as working- and middle-class people, all on the ground of popular culture in this distinctive regional format.

Unlike Blackhawk, Blues Nation plays up its Native American roots in its dress, lyrics, and promotional materials.[21] The cover picture on their self-released CD portrays the five male musicians in everyday informal Native-accented dress in the foreground, but with them in full tribal regalia in the background. Each member's tribal identity is listed in the album liner notes (Kiowa; Comanche; Creek; Kiowa-Comanche; and Kiowa-Comanche-Apache). This band plays primarily Native American festivals and events locally and regionally, also including some travel abroad. Their album, *Blues Nation*, one of five finalists in the "Best Blues Recording" category of the 2000 Native American Music

Figure 10 Blues Nation CD Front Cover

Awards,[22] is dedicated to the "youth of all tribes." Of the 11 songs on the CD, all originals and most cowritten, eight deal with complications of love relationships, and three focus on an array of topics, ranging from the coming of Christian Armageddon to the problems of being a traveling musician to the right of Native Americans to sing the blues. Half of the songs have clear Native American inflections: for instance, "Empty Tipi Blues" makes it plain that the forgiving male lover is Native American; "Stayin' Home" stages a dispute between a stay-at-home woman and a longing-to-roam man who is on his way to a "dance," that is, a "Pow-Wow"; and "East Bound Greyhound" laments the departure on a bus of a woman, a long-haired, brown-eyed "Indian girl."

The most moving song on Blues Nation's disc, "My People," features a sad and angry declaration by the Native American singer-bluesman accompanied by weeping slide guitar, solemn electric piano, and mournful bass (itself backed by a driving, thumping bass drum):

My people have a right to sing the blues,
My people have a right to sing the blues,
The places we got lied to, oh we got the blues.

Used to live in tipis and hunt the buffalo,
Now we live in projects and use food cards for dough,
The place we got dumped off, oh we got the blues.

Used to speak our language and teach it to our kids,
Now we teach them English and have no money to live,
Boy, the places we got dumped off, oh we got the blues.

The remaining verses are equally strong on Native American issues, most notably broken treaties. I have heard this song in performance twice, both times in the presence of Native American as well as other blues fans, and I have entertained the thought that the "Indian" subaltern can speak, using the blues as medium. At both performances, separated by eighteen months, Blues Nation was the host band of the monthly OBS jam, a site where races and classes mix indiscriminately in enjoyment of the blues. Native Americans occupy an equal spot in the subculture, although demonstrably not in the regional culture at large.

There are several gay and lesbian bars in OKC, and one of them, the HiLo, has a long-standing monthly blues night at which Act Casual with Miss Blues plays. This integrated quartet consists of a white guitar player-vocalist; a white drummer; a black bass player-vocalist-band leader; and a black lead vocalist-washboard player (Miss Blues). Miss Blues, in her late sixties, an African-American woman, has been singing blues in and around OKC on and off for more than fifty years (Figure 11). She performs in excess of a one hundred dates a year in OKC, Tulsa, and North Texas with occasional trips out of the region. She usually works with Act Casual, but sometimes with other bands. She is a member of the OBS Board and an esteemed member of the subculture. When she appears monthly at HiLo, she brings along some of her fans (nongay), connecting normally separate social worlds.

In 2001 Miss Blues brought out a joint CD with an all-white quintet of young blues-rock musicians from Laramie, Wyoming, Blinddog Smokin', whom she met and casually jammed with at a regional festival eighteen months earlier. The chemistry was good, and Blinddog conceived, nurtured, and self-released the project, which was recorded in their basement studio without headphones, overdubs, or other technical devices, capturing the relaxed feel of a live Miss Blues performance, usually an informal raucous happening with commentary between songs.

February '0(?) Volume 3 Edition 27

southwest

featuring

MISS BLUES

Kathy Prather

Lil' Son Jackson

Pull-out Calendar

Figure 11 Cover Drawing of Miss Blues from *Southwest Blues*

Of the nine songs on Miss Blues' full-length *Sittin' In with Blinddog Smokin'*, three are written and sung by her, two by Blinddog Smokin', and the remaining four are covers of blues classics.[23]

The most moving of Miss Blues' three originals on her CD is arguably "Sinkin', Sinkin', Sinkin'," which poignantly tells the story of her 28-year-old stepmother who worked hard and took care of her man, providing shelter, clothing, and food, but in the end, when he ran off, losing everything including the house and the five children taken by the state. The song uses a classic blues form and is punctuated with weeping harmonica and two somber guitar solos accompanied by a continuous funereal bass line. The chorus, which starts and ends the song, appears between each of the five verses, gaining incrementally in poignancy as it is repeated:

I'm sinkin', sinkin', sinkin':
I want you to look at the hole I'm in.
I've been in this doggone hole,
Ever since me and this man began.

In the middle of the song, Miss Blues, in the role of a dispossessed, despairing, yet outraged and enduring young black woman, tells:

I gave him some money to go pay my bills.
You know what? The bastard spent it all.
On what? His friends.

The implication of "friends" is "women friends," since in the preceding verse he is caught cheating in the house. Miss Blues often sings shout style, a nearly forgotten mode first popularized during the early postwar period when she began singing publicly, and in this verse "bastard" is shouted loudly and angrily. In many of her songs there is an unpredictable, dangerous quality, stemming from this sparsely used but ever-present startling possibility of a shout. Being six feet tall and 230 pounds, Miss Blues rivets attention when she shouts.

As in "Sinkin', Sinkin', Sinkin'," "Trapped," another original on the CD, offers a black woman's life story and personal lament, only this time it is from an old woman looking back over a forty-year marriage and a husband who complains now of her increasing weight and slowness. She threatens to fix herself up, to buy a car and go cruising, and to stop pining and find a good man. Yet the chorus that starts and closes the song has her "trapped in a bad situation," worrying "what in the world is going to be my fate." This song is addressed, as is so often the case in blues music, to "people": "I'm going to quit worrying, people," says one key line. The standout pieces on this CD are these two original songs about vulnerable but strong-willed women in bad situations, addressed explicitly to the community, sung and shouted by an old black female spokesperson, yet pertaining as much to white as to black women today, since marriage and family in white society have in recent decades become more precarious.

Within the OKC blues subculture, the only criticisms of Miss Blues concern her letting lyrics get blurred through poor handling of the microphone and inaudible pronunciation (common problems) and her unevenness (some performances are better than others). But other than that, there is much admiration, respect, and reverence.

Although people enjoy Miss Blues' dramatic renditions of songs, especially her shouts, they are mostly unaware of her background and her other accomplishments, not to mention her song-writing abilities. (Blues fans largely ignore composing skill, and blues artists rarely mention when they are about to sing a song that they happened to write it.) According to an informative and surprising interview published in *Southwest Blues* 27 (February 2000), Dorothy Ellis (Miss Blues) was born and raised during the Depression in Direct, Texas near the Red River, the boundary line between Texas and Oklahoma.[24] Those in her family were sharecroppers, and she holds vivid memories of picking and chopping cotton as a child. She moved to Oklahoma City in the late 1940s to live with a cousin. The day jobs she held before retiring in the 1990s include teacher, school administrator, and nursing home administrator. She holds an M.Ed. in Counseling Psychology. She is most proud of two self-published books, one of which, the cookbook *Hoecakes and Collard Greens* (1995), is reprinted menu-by-menu in each monthly issue of *Southwest Blues* (headquartered in Dallas). Her current project is a CD with a selection of songs that her fans most enjoy, which, she told me during an informal interview, "they can have after I'm gone." (Thanks to invitations from Miss Blues, I as well as other white blues people have been to a number of black clubs and community musical events in OKC [see Figure 12, for example], which we would otherwise not have attended.) When I think of Miss Blues' well-crafted dramatic songs like "Sinkin', Sinkin', Sinkin'," "Trapped," and others, I am put in mind of Angela Davis' observation concerning black blues women: "public articulation of complaint—of which there are many instances in the blues—must be seen as a form of contestation of oppressive conditions, even when it lacks a dimension of organized political protest" (*BL*, 101).

I have barely scratched the surface with these brief profiles of the OKC blues scene, singling out only a handful of leading local musicians and bands, albums and songs. There are several dozen other bands and singer-songwriters, such as Scott Keeton & the Deviants (a trio of thirty-something white males), the most productive and talented songwriter-singer-guitarist, polished professional traveling band, and experienced recording artists (six CDs). There are also several astonishingly accomplished young white male guitar players (who sing and write songs), still in their teens, namely, Garrett Jacobson, Dustin Pittsley, and Shane Henry (each has self-released one or more CDs), a phenomenon in evidence all over the country, not just OKC,

Figure 12 Blues Show Poster—Oklahoma City Black Liberated Arts Center

boding well for the future of the blues. And there is a promising crop of young (under thirty-five) women lead blues singers in OKC (Miss Amy, Nikki Nicole, and De Anna Britt). In addition, there is D. C. Minner, a sixty-something black songwriter-singer-guitarist, band-leader, club owner, award-winning blues educator, and perhaps most well-known as a festival organizer who, along with his wife, Selby, a white bassist-singer-songwriter, hosts 5,000 blues fans and thirty acts during three days each Labor Day weekend.

Other important factors in the scene include a dozen or more clubs, several studios, a key radio host (Hardluck Jim Johnson), and major regional festivals, the latter including the OBS Blues Bash and the Bricktown Blues & BBQ Festival in OKC, D. C. and Selby Minner's Dusk Til Dawn in Rentiesville (Figure 13), Tulsa's Oklahoma Blues Festival, Edmond's Jazz and Blues Festival, Stillwater's Bikes 'n Blues, and then just beyond Oklahoma to Memphis in May, Kansas City Blues and Jazz Festival, Bedford Blues Festival and Art Fair (Dallas), and the granddaddy in Helena, Arkansas, King Biscuit Blues Festival.[25] (Incidentally, I, like other OKC blues fans, have attended many of these annual festivals, which resemble something like yearly journeys to Mecca.) Beyond immediate performance, there are the technical details and economics of CD production: copyright fees, studio time expenses, wholesale costs of jewel boxes and compact discs, and so on. Still, I believe I have provided enough description and detail in these profiles to suggest the dimensions and depth of the OKC blues subculture.

BRINGING IT ON HOME

The blues subculture in OKC is structured in large part as a "weekend world" of leisure and partying separated from the everyday world of work and worry. It offers many pleasures, music, dancing, drinking, smoking, eating, plus meeting new people (potential partners). It is a realm of freedom, comparatively speaking, and of entertainment and art. It is implicitly critical of, and explicitly an antidote to, certain major social problems: racism among and between whites, blacks, and Native Americans; segregation of age cohorts; oppression and silence of women; and separation of the middle and working classes. Functioning socially like carnival, it regularly brings together different groups of people whose meeting would otherwise be hard to imagine. Dancing is an especially egalitarian force. The blues subculture provides ecstatic and peak moments through music and dance. Although it is not without more or less strict conventions and taboos and limitations, both social and artistic, and although it adheres to various business imperatives and processes of commodification, this local blues subculture effectively subverts key social barriers, which makes it of special interest for cultural studies research and teaching.

To consider the OKC blues scene from another angle, I happen to be part of a very different adult community in the area, the art world,

Figure 13 Flyer for 2001 Dusk Til Dawn Blues Festival

which consists not only of painters, sculptors, photographers, video makers, mixed media artists, and art lovers, but also gallery owners/ dealers, museum personnel, arts administrators and educators, critics, collectors, donors, and patrons. In the OKC area there are three dozen galleries, a dozen museums, and several large eclectic organizations such as Individual Artists of Oklahoma and Oklahoma Visual Arts Coalition, as well as museum associations. Not surprisingly, there is a regular flow of gallery openings, museum shows, lectures, special events, and varied fundraisers, the last-mentioned ranging from studio tours, garage sales, picnics, and dinner dances to an annual erotic ball. I do not intend to profile the contemporary OKC art world, but to indicate that it is a remarkably different world from that of the blues subculture. The most immediate differences in my experience appear in dress codes, food and drink, venues, and social class membership. For instance, I have never experienced (or heard of) in the local blues subculture a catered black-tie country club dinner-dance complete with canapés, champagne, and gourmet nouvelle cuisine at $150 per plate, a not uncommon occasion in the art world, a type of event characteristically attended by community leaders (politicians, doctors, lawyers, bankers, corporate executives, etc.). Furthermore, Native American and African American art are each treated as specialties, having their own dealers, collectors, venues, newsletters/ magazines, and traditions, only very partially hooked into the mainstream art world, unlike their fully integrated position in the blues subculture. Finally, gays, lesbians, and bisexuals are more or less out and part of the art world, which is not at all the case in the local blues scene.[26]

The OKC blues subculture is, to return in closing to a recurring concern of this book, part of the broad postmodernization of culture insofar as it is multiracial, heterogeneous, and decentralized. But let me illustrate this last point with a story. In the spring of 2002 Oklahoma City was treated to a concert by B. B. King and Bobby Blue Bland, two venerable blues icons who first emerged out of early postwar blues developed in Memphis. Tickets for the show ranged from $45 to $70. (By contrast, the nightly cover charge in OKC jukes ranges from $2 to $8, averaging $5, and festival gate charges usually cost $15 per day.) The concert took place at the newly refurbished downtown Civic Center in the sumptuous Music Hall where the Oklahoma City Philharmonic Orchestra plays. Thousands of well-dressed people attended; it was a success. Each star brought his own formally dressed big band (brass and all), and the audience listened respectfully for four hours with the usual brief intermission (no smoking, drinking, dancing, food, or noise in the audience). From time to time a certain small segment of blues music crosses over into high culture. It is, in such cases, a matter of large volume sales, major record labels, longevity and respectability, international tours, philharmonic halls, upscale well-dressed and behaved audiences, and so on.[27] But all this has very little to do with the local blues scene. Even the one or two big successful regional blues festivals, for example, the annual Bricktown Blues & BBQ Festival in OKC (which had an attendance of 40,000 during its two days in 2002), offering a bill with local bands as openers for national acts, extends far beyond the local subculture into something like a mass culture phenomenon. There are relatively autonomous tiers in the broad blues world, falling out roughly along local, regional, national, and international lines. When an international blues concert comes to town, the local blues subculture with all its rites and rituals seems far away. That is what postmodern disorganization of the blues looks like.

12

POSTMODERN INTERDISCIPLINARITY

IN THIS FINAL CHAPTER, addressed to academic intellectuals, I argue four somber propositions: that university professors are "disciplinary subjects"; that academic interdisciplinary work, including cultural studies, does not alter the existing disciplines; that the university is a "disciplinary institution" located in disciplinary societies; and that the conception of interdisciplinarity is currently undergoing significant change. My main goal here is to offer neither encouraging nor discouraging words about the disciplines today and their interdisciplinary offshoots, but to shed new light on the changing dynamics of interdisciplinarity during postmodern times. There is, I argue, a postmodern mode of interdisciplinarity which is different from and antagonistic to its modern forerunner and whose future is uncertain. All of this has important bearing on the position of both literary theory and cultural studies today.

PROFESSORS AS DISCIPLINARY SUBJECTS

My first proposition is that university professors are disciplinary subjects, which I take to be a noncontroversial claim. Although we all occupy multiple subject positions, we as credentialed professionals typically hold primary identities as specialists in a specific field or occasionally two fields. If we work, for example, in a U.S. English Department, although we may teach composition and introductory literature courses to nonmajors, we self-identify by the specialty courses we teach to majors. Such courses are normally in the area in which we did our specialized graduate course work, our doctoral examinations, our dissertations, possibly some postdoctoral study, and our research and publications. We often hold memberships in specialty associations and attend their meetings and stay current with research in the area, regularly monitoring the key journals and book publications in the special field, keeping an eye out for specialized grants and other opportunities, and informing ourselves about the latest textbooks and course materials. Were you to meet someone early in the morning in an empty elevator at the annual convention of the Modern Language Association, and were he or she to ask what you do, your answer, necessarily succinct, would contain a word or two naming a specialty followed, if time permits, by a few quick specifics: something like— American modernism; poetry; Eliot and Pound, or English Renaissance; Shakespeare; early comedies. It is generally a nation, a recognized historical period, a genre or major figure (or both), and a theme or topic. (All of these common categories, namely, nation, period, major figure, and theme, are highly problematic.) Of course, university regulars know all this, it is part of our professional unconscious, but I want to underscore two points here, however obvious they may seem. Colleges and universities consist of academic departments that house disciplines which train and credential students and faculty in the disciplines.[1] Knowledge is divided up in certain ways, which is to say knowledge consists of social constructs and practices bearing specific disciplinary histories.[2]

When I say university professors are disciplinary subjects, I mean to foreground several things. To begin with, whatever professional identities and standpoints we professors develop, they make sense (contradictions included) within the framework of the disciplines. There is no place outside disciplines.[3] Moreover, we all continuously do boundary work or border patrol, sometimes unconsciously. We rule in and out, for instance, certain research topics, courses, program proposals, and job applications, using more or less strict disciplinary criteria in doing so.[4] Despite rumors and right-wing propaganda, the attitude "anything goes" does not exist. Certain topics, methods, and subjects "simply" appear beyond the pale. The disciplines are at once enabling and productive *and* restrictive and confining. Not surprisingly, they engender interdisciplinary projects as well as cross-disciplinary, transdisciplinary, counterdisciplinary, multidisciplinary, and antidisciplinary enterprises, all of which characteristically conceive themselves as resistant to both disciplinarity and departmentalization.

THE ENDS OF INTERDISCIPLINARY WORK

My second proposition is that most interdisciplinary work supports or modifies, but does not transform, that is, change, existing disciplines. This claim is based on several decades of interdisciplinary work of various kinds: in a large humanities department, in a small honors Great Books program, in a medium-sized graduate comparative literature program, in a small doctoral program in philosophy and literature, and in a small graduate concentration in theory and cultural studies. Each of these endeavors has a complicated history, but each bears witness to the endurance of the disciplines and a certain fragility of interdisciplinary enterprises. As long as there are disciplines (in the current sense), there will be interdisciplinary formations framed as minor offshoots and faced with precarious futures. And these futures will be structurally marked by the possibility of becoming disciplines and departments. The origin and end of interdisciplines is the discipline.

I can make this point another, more poignant way. Cultural studies, an interdiscipline if there ever was one, has been around for fifteen years in the United States, and not one full-blown department of cultural studies exists in the United States. There are numerous programs, centers, institutes, concentrations, and tracks, but no departments per se. Neither literary studies, nor sociology, nor communications, nor film studies are about to reconfigure themselves around this emerging "discipline." We all know how this works. Many self-identified cultural studies people are currently in drag, holding posts in English and communications departments, teaching the usual array of standard disciplinary courses with the odd cultural studies course in the mix and the standard courses inflected toward cultural studies concerns. This institutional bottlenecking of cultural studies in the United States will probably last another decade or so until the current generation of cultural studies scholars assumes enough administrative clout to departmentalize cultural studies and escape from more or less hostile environments and ineffective arrangements. At the end of the road, as well as along the way, is discipline with the usual array of requirements, examinations, and certifications; with training in specialized skills, vocabularies, canons, problematics, and traditions; with more or less clear criteria for admission and advancement; with relative autonomy in setting goals, standards, and rankings; and with border work. This disciplinary border labor entails protecting the inside from the outside, ensuring the distinctiveness of the discipline and thereby solidifying the division of knowledge. Cultural studies needs to undertake all of these disciplinary tasks, which illustrates my point that interdisciplinary work supports or modifies, but does not change, existing disciplines.

DISCIPLINARY INSTITUTIONS AND SOCIETIES

Thus far I have asserted that university professors are disciplinary subjects and that interdisciplinary projects shore up the disciplines. As part of overarching national school systems, colleges and universities are themselves disciplinary institutions situated in disciplinary societies. This observation, my third proposition, derives from Michel Foucault's *Discipline and Punish,*[5] and is, I take it, noncontroversial in its broad outlines. Foucault's main point in this book, it will be recalled, is that from the 1760s to the 1960s—the modern era—societies became increasingly regulated by norms directed at the "docile body" and disseminated through a network of cooperating "disciplinary institutions," including the judicial, military, educational, workshop, psychiatric, welfare, religious, and prison establishments, all of which entities enforce norms and correct delinquencies, using identical techniques of insertion, distribution, surveillance, and punishment. The university, like the prison, "continues, on those entrusted to it, a work begun elsewhere, which the whole of society pursues on each individual through innumerable mechanisms of discipline" (*DP*, 302–03). In casting the school as a "disciplinary institution," Foucault has in mind specifically the use of dozens of so-called disciplines, that is, microtechniques of registration, organization, observation, correction, and control, all maximally synergized. Among these tiny ubiquitous "disciplines" are, to name a dozen or so, examinations, case studies, records, partitions and cells, enclosures, rankings, objectifications, monitoring systems, assessments, hierarchies, norms, tables (such as timetables), and individualizations. The disciplines, invented by the Enlightenment, facilitate the submission of bodies and the extraction from them of useful forces. These small everyday physical mechanisms operate beneath our established egalitarian laws and ideals, producing a counterlaw that subordinates and limits reciprocities. Of teaching, Foucault observes: "A relation of surveillance, defined and regulated, is inscribed at the heart of the practice of teaching, not as an additional or adjacent part, but as a mechanism that is inherent to it . . ." (*DP*, 176). Universities and colleges deploy the micro disciplines to train and discipline the students in preparation not only for jobs and professional disciplines, but for disciplinary societies. For Foucault this is the legacy of the post-Enlightenment era and a grim birthright of modernity.

Foucault's *Discipline and Punish* is one of the most celebrated of interdisciplinary works of postmodern times. It invents new objects of inquiry, such as the "disciplines," the "docile body," "Panoptic power," the "knowledge/power" nexus, and "disciplinary society." It works in between the fields of history, philosophy, sociology, political science, criminology, and discourse theory, combining their methods and problematics in an original way while resisting classification. Paradoxically, Foucault's book provides a model of how to do interdisciplinary work as well as of what to fear in the convergence and cooperation of disciplines. The concatenation of disciplines promises more knowledge/power, more organization and efficiency, more monitoring and docility, more records and objectifications, more rankings and norms, and more sinister enlightenment, solidifying disciplinary societies while assuring the continuation of disciplinary institutions like the prison and the university.

TWO MODES OF INTERDISCIPLINARITY

In keeping with a major concern of this book, I want at this point to resituate the question of disciplinarity and its complications within an explicitly postmodern frame.[6] My fourth proposition is this: during postmodern times interdisciplinarity has been undergoing a process of reconceptualization, and this is happening in a period when the aging modern university still dominates the educational landscape. While disciplinarity survives intact, interdisciplinarity has lately been changing its character and focus.

In its present departmentalized form, the university appears a throwback modern organization designed in the nineteenth century, crystallized in the mid-twentieth century, and in many ways frozen in that time of big business, big government, and big labor.[7] From the perspective of today's traditional disciplines and departments, postmodern implosion and fragmentation or, more pointedly, disaggregation have been fairly well resisted and finessed.[8] The proliferation in recent decades of challenging new (inter)disciplines, often housed in insecure programs and centers, not in well-funded departments, bears witness to the finessing. Among these many "new" (inter)disciplines, I list here only a few in the humanities and social sciences, skipping over the sciences and professions: women's and gender studies, black studies as well as other ethnic studies, film and media studies, body studies, Third World studies, and cultural studies. I have listed several dozen in the Preface. These are all postmodern (inter)disciplines, formed in the late twentieth century, and in certain specific ways also counterdisciplines, that is, constructed self-consciously against the oversights, blindspots, or ingrained prejudices of the modern disciplines. They are also, in part, "multidisciplines," meaning built on the assumption that close cooperation among many different disciplines is a wholesome thing. Proponents of the new (inter)disciplines exhibit mixed emotions about departmentalization, but in my experience they readily submit to disciplinarity with its special training, requirements, standards, and certifications, and they readily rely on the microdisciplines as well, that is, exams, exercises, records, rankings, monitorings, norms, and the like: Discipline endures.

Yet as the Cultural Wars of recent times, pitting neoconservatives against liberals, demonstrate, the postmodern (inter)disciplines threaten the moral and political order of the conservative establishment, although not disciplinarity per se. For neoconservatives, university disciplines, new or old, must meet the litmus test of "objectivity," an objectivity fetishized in the early Cold War era, a time of both the "end of ideology" and of vicious political purges. The postmodern university (inter)disciplines, then, threaten not disciplinarity, but the moribund modernist image of the university as ivory tower, peaceful, well-organized, and disengaged, a place where the Great Books ideally crown the curriculum.

From a postmodern perspective, "interdisciplinarity" has two very different forms. In its most ambitious modern version, it dreams of the end of the disciplines with their hideous jargons and false divisions of knowledge; it wants to unify the disciplines, rendering them transparent.[9] But insofar as postmodern thinking seeks to multiply the differences and respect heterogeneities,[10] the recent proliferation of (inter)disciplines is an encouraging turn. The postmodern version of interdisciplinarity seeks, therefore, not to unify or totalize, but to respect the differences. And, significantly, it predicates internal and external differences as ineradicable. Here is how Jacques Derrida puts this latter point: "What happens is always some *contamination*."[11] In this context, each discipline itself is always already infiltrated by some other discipline(s). Physics has mathematics, astronomy, and chemistry not only as neighbors but as guests. Literary studies, a more permeable discipline than most, is entangled with history, mythology and religion, psychology, linguistics, philosophy (especially aesthetics), folklore and anthropology, and political economy. And I have omitted areas at that (theater, sociology, gender studies, cultural studies, etc.). In this postmodern conceptualization, there is no denying the existence, necessity, and value of the disciplines, nor of their boundaries and struggles. Interdisciplinarity during postmodern times designates the de facto intermixture of the disciplines, new and old, plus recognition of their differences and conflicts. One can understand why Foucault ended up famously promoting the "specific intellectual" over the general intellectual:[12] he understood the dangers of modern interdisciplinarity, and the benefits of its postmodern transformation.

Let me end this book on a less somber note. Although I believe that college and university professors are disciplinary subjects, that our universities are disciplinary institutions serving disciplinary societies, and that interdisciplinary enterprises tend ironically to buttress the disciplines, I also know that innumerable local subversions, creative misuses, and antidisciplinary moves continuously loosen the rigidities and holds of the modern disciplinary system. And too, interdisciplinary projects—whether inside, between, or among disciplines—frequently increase permeabilities and deterritorialize fixed cognitive maps. There is, in addition, among university professors and students everywhere during postmodern times an unacknowledged party of interdisciplinarity, whose existence and size are unknown, whose programs are unclear or unformulated, but whose underground members seem to recognize one another. I am among these postmodern nightcrawlers. It is not clear, however, what connections might exist between the aims of this party and the logic of today's market economy, with its need for rapid change and renewal, its disregard for established ways and traditions, its preference for flexibility and temporary contracts, and its devotion to productivity. Nor is it always clear when a particular interdisciplinary initiative is intellectual vanguardism, obsessed with the new and the cutting edge whatever they may be. But for all that, I take my stand with interdisciplinary projects, particularly cultural studies nowadays, only without the dispiriting hopes of putting an end to disciplinary rituals and interests or of unifying the fragmented disciplines and faculties, in damaging pursuits of elusive harmonies.

Appendix

PROTOCOLS FOR ANTHOLOGY HEADNOTES

The Norton Anthology of Theory and Criticism

The headnotes for each figure will be in essay form and range between 750 to 2,000 words. The protocols below will be used flexibly so as to generate uniformity across the headnotes without them becoming predictable or perfunctory.

PROTOCOLS FOR HEADNOTES

1. Author's name, dates, and, where possible, catchy quotation by or about the author;
2. highlighting of relevant biographical details;
3. reference to author's other key theoretical or critical publications;
4. sketch of sources and forerunners;
5. inclusion of pertinent factors of social history;
6. précis of selection(s)'s main concepts, arguments, and issues, keeping in mind that selections are invariably interventions in complex arguments;
7. statement on present-day relevance, importance, or use of selection(s);
8. comparison and contrast with selected pertinent figures in the anthology;
9. critique of problems in the selection(s);
10. discussion of reception (friendly and hostile) and progeny;

11. information on historical trends, including especially related critical schools and movements;
12. concise explanations of key technical and theoretical terms and concepts;
13. stress on relevant perennial problems in the history of theory;
14. evaluative prose paragraphs(s) (not a list), covering (a) standard editions or texts of author; (b) biographies; (c) pertinent secondary sources on author; and (d) bibliographies of author's writings.

NOTES

Preface

1. Scott Lash and John Urry, *The End of Organized Capitalism* (Madison: University of Wisconsin Press, 1987).
2. See, for example, Cary Nelson, "Always Already Cultural Studies: Two Conferences and A Manifesto," *Journal of the Midwest Modern Language Association* 24 (Spring 1991): 24–38. Compare Herman Rapaport's *The Theory Mess: Deconstruction in Eclipse* (New York: Columbia University Press, 2001), which depicts the disorganization of theory during the 1990s as a tragic "mess."
3. See, for example, Bill Readings, *The University in Ruins* (Cambridge, MA: Harvard University Press, 1996).
4. Gayatri Chakravorty Spivak, *In Other Worlds: Essays in Cultural Politics* (New York: Methuen, 1987).

Chapter 1

1. Let me note for the record that in recent years "restructuring" has had an impact on university departments of literary study in devastating economic ways: faculty lines have been reduced; older faculty members have been enticed to retire; many retirees have not been replaced; tenure-accruing positions have dried up; the percentage of low-paid adjuncts and part-timers (who typically receive no benefits) has increased dramatically; and Ph.D. study has lengthened, causing students to go into debt while waiting out a job market that offers to many candidates unemployment, part-time work, or visiting appointments.
2. I outline the thesis about disaggregation being characteristic of postmodern culture in my *Postmodernism—Local Effects, Global Flows* (Albany: State University of New York Press, 1996), especially chapter 12.
3. On this topic, see Gerald Graff, *Professing Literature: An Institutional History* (Chicago: University of Chicago Press, 1987).
4. Here I am summarizing observations made by both Fredric Jameson, *Postmodernism, or, the Cultural Logic of Late Capitalism* (Durham, NC: Duke University Press, 1991), and David Harvey, *The Condition of Postmodernity* (Cambridge, MA: Blackwell, 1990).

5. I detail segments of the complex modern history of shifting reading practices and theories in my *American Literary Criticism from the 1930s to the 1980s* (New York: Columbia University Press, 1988).

6. On the different branches of early U.S. poststructuralism, see my *Deconstructive
   Criticism* (New York: Columbia University Press, 1983), which also underscores significant differences among first-generation members of the Yale school of deconstruction. (This book was published in autumn 1982, but the book's editor decided
   to date it 1983 in order "to extend its shelf life," a common practice.)

7. I am echoing an argument often made by Edward Said; see, for example, "Secular
   Criticism." In *The World, the Text, and the Critic* (Cambridge, MA: Harvard University Press, 1983).

8. On the problematic of "production," see my *Cultural Criticism, Literary Theory, Poststructuralism* (New York: Columbia University Press, 1992), chap. 8 and pp. 165–67;
   and also Jean Baudrillard, *The Mirror of Production*, trans. Mark Poster (St. Louis:
   Telos, 1975).

   For a useful overview of recent U.S. cultural studies, see the editors' "The Culture
   That Sticks to Your Skin: A Manifesto for a New Cultural Studies," *Hop on Pop: The
   Politics and Pleasures of Popular Culture*, ed. Henry Jenkins, Tara McPherson, and
   Jane Shattuc (Durham: Duke UP, 2002), pp. 3–26.

9. "Theory," as I explain in subsequent chapters, has expanded in recent decades to include
   not just poetics, aesthetics, and interpretation theory, but also rhetoric, semiotics, media
   and discourse theory, gender theory, and visual and popular culture theory. On the
   changing definitions of "theory," see also the Preface, *The Norton Anthology of Theory
   and Criticism*, gen. ed. Vincent B. Leitch, ed. William E. Cain, Laurie A. Finke, Barbara E.
   Johnson, John P. McGowan, and Jeffrey J. Williams (New York: W. W. Norton, 2001).

Chapter 2

1. Such as Teachers for a Democratic Culture, National Association of Scholars, and Association of Literary Scholars and Critics.

2. For the problems with a schools-and-movements approach to contemporary criticism and theory, see chapter 4, "Framing Theory," on the disorganization of historiography; and James Sosnoski, *Token Professionals and Master Critics* (Albany: State
   University of New York Press, 1994).

3. Two landmark texts, the multicultural *Heath Anthology of American Literature*, 2 vols.,
   ed. Paul Lauter et al. (Lexington, MA: D. C. Heath, 1990) and the star-studded *Cultural Studies*, ed. Lawrence Grossberg, Cary Nelson, and Paula Treichler (New York:
   Routledge, 1992).

4. Michel Foucault, *Discipline and Punish: The Birth of the Prison*, trans. Alan Sheridan
   (New York: Vintage, 1979), p. 200.

5. Harold Bloom, *The Anxiety of Influence: A Theory of Poetry* (New York: Oxford University Press, 1973), p. 94.

6. Ngugi wa Thiong'o (James Ngugi), *Homecoming: Essays on African and Caribbean
   Literature, Culture, and Politics* (New York: Lawrence Hill, 1972), pp. 145–50.

7. Elaine Showalter, *A Literature of Their Own: British Women Novelists from Brontë to
   Lessing* (Princeton: Princeton University Press, 1977), chap. 1, which lists several phases
   of British women's literature: (1) Feminine, 1840 to 1880; (2) Feminist, 1880 to 1920;
   and (3) Female, 1920 to 1960. Unnamed and uncharacterized by Showalter, the period
   after 1960 clearly constitutes a new fourth (postmodern) phase of development.

8. Sandra M. Gilbert and Susan Gubar, *The Madwoman in the Attic: The Woman Writer
   and the Nineteenth-Century Literary Imagination* (New Haven: Yale University Press,
   1979), p. 53.

9. Lionel Trilling, *Beyond Culture: Essays on Literature and Learning* (1965; New York:
   Viking, 1968), p. 3.

10. Robert Scholes, *Textual Power: Literary Theory and the Teaching of English* (New Haven: Yale University Press, 1985), p. 24.
11. John Urry, "The End of Organised Capitalism." In *New Times: The Changing Face of Politics in the 1990s,* ed. Stuart Hall and Martin Jacques (London: Verso, 1990), p. 99.
12. Donna Haraway, "A Manifesto for Cyborgs: Science, Technology, and Socialist Feminism in the 1980s." In *Feminism/Postmodernism,* ed. Linda J. Nicholson (New York: Routledge, 1990), p. 209.
13. Stanley Aronowitz and Henry Giroux, *Postmodern Education: Politics, Culture, and Social Criticism* (Minneapolis: University of Minnesota Press, 1991), p. 70.

Chapter 3

1. Having completed a summer of training at the School of Criticism and Theory in the late 1970s, I, like many in my cohort at the time, felt "certified" as a theorist. Since then, I have owned the label.
2. For a discussion of major issues in today's critical fashion studies, see chapter 10, "Postmodern Fashion."
3. This observation about global commercialization appears in numerous forms and places, for instance, Jean Baudrillard, *Simulations,* trans. Paul Foss, Paul Patton, and Philip Beitchman (New York: Semiotext[e], 1983), and Fredric Jameson, *Postmodernism, or, the Cultural Logic of Late Capitalism* (Durham, NC: Duke University Press, 1991).

Chapter 5

1. Vincent B. Leitch, gen. ed., *The Norton Anthology of Theory and Criticism,* ed. William E. Cain, Laurie A. Finke, Barbara E. Johnson, John P. McGowan, and Jeffrey J. Williams (New York: W. W. Norton, 2001).
2. See Robert Scholes' useful discussion of critique in his *Textual Power: Literary Theory and the Teaching of English* (New Haven: Yale University Press, 1985), chap. 2.
3. See Roland Barthes, "Death of the Author," *Image—Music—Text,* ed. and trans. Stephen Heath (New York: Hill and Wang, 1977), pp. 142–48; and J. Hillis Miller, *Versions of Pygmalion* (Cambridge, MA: Harvard University Press, 1990), pp. 136–37. Here I extend the scope of ideology to include such logocentric concepts as author, oeuvre, canon, supplement, and context.
4. The "dangerous/beneficial supplement" alludes to Jacques Derrida, *Of Grammatology,* trans. Gayatri Chakravorty Spivak (Baltimore: Johns Hopkins University Press, 1976), pp. 144–57.
5. An observation enabled by the work of Pierre Bourdieu but particularly Louis Althusser; see Althusser, "Ideology and Ideological State Apparatuses." In *"Lenin and Philosophy" and Other Essays,* trans. Ben Brewster (New York: Monthly Review Press, 1971), especially pp. 127–57.
6. Anthologies, also in ancient times called collations, excerpts, or *florilegia,* derive both from collections of epigrams first compiled around 100 B.C.E and from later excerpted commentaries on the Bible as well as from medieval collections of letters, poems, recipes, and citations of authors. Put together for public circulation and for private use, early anthologies often begin with compilers' prologues (modern "headnotes"), which from late classical and early medieval times followed and developed the conventions of the well-known *prelectio* and *accessus ad auctores,* addressing systematically the life of the poet, the quality of the work, the intention of the writer, the number and order of books, and the text's meaning. Other key topics addressed include utility of the work, branch of learning, and time, place, and circumstances of composition. See A. J. Minnis, *Medieval Theory of Authorship,* 2d ed. (Philadelphia: University of Pennsylvania Press, 1988), especially chap. 1.

7. M. H. Abrams, *The Mirror and the Lamp: Romantic Theory and the Critical Tradition* (New York: Oxford University Press, 1953), p. 6.

8. On the strategy of deterritorialization, see Gilles Deleuze and Félix Guattari, *Anti-Oedipus: Capitalism and Schizophrenia,* trans. Robert Hurley, Mark Seem, and Helen R. Lane (Minneapolis: University of Minnesota Press, 1983), pp. 192–200, 244–62.

Chapter 6

1. Vincent B. Leitch, gen. ed., *The Norton Anthology of Theory and Criticism,* ed. William E. Cain, Laurie A. Finke, Barbara E. Johnson, John P. McGowan, and Jeffrey J. Williams (New York: W. W. Norton, 2001).

2. David H. Richter, *The Critical Tradition,* 2d ed. (Boston: Bedford, 1998).

3. Hazard Adams, ed., *Critical Theory Since Plato,* rev. ed. (Fort Worth: Harcourt, Brace, Jovanovich, 1992).

4. John Ellis, *Literature Lost: Social Agendas and the Corruption of the Humanities* (New Haven: Yale University Press, 1997).

5. J. Linn Allen, "Swiftly! Fetch the Pea-Filled Bladders!," *Chicago Tribune,* 1 July 2001: 1+.

6. Vincent B. Leitch, *American Literary Criticism from the 1930s to the 1980s* (New York: Columbia University Press, 1988).

7. J. C. Flügel, *The Psychology of Clothes* (London: Hogarth, 1930).

8. Vincent B. Leitch, *Deconstructive Criticism* (New York: Columbia University Press, 1983).

9. Vincent B. Leitch, *Cultural Criticism, Literary Theory, Poststructuralism* (New York: Columbia University Press, 1992); *Postmodernism—Local Effects, Global Flows* (Albany: State University of New York Press, 1996); and *American Literary Criticism* cited above in note 6.

10. Sarah Boxer, "How Crit Finally Won Out Over Lit," *New York Times,* 19 May 2001: B9+.

11. Scott McLemee, "Making the Cut," *Chronicle of Higher Education,* 4 May 2001: A16–18.

12. William K. Wimsatt, Jr., and Cleanth Brooks, *Literary Criticism: A Short History* (New York: Knopf, 1957).

13. René Wellek, *A History of Modern Criticism: 1750–1950,* 8 vols. (New Haven: Yale University Press, 1955–1993).

Chapter 8

1. David Schwartz, *Culture & Power: The Sociology of Pierre Bourdieu* (Chicago: University of Chicago Press, 1997), p. 293.

2. Bridget Fowler, *Pierre Bourdieu and Cultural Theory: Critical Investigations* (London: Sage, 1997), p. 84n10.

3. Richard Jenkins, *Pierre Bourdieu* (London: Routledge, 1992), p. 91. Hereafter *PB.*

4. Loïc J. D. Wacquant, "Toward a Social Praxeology: The Structure and Logic of Bourdieu's Sociology." In *An Invitation to Reflexive Sociology* by Pierre Bourdieu and Loïc J. D. Wacquant (Chicago: University of Chicago Press, 1992), p. 56. See pp. 50–59 for a nuanced analysis of Bourdieu's politics.

5. Nicholas Garnham, "Bourdieu, the Cultural Arbitrary, and Television." In *Bourdieu: Critical Perspectives,* ed. Craig Calhoun, Edward LiPuma, and Moisha Postone (Chicago: University of Chicago Press, 1993), p. 183.

6. "Conclusion: Critique." In *An Introduction to the Work of Pierre Bourdieu: The Practice of Theory,* ed. Richard Harker, Cheleen Mahar, and Chris Wilkes (New York: St. Martin's, 1990), p. 201. In his "Bourdieu's Refusal," in *Pierre Bourdieu: Fieldwork in*

Culture, ed. Nicholas Brown and Imre Szeman (Lanham, MD: Rowman & Littlefield, 2000), John Guillory notes that criticism of Bourdieu's "pessimism" sometimes comes from cultural studies academics unself-consciously committed to voluntarism and individualistic moralism (pp. 20–21).

7. See especially Pierre Bourdieu, "A Reasoned Utopia and Economic Fatalism," *New Left Review* 227 (January–February 1998), 125–30, and his "The Essence of Neoliberalism: Utopia of Endless Exploitation," *Le Monde Diplomatique* (December 1998).

8. See Pierre Bourdieu, *Outline of a Theory of Practice*, trans. Richard Nice (Cambridge, UK: Cambridge University Press, 1977), chap. 2.

9. Jenkins, p. 83. Among the leading introductions to Bourdieu's work, Jenkins' book is the most critical, pointing out contradictions and inconsistencies along the way. The opening chapter on Bourdieu's life and work, for example, states, "despite the best efforts to transcend the dualistic divide between 'objectivism' and 'subjectivism,' his model of humanity . . . remains caught in an unresolved contradiction between determinism and voluntarism, with the balance of his argument favouring the former" (*PB*, 21).

    On Bourdieu's place in the intellectual history of French structuralism during the period from 1945 to 1990, see François Dosse, *History of Structuralism*, vol. 2, trans. Deborah Glassman (Minneapolis: University of Minnesota Press, 1997), chaps. 6 and 29.

10. See Pierre Bourdieu, "The Forms of Capital." In *Handbook of Theory and Research for the Sociology of Education*, ed. John G. Richardson (New York: Greenwood, 1986), pp. 241–58, especially p. 243. From time to time Bourdieu refers to other forms such as family, political, religious, moral, and state capital.

11. Pierre Bordieu, *Distinction: A Social Critique of the Judgment of Taste*, trans. Richard Nice (Cambridge, MA: Harvard University Press, 1984). *Distinction* provides 36 tables and 21 figures (graphic illustrations) correlating class standing and taste in music, literature, art, film, home architecture, furniture, food, sports, media outlets, and beauty products, all elements of cultural capital (a mode of capital, of course, well suited to cultural studies inquiry).

12. For an account of the *social* foundations of economics, see Pierre Bourdieu, *Les structures sociales de l'économie* (Paris: Seuil, 2000), which argues that sociology and economics constitute one discipline given to analyzing social facts where economic transactions are only one aspect of social life. This book is focused on the housing field. In *Acts of Resistance*, Bourdieu observes "sociologists are often asked to repair economists' breakages" (45), and "Economics is, with a few exceptions, an abstract science based on the absolutely unjustifiable separation between the economic and the social which defines economism" (51). My translation. The critique of economics as a discipline is examined more fully in chapter 9.

13. Pierre Bourdieu, *Homo Academicus*, trans. Peter Collier (Stanford: Stanford University Press, 1988), pp. 48, 69.

14. Pierre Bourdieu, *The Rules of Art: Genesis and Structure of the Literary Field*, trans. Susan Emanuel (Stanford: Stanford University Press, 1995), pp. 114, 217 ff.

    Perhaps no contemporary artist has been more critical of the questionable economic and political ties of the mainstream art world than Hans Haacke, a fearless opponent of big business patronage and of political censorship. See his conversations with Bourdieu in Pierre Bourdieu and Hans Haacke, *Free Exchange* (Stanford: Stanford University Press, 1995).

15. See also his "The Essence of Neoliberalism" cited above in note 7.

16. Here I follow the usage of Jeremy Brecher and Tim Costello, *Global Village or Global Pillage: Economic Reconstruction from the Bottom Up* (Boston: South End, 1994).

17. Pierre Bourdieu, *Contre-feux 2: Pour un mouvement social européen* (Paris: Raisons d'Agir, 2001), pp. 45–46. Hereafter *Cf2*. My translation.

18. The role of the collective intellectual is discussed succinctly not only in *Contre-feux* and *Contre-feux 2*, but in Bourdieu's "Postscript: For a Corporatism of the Universal," in *The Rules of Art*, pp. 337–48, where he movingly urges intellectuals to defend the autonomy of their respective fields.

19. Pierre Bourdieu, *On Television*, trans. Priscilla Parkhurst Ferguson (New York: New Press, 1998), p. 53.

20. Pierre Bourdieu, *Acts of Resistance: Against the Tyranny of the Market*, trans. Richard Nice (New York: New Press, 1999), p. 57. Hereafter *AR*. This book was first published in France as *Contre-feux: Propos pour servir à la résistance contre l'invasion néo-libérale* (Paris: Raisons d'Agir, 1998).

21. Bourdieu, "A Reasoned Utopia . . . ," 128.

22. "People often have a tendency to think that intellectual life is spontaneously international. Nothing could be further from the truth. Intellectual life, like all other social spaces, is a home to nationalism and imperialism . . ."—Pierre Bourdieu, "The Social Condition of the International Circulation of Ideas." In *Bourdieu: A Critical Reader*, ed. Richard Shusterman (Malden, MA: Blackwell, 1999), p. 220.

23. Among occasional asides criticizing cultural studies, consider Pierre Bourdieu and Loïc Wacquant, "On the Cunning of Imperialist Reason." In *Theory, Culture and Society* 16:1 (1999), 47: "Cultural Studies, this mongrel domain, born in England in the 1970s, which owes its international dissemination (which is the whole of its existence) to a successful publishing policy." Interestingly, Bourdieu's work was translated and taught during the 1970s at the University of Birmingham's pioneering Centre for Contemporary Cultural Studies where Richard Nice, Bourdieu's main English translator, was on staff. Also Bourdieu published at that time British cultural studies work by Raymond Williams, E. P. Thompson, and Paul Willis in his journal *Actes de la recherche en sciences sociales* (founded 1975). On this connection to British cultural studies, see Derek Robbins, *Bourdieu and Culture* (London: Sage, 2000), pp. 123–25.

24. See the landmark account of postmodern culture by Fredric Jameson, *Postmodernism, or, the Cultural Logic of Late Capitalism* (Durham, NC: Duke University Press, 1991); and my own *Postmodernism—Local Effects, Global Flows* (Albany: State University of New York Press, 1996).

25. On one hand, Bourdieu was fully committed to the scientific project and its value for the future, but he also conceived "science" in a contemporary Kuhnian sense as a historically relative construction of fields. See, for example, Pierre Bourdieu, *Pascalian Meditations*, trans. Richard Nice (1997; Stanford: Stanford University Press, 2000), which is a full-blown critique of "scholastic reason."

Chapter 9

1. Ulla Grapard, "Robinson Crusoe: The Quintessential Economic Man?," *Feminist Economics* 1 (1995): 33–52. A much-discussed strand of "critical economics," not treated in this chapter, is the discourse analysis launched by Donald (Deirdre) McCloskey in *The Rhetoric of Economics* (Madison: University of Wisconsin Press, 1985) and continued in several subsequent books and many articles, all critical of mainstream economic modeling and discourse from a reformist anti-foundationalist perspective. Pioneering selections of feminist critical economics appear in *Beyond Economic Man: Feminist Theory and Economics*, ed. Marianne A. Ferber and Julie A. Nelson (Chicago: University of Chicago Press, 1993), and *Out of the Margin: Feminist Perspectives in Economics*, ed. Edith Kuiper and Jolande Sap (New York: Routledge, 1995). To sample critical economics from a Marxist vantage point, see *Rethinking Marxism: A Journal of Economics, Culture, and Society*, ed. Jack Amariglio, David Ruccio, and Stephen Cullenberg, economists who have themselves published representative articles, chapters, and books.

2. Susan F. Feiner, "A Portrait of *Homo Economicus* as a Young Man." In *The New Economic Criticism: Studies at the Intersection of Literature and Economics,* ed. Martha Wood-mansee and Mark Osteen (New York: Routledge, 1999), pp. 193–209. Hereafter *NEC.*
3. Hazel Henderson, *Paradigms in Progress: Life Beyond Economics* (Indianapolis: Knowledge Systems, 1991), p. 30. In "Clothes Encounters: Activists and Economists Clash over Sweatshops," *Lingua France: The Review of Academic Life,* 11 (March 2001), Lisa Featherstone and Doug Henwood observe: "As a field, economics has become increasingly hostile to unorthodox opinion in recent years, and virtually no serious left-of-center economist has been hired by a major department in more than two decades" (31).
4. See, for example, the suggestive proceedings of the Le Monde–Le Mans Forum, *What is the Meaning of Money,* ed. Roger-Paul Droit (Boulder: Social Science Monographs, 1998), especially Jacques Derrida, "The Principles of Pricelessness," where he observes: "Above all, the fact that money belongs to the limitless world of language and the written word—the inscription—means that it cannot be contained in monetary accounting or objective economics. Money drives the enterprise in the direction of the infinite or towards regions unknown to accountants, to the edge of an abyss of speculation which lies outside the field of the Stock Exchange or the limits of institutions regulating economic transactions" (67).
5. Major texts of French gift theory include Marcel Mauss, *The Gift: Forms and Functions of Exchange in Archaic Societies,* trans. Ian Cunnison (New York: Norton, 1967); Georges Bataille, *The Accursed Share: An Essay on General Economy,* trans. Robert Hurley (New York: Zone, 1988); Jean-François Lyotard, *Libidinal Economy,* trans. Iain Hamilton Grant (Bloomington: Indiana University Press, 1993); and Jacques Derrida, *Given Time: I. Counterfeit Money,* trans. Peggy Kamuf (Chicago: University of Chicago Press, 1992), and his *The Gift of Death,* trans. David Wills (Chicago: University of Chicago Press, 1995).
6. The composition of the British rentier class is discussed by E. J. Hobsbawm in *Industry and Empire: The Making of Modern English Society, Vol. II, 1750 to the Present Day* (New York: Pantheon, 1968), pp. 96–97.
7. Anthony Giddens, "On Globalization," *UNRSID News* 15 (Autumn 1996/Winter 1997), 4. For Giddens, pro and contra positions on economic globalization are represented, respectively (and accurately, I might add), by Kenichi Ohmae, *The Borderless World: Power and Strategy in the Interlinked Economy* (New York: Harper Business, 1990) and his *The End of the Nation State: The Rise of Regional Economies* (New York: Free Press, 1995) and by Paul Hirst and Grahame Thompson, *Globalization in Question: The International Economy and the Possibilities of Governance* (Cambridge: Polity, 1996).
      Globalization discourse, as I see it, is currently segmented into six discrete but overlapping areas: economics, sociology, culture, politics, ecology, and history. Needless to say, each domain has an extensive and growing bibliography. On a related model of segmentation, see David Held, et al., *Global Transformations: Politics, Economics and Culture* (Stanford: Stanford University Press, 1999), especially Introduction. For a useful introduction, see *Globalization: The Reader,* ed. John Beynon and David Dunkerly (New York: Routledge, 2000), especially pp. 1–38.
8. George Soros, "Toward a Global Open Society," *The Atlantic Monthly,* 281 (January 1998): 21–22, 24, 32. Soros has since then published several books, elaborating his concerns about globalization. Another exemplary neo-Keynesian reformer is Joseph E. Stiglitz, Nobel Prize winner in Economics (2001), former Chairman of the Council of Economic Advisers during the Clinton administration, and Chief Economist at the World Bank (1997 to 2000), whose *Globalization and Its Discontents* (New York: W. W. Norton, 2002) documents many problems with economic globalization, targeting the IMF in particular.

9. Robin Hahnel, *Panic Rules! Everything You Need to Know about the Global Economy* (Cambridge, MA: South End, 1999), p. 92. Hereafter *PR*.

10. Immanuel Wallerstein earlier and more broadly defined the project of these "anti-systematic" movements in, for example, his *Geopolitics and Geoculture: Essays on the Changing World-System* (Cambridge, UK: Cambridge University Press, 1991), especially pp. 229–30. See also Michael Hardt and Antonio Negri, *Empire* (Cambridge, MA: Harvard University Press, 2000), pp. 272–76, who reflect on the creativity and the cooption of Lilliputian groups.

11. The World Trade Organization meeting in Seattle during the week of November 28, 1999, an event protested by a broad array of some thousands of Lilliputians, canceled its opening and closing ceremonies as well as its gala evening address from President Bill Clinton due to street protests marked by excesses from police and the National Guard. The meeting adjourned in chaos and acrimony with no agenda set for the subsequent round. This was arguably the most successful public protest and multinational popular resistance against the negative consequences of economic globalization during the 1990s. For a firsthand account, see Jeffrey St. Clair, "Seattle Diary: It's a Gas, Gas, Gas," *New Left Review* 238 (November/December 1999), 81–96. On a similar protest staged three years later at the World Social Forum, see Michael Hardt, "From Porto Alegre," *New Left Review*, 14 (March/April, 2002), 112–18.

12. In his *The Global Age: State and Society Beyond Modernity* (Stanford: Stanford University Press, 1996), Martin Albrow states: "If we try to rank economic organization and processes in terms of their importance for globalization, the transnational corporation would have to come first, then production technology, consumption patterns and lifestyles, mobility of capital, international financial institutions, followed by mobility of labour and finally dismantling of trade barriers" (p. 130). But compare Hirst and Thompson who consider hyperglobalization to be a myth and the growing dominance of transnational corporations likewise mythical. On global capitalism as a hegemonic myth, see also *Re/Presenting Class: Essays in Postmodern Marxism*, ed. J. K. Gibson-Graham, Stephen Resnick, and Richard D. Wolff (Durham, NC: Duke University Press, 2001), especially chaps. 1 and 7: "We would like to deploy our language of class in a project of undermining capitalocentrism and unmaking the global capitalist economy as a discursively hegemonic entity" (p. 170).

13. Jeremy Brecher and Tim Costello, *Global Village or Global Pillage: Economic Reconstruction from the Bottom Up* (Boston: South End, 1994), p. 16. Hereafter *GV*.

14. One dramatic example is Jacques Derrida's opening up deconstruction to the critique of globalization and the rise of the Lilliputian strategy in his *Specters of Marx: The State of the Debt, the Work of Mourning and the New International*, trans. Peggy Kamuf (New York: Routledge, 1994), pp. 77–86. Derrida's critique of the New World Order centers on Francis Fukuyama's *The End of History and the Last Man* (New York: Free Press, 1992). For a ground-breaking post-Marxist feminist deconstruction of Marxian political economy, see J. K. Gibson-Graham, *The End of Capitalism (as We Knew It): A Feminist Critique of Political Economy* (Cambridge, MA: Blackwell, 1996), especially chap. 6 on globalization theory in which the two authors set out "to reject globalization as the inevitable inscription of capitalism . . ." (p. 139).

15. For a suggestive model of global cultural dynamics, see Arjun Appadurai, *Modernity at Large: Cultural Dimensions of Globalization* (Minneapolis: University of Minnesota Press, 1996), chap. 2.

16. Fredric Jameson, Preface, *The Cultures of Globalization*, ed. Fredric Jameson and Masao Miyoshi (Durham, NC: Duke University Press, 1998), p. xvi. See also Roland Robertson, *Globalization: Social Theory and Global Culture* (London: Sage, 1992), p. 76: "responses to *globality* are very likely to frame the character of social theory, doc-

trine, ideology and political culture in the decades ahead." For examples of this growing preoccupation, see "Globalization?," special issue of *Social Text* 17.3 (1999), and "Globalizing Literary Studies," special issue of *PMLA* 116 (January 2001).

17. On the concept and the globalizing dynamics of "world music," see Steven Feld, "A Sweet Lullaby for World Music," *Public Culture* 12.1 (Winter 2000): 145–171, special issue on "Globalization."

Chapter 10

1. Dick Hebdige, *Subculture: The Meaning of Style* (London: Routledge, 1979). Compare Barthes, who examines the ʿashion system as embodied in French fashion magazines of the 1950s, a time before the explosion of fashion conventions in the 1960s, *The Fashion System*, trans. Matthew Ward and Richard Howard (New York: Hill and Wang, 1983).

2. On the rebirth of the sweatshop during postmodern times, see the informative collection *No Sweat: Fashion, Free Trade, and the Rights of Garment Workers*, ed. Andrew Ross (New York: Verso, 1997).

3. Shari Benstock and Suzanne Ferriss, ed., *On Fashion* (New Brunswick, NJ: Rutgers University Press, 1994). Hereafter OF.

4. See Sarah Berry, "Fashion," *A Companion to Cultural Studies*, ed. Toby Miller (Malden, MA: Blackwell, 2001), pp. 454–70, which offers a succinct overview of fashion studies, comparing different approaches including cultural studies and providing an excellent bibliography.

5. See, for example, Susan Willis' reflections on gendering and the mass toy market, *A Primer for Daily Life* (London: Routledge, 1991), chap. 2.

6. See also Ann duCille, "Dyes and Dolls: Multicultural Barbie and the Merchandizing of Difference." In *A Cultural Studies Reader*, ed. Jessica Munns and Gita Rajan (London: Longman, 1995), pp. 551–67.

7. For reviews of fashion research, see Jane Gaines and Charlotte Herzog, ed., *Fabrications: Costume and the Female Body* (New York: Routledge, 1990), chap. 1; and Jennifer Craik, *The Face of Fashion: Cultural Studies in Fashion* (London: Routledge, 1994). Recall Georg Simmel, who concludes grandly that "fashion expresses and at the same time emphasizes the tendency towards equalization and individualization, and the desire for imitation and conspicuousness . . ." (143)—"Fashion," *International Quarterly* 10 (1904): 130–55.

8. For a fine article on retro fashion, see Angela McRobbie, "Second-Hand Dresses and the Role of the Ragmarket." In *Zoot Suits and Second-Hand Dresses: An Anthology of Fashion and Music*, ed. Angela McRobbie (Boston: Unwin Hyman, 1988), pp. 23–49. Compare the chapter on haute couture retro in Colin McDowell, *Fashion Today* (London: Phaidon, 2000), pp. 282–317.

9. Anne Hollander, *Seeing Through Clothes* (New York: Viking, 1978), p. xiii. The Euro-aesthetic bias in this book, however, is troubling.

10. On postmodern pastiche see, for instance, Julia Emberley, "The Fashion Apparatus and the Deconstruction of Postmodern Subjectivity." In *Body Invaders: Panic Sex in America*, ed. Arthur Kroker and Marilouise Kroker (New York: St. Martin's, 1987), p. 59; and Jean Baudrillard, *The Transparency of Evil*, trans. James Benedict (London: Verso, 1993), pp. 11–17.

11. The *classicus locus* on the "great male renunciation," the moment in the late eighteenth century (the onset of modernity) when male clothing became austere, utilitarian, and uniform, is, of course, J. C. Flügel, *The Psychology of Clothes* (London: Hogart, 1930), especially pp. 110–21.

12. For a critical casebook on Madonna, which spends much time on the question of postmodernity and Madonna, see Cathy Schwichtenberg, ed., *The Madonna Connection: Representational Politics, Subcultural Identities, and Cultural Theory* (Boulder: Westview, 1993). ˙

13. See, for example, Giovanni Arrighi, *The Long Twentieth Century: Money, Power, and the Origins of Our Time* (London: Verso, 1994).

Chapter 11

1. For a succinct overview, see Patrick Ragains, "Blues: An Assessment of Scholarship, Reference Tools, and Documentary Sources," *Reference Services Review* (Winter 1993), 13–28, 66, which provides evaluative annotations on historical studies of the blues, reference works, biographies, songbooks, archives, and instructional and audiovisual materials. See also Robert Ford, *A Blues Bibliography: The International Literature of an Afro-American Music Genre* (Bromley, England: Paul Pelletier, 1999).

2. John Fiske, *Reading the Popular* (1989; rpt. London: Routledge, 1991), p. 2.

3. Whether early blues of the period 1912 to 1945 is folk or mass (commercially recorded) culture is subject to debate. See, for example, Francis Davis, *The History of the Blues* (New York: Hyperion, 1995), p. 257: "I believe that what we call the blues mutated into a form of pop the moment it was first commercially recorded" [during the 1920s]. Phonograph records, according to Davis, are emblems of mass culture that render folk culture "obsolete" (p. 8). "In capitalist societies," argues John Fiske, "there is no so-called authentic folk culture against which to measure the 'inauthenticity' of mass culture, so bemoaning the loss of the authentic is a fruitless exercise in romantic nostalgia."—*Understanding Popular Culture* (London: Routledge, 1989), p. 26.

4. Minelle Mahtani and Scott Solmon, "Site Reading?: Globalization, Identity, and the Consumption of Place in Popular Music." In *Popular Culture: Production and Consumption*, ed. C. Lee Harrington and Denise D. Bielby (Malden, MA: Blackwell, 2001), p. 175. Compare Arif Dirlik, "Place-based Imagination: Globalism and the Politics of Place," *Review* 22.2 (1999), 151–87.

5. On "white blues," a subgenre of early country music during the period 1925 to 1940, see Charles Wolfe, "A Lighter Shade of Blue: White Country Blues," *Nothing But the Blues: The Music and the Musicians*, ed. Lawrence Cohn, et al. (New York: Abbeville, 1993), pp. 233–63.

6. William Barlow, *"Looking Up at Down": The Emergence of Blues Culture* (Philadelphia: Temple University Press, 1989), p. 346. Starting in the late 1950s, there has been a sequence of major books on the blues and Barlow's is one of them (see the article by Ragains on this sequence).

7. Compare Wendy Fonarow, "The Spatial Organization of the Indie Music Gig." In *The Subcultures Reader*, ed. Ken Gelder and Sarah Thornton (London: Routledge, 1997), pp. 360–69, which examines the audience layout of young British fans of "independent music." On different modes of fan listening/reception, undivided concentration, selective attention, social interaction, and so on, see Henry Jenkins, "'Strangers No More, We Sing': Filking and the Social Construction of the Science Fiction Fan Community." In *The Adoring Audience: Fan Culture and Popular Media*, ed. Lisa A. Lewis (London: Routledge, 1992), pp. 209–10.

8. On the significance of "noise" (vs. silence), see Jacques Attali, *Noise: The Political Economy of Music*, trans. Brian Massumi (Minneapolis: University of Minnesota Press, 1985), especially pp. 120–24.

9. "There's a blues revival every ten or twenty years . . ." (Davis, p. 13). Each revival has its own singular history and configuration. See, for an exemplary nuanced account,

Jim O' Neal, "I Once was Lost, But Now I'm Found: The Blues Revival of the 1960s," *Nothing But the Blues*, pp. 347–87.

10. "This proclivity to break down cultural barriers and to refashion race and social relations along more egalitarian lines gives the blues culture its utopian potential and positions it as a radical alternative to the color-coded, hierarchical dominant culture." (Barlow, p. 346).

11. Aletha Dewbre, "OBS 1999 Unsigned Blues Talent Contest," *Back Beat*, July-September 1999, 1–2. The SnakeShakers victory in the annual OBS Contest qualified them to compete against fifty bands in the annual International Unsigned Blues Talent Contest hosted in Memphis each winter by the Blues Foundation. The prize money was $500 from the OBS.

12. Pinkie & the SnakeShakers received "Best Performer of the Year" in March 2002 from *The Oklahoma Gazette*, the weekly alternative paper widely read throughout the OKC metroplex.

13. See, for example, Lonnie Brooks, Cub Koda, and Wayne Baker Brooks, "The 25 All-Time Classic Blues Numbers" in their *Blues for Dummies* (Chicago: IDG, 1998), pp. 243–44, among which are "Back Door Man" (Howlin' Wolf), "Boogie Chillen" (John Lee Hooker), "Everyday I Have the Blues" (B.B. King), "Got My Mojo Workin'" (Muddy Waters), "Hoochie Coochie Man" (Muddy Waters), "Stormy Monday" (T-Bone Walker), "Sweet Home Chicago" (Robert Johnson), "The Thrill is Gone" (B.B. King), and "Wang Dang Doodle" (Koko Taylor).

14. For material on a related matter (a subgenre), see Graham Marsh and Barrie Lewis, ed., *The Blues Album Cover Art* (San Francisco: Chronicle, 1996), which surveys cover art of the great period from the 1950s to the 1960s in full color. The SnakeShakers' harmonica player, Robert Riggs, a professional photographer and their lead guitarist, Chris Henson, a professional illustrator and designer, along with lead singer Pinkie West, designed this CD cover art, counterposing musical and gambling items with everyday items (candles, lipstick, ashtray, sunglasses), *Shake These Blues* (Platinum Factory Studio, 2001).

15. Tom Chaney, "Pinkie," *Southwest Blues* 30 (May 2000), 13. *Southwest Blues*, a monthly publication using a large newspaper format of sixteen pages, covers the Dallas and Ft.Worth blues scenes with frequent articles on the OKC blues scene as well.

16. Dennis Jarrett, "The Singer and the Bluesman: Formulations of Personality in the Lyrics of the Blues," *Southern Folklore Quarterly* 42.1 (1978): 31–37.

17. Steven C. Tracy, ed., *Write Me a Few of Your Lines: A Blues Reader* (Amherst: University of Massachusetts Press, 1999), p. 7. This landmark reader offers selected bibliographies, discographies, and videographies as well as fifty informative selections from leading scholars of the blues. See also Hazel Carby, "It Jus Be's Dat Way Sometime: The Sexual Politics of Women's Blues." In *Gender and Discourse: The Power of Talk*, ed. Alexandra Dundas Todd and Sue Fisher (Norwood, NJ: Ablex, 1988), p. 241: "The [earliest] blues singers had assertive and demanding voices; they had no respect for sexual taboos or for breaking through the boundaries of respectability and convention, and we hear the 'we' when they say 'I.'"

18. Angela Y. Davis, *Blues Legacies and Black Feminism: Gertrude "Ma" Rainey, Bessie Smith, and Billy Holiday* (New York: Pantheon, 1998), p. 41. Hereafter *BL*.

19. "In terms of content, most blues lyrics provide the listener with a poetic yet starkly realistic look at relationships between the sexes," Charles Keil, *Urban Blues* (Chicago: University of Chicago Press, 1966), p. 53. But approximately one-third of blues lyrics examine other topics. See, for example, Brian Robertson, *Little Blues Book* (Chapel Hill: Algonquin, 1996), which lists seventeen themes ranging from bad luck, magic, and life on the road to religion, poverty, crime, and old age.

20. Blackhawk Blues Band, *Gypsy Blue* (Isorhythmic Studio and Studio Seven, 2000), and *Rainy* (Isorhythmic Studio, 2002).

21. Blues Nation, *Blues Nation* (R.H.O.M., 1999).
22. See the album review "Blues Nation Music Review," *Oklahoma Indian Times* (September/October 2000).
23. Miss Blues, *Sittin' In with Blinddog Smokin'* (Crying Tone, 2001).
24. A. Dewbre, "Miss Blues: Blues with an Attitude," *Southwestern Blues* 27 (February 2000), 8–9.
25. See "Blues Festivals 2002," *Blues Revue* 75 (April/May 2002), pp. 17–21, 88, which lists 250 blues festivals worldwide between March and October, 2002.
26. "Oppression in the form of 'invisibilization' comes through a refusal of legitimate, public existence, i.e. of an existence that is known and recognized . . . ," points out Pierre Bourdieu in *Masculine Domination*, trans. Richard Nice (Stanford: Stanford University Press, 2001), p. 119.
27. For a succinct and informative overview of the very complicated history of major versus independent record companies, see "Blues Labels," *All Music Guide to the Blues*, 2d. ed., ed. Michael Erlewine, et al. (San Francisco: Miller Freeman, 1999), pp. 612–18.

Chapter 12

1. See Julie Thompson Klein, *Crossing Boundaries: Knowledge, Disciplinarities, and Interdisciplinarities* (Charlottesville: University Press of Virginia, 1996). University disciplines and departments are two different things that may overlap or not (Klein, pp. 53–54). An example of discontinuity would be a large English department that housed programs in linguistics and comparative literature as well as creative writing, rhetoric and composition, English as a second language, and British and American literatures. Here we see a combination of disciplines and subdisciplines joined together in one department.
2. Ellen Messer-Davidow, David R. Shumway, and David J. Sylvan, ed., *Knowledges: Historical and Critical Studies in Disciplinarity* (Charlottesville: University Press of Virginia, 1993), pp. vii–viii. The disciplines, therefore, need constant care and attention, being more like Althusser's Ideological State Apparatuses than Plato's Ideal forms. See Louis Althusser, "Ideology and Ideological State Apparatuses," *"Lenin and Philosophy" and Other Essays*, trans. Ben Brewster (New York: Monthly Review, 1971), pp. 127–86. See also Plato, *Republic*, trans. Robin Waterfield (New York: Oxford University Press, 1993).
3. I echo Derrida here. See his "The Principal of Reason: The University in the Eyes of its Pupils," trans. Catherine Porter and Edward P. Morris, *Diacritics* 13.3 (1983): 3–20, especially p. 17, where he maps the place of deconstruction vis-à-vis the tradition of disciplines. Here is a modulated version of my point from the opening page of *Disciplinarity at the Fin de Siècle*, ed. Amanda Anderson and Joseph Valente (Princeton: Princeton University Press, 2002): "Recognizing the claims of interdisciplinarity, many universities have inaugurated special humanities institutes, which typically bring together scholars from different disciplines working on similar issues or themes. Yet the overall budget structure of the university also shows deep intellectual, financial, and structural investments in traditional disciplinary boundaries . . ." (1).
4. David R. Shumway and Ellen Messer-Davidow, ed., Introduction, *Disciplinarity*, special issue of *Poetics Today* 12 (1991): 201–25.
5. Michel Foucault, *Discipline and Punish: The Birth of the Prison*, trans. Alan Sheridan (New York: Vintage, 1979). Hereafter *DP*.
6. For my take on postmodernism, see also Vincent B. Leitch, *Postmodernism—Local Effects, Global Flows* (Albany: State University of New York Press, 1996), especially chap. 10, which assesses Fredric Jameson's landmark *Postmodernism, or, The Cultural Logic*

of Late Capitalism (Durham, NC: Duke University Press, 1991), a book to which I am indebted. See also Jameson's provocative comments concerning (inter)disciplinarity and Marxism in "Interview with Fredric Jameson," *Diacritics* 12.3 (1982): 72–91, especially p. 89.

7. I am synthesizing here the influential accounts of modernity developed in Scott Lash and John Urry, *The End of Organized Capitalism* (Madison: University of Wisconsin Press, 1987); Stuart Hall and Martin Jacques, ed., *New Times: The Changing Face of Politics in the 1990s* (London: Verso, 1990); and Bill Readings, *The University in Ruins* (Cambridge: Harvard University Press, 1996).

8. Jean Baudrillard's many fin-de-siècle books develop the theme of postmodern social implosion; see, for one intense and memorable example, his *The Transparency of Evil: Essays on Extreme Phenomena*, trans. James Benedict (London: Verso, 1993), pp. 9–10.

9. Stanley Fish, *Professional Correctness: Literary Studies and Political Change* (Cambridge: Harvard University Press, 1995), pp. 135–40.

10. Jean François Lyotard, *The Postmodern Condition: A Report on Knowledge*, trans. Geoff Bennington and Brian Massumi (Minneapolis: University of Minnesota Press, 1984), pp. 81–82.

11. Jacques Derrida, " 'This Strange Institution Called Literature': An Interview with Jacques Derrida," trans. Geoffrey Bennington and Rachel Bowlby, *Acts of Literature*, ed. Derek A. Attridge (New York: Routledge, 1992), p. 68.

12. Michel Foucault, "Truth and Power," *Power/Knowledge: Selected Interviews and Other Writings 1972–77*, ed. Colin Gordon, trans. Gordon, et al. (New York: Pantheon, 1980), pp. 126–33.

INDEX